INCLUSIVE SCREENWRITING FOR FILM AND TELEVISION

Breaking down the traditional structures of screenplays in an innovative and progressive way, while also investigating the ways in which screenplays have been traditionally told, this book interrogates how screenplays can be written to reflect the diverse life experiences of real people.

Author Jess King explores how existing paradigms of screenplays often exclude the very people watching films and TV today. Taking aspects such as characterization, screenplay structure, and world-building, King offers ways to ensure your screenplays are inclusive and allow for every person's story to be heard. In addition to examples ranging from *Sorry to Bother You* to *Portrait of a Lady on Fire*, four case studies on *Killing Eve*, *Sense8*, *I May Destroy You*, and *Vida* ground the theoretical work in practical application. The book highlights the ways in which screenplays can authentically represent and uplift the lived experiences of those so often left out of the narrative, such as the LGBTQIA+ community, women, and people of color. The book addresses a current demand for more inclusive and progressive representation in film and TV and equips screenwriters with the tools to ensure their screenplays tell authentic stories, offering innovative ways to reimagine current screenwriting practice towards radical equity and inclusion.

This is a timely and necessary book that brings the critical lenses of gender studies, queer theory, and critical race studies to bear on the practice of screenwriting, ideal for students of screenwriting, aspiring screenwriters, and industry professionals alike.

Jess King is an Instructor of Screenwriting and Cinema Production at DePaul University, USA. Jess is an educator, scholar, and interdisciplinary filmmaker, teaching courses in screenwriting, independent television, and film analysis. King's creative scholarship revolves around frameworks for reimagining screenwriting for inclusion and social justice.

INCLUSIVE SCREENWRITING FOR FILM AND TELEVISION

Jess King

Routledge
Taylor & Francis Group

LONDON AND NEW YORK

First published 2022
by Routledge
4 Park Square, Milton Park, Abingdon, Oxon OX14 4RN

and by Routledge
605 Third Avenue, New York, NY 10158

Routledge is an imprint of the Taylor & Francis Group, an informa business

British Library Cataloguing-in-Publication Data
A catalogue record for this book is available from the British Library

Library of Congress Cataloging-in-Publication Data
A catalog record for this book has been requested

ISBN: 978-0-367-77220-8 (hbk)
ISBN: 978-0-367-77218-5 (pbk)
ISBN: 978-1-003-17031-0 (ebk)

DOI: 10.4324/9781003170310

Typeset in Bembo
by Apex CoVantage, LLC

For Julie

CONTENTS

ACKNOWLEDGEMENTS

I am immensely grateful for the thoughtful feedback, enthusiastic encouragement, and generous support of many of my colleagues at DePaul University, including David Gitomer, Dustin Goltz, Anna Hozian, Susan McGury, and Brad Riddell, all of whom read and gave feedback on early drafts of this book. I'd also like to thank Fatou Samba for our many generative conversations about problematic media representation and how screenwriters can do better to upend it.

Throughout this process I've been consistently delighted by my students' earnest engagement with and practical application of the ideas presented throughout this book in classes like The Female Gaze, Writing the Independent Television Series, and Queer(ing) Narratives. Thank you to Dominique Prince-Points and Karan Sunil for talking with me about writing characters who code-switch. And I'm overwhelmingly grateful to Liv Krusinski and Tessa Melvin, who, as undergraduate research assistants, provided limitless questions, additional relevant examples, and thoughtful suggestions from a student perspective.

In addition to my colleagues and students, I'd like to thank Claire Margerison and Sarah Pickles at Routledge for being champions of this book and demystifying the publishing process with grace and kindness.

And, finally, to Julie, my love. I could not have done this without you. You encouraged me every step of the way. You read and commented on so many drafts without ever acting like it was a chore. But I know it was. Thank you.

INTRODUCTION

Over the past decade, there has been a shift in on-screen and behind-the-scenes representation in popular entertainment. Along with the rise of affordable technology for the production and distribution of independent film and television, the generative power of social media movements like #MeToo, #TimesUp, and #OscarsSoWhite has forced Hollywood to reckon with longstanding issues around the representation of women, BIPOC, queer and trans folks, disabled people, and more. At the forefront of efforts towards equity and inclusion on television—where some of the most noticeable strides are being made—are show runners like Steven Canals (*Pose*), Michaela Coel (*Chewing Gum* and *I May Destroy You*), Ava DuVernay (*Queen Sugar* and *When They See Us*), Tanya Saracho (*Vida*), and Phoebe Waller-Bridge (*Fleabag* and *Killing Eve*), all of whom have been lauded for centering series on women with intersectional identities, hiring mostly female and/or of color directors, and creating unprecedentedly inclusive writing rooms. Further, their work has been held up as exemplary of progressive female/of color/queer and trans representation.

Though more inclusive media now exists for audiences hungry for diverse representation, the *Comprehensive Annenberg Report on Diversity in Entertainment* shows that we have a long way to go in both on-screen and behind-the-scenes representation. In an examination of major studio releases and television series, the report finds that racial, gender, and LGBTQ+ parity is much less than what anecdotal evidence suggests, most likely on account of the increased volume of media production for the streaming market, which yields proportionately more media created by and focused on white men. From film to broadcast to streaming, the ratio of males-to-females with speaking parts is 2:1, and the numbers get worse for LGBTQ+ people and people of color. On television, for instance, only "26.6% of series regulars were from underrepresented racial/ethnic groups;" less than 2% of characters were identifiable as LGBTQ+, and of those, most were white.[1] In terms

DOI: 10.4324/9781003170310-1

of LGBTQ+ representation, GLAAD's 2020 "Where We Are on TV Report" shows additional declines in the area of queer representation overall, which was expected due to pandemic-related series cancellations. For example,

> of the 773 series regular characters scheduled to appear on broadcast scripted primetime television this season, 70 (9.1 percent) are LGBTQ+. This is a decrease from the previous year's record high percentage of 10.2 percent, and the first season to see a decrease since the 2013–14 report.[2]

This dip in numbers is consistent across broadcast, cable, and streaming platforms. Behind the scenes, in terms of screenwriters, the numbers are equally bleak. The WGAW's 2020 *Inclusion Report* shows that when broken down by ethnicity, "Latinx, Black, and Asian-American Pacific Islander screenwriters hav[e] less representation relative to their share of the overall U.S. population—and Native/Indigenous and Middle Eastern screenwriters hav[e] almost no representation at all."[3]

All is not lost, however, as identifiable gains behind the scenes are occurring. It's simply that when the data shows increases in representation, they are usually modest. As the WGA reports "[i]n T.V., women and people of color held 5% more jobs than in the previous year. In motion pictures, women gained 4% and people of color gained 2%."[4]

While small improvements are worth celebrating, the overall dominance of white, cis, straight male-centered media remains largely unchanged. It seems that despite the critical success of series like *Fleabag, Pose*, and *Insecure*—and the ways in which those series and others like them have fostered sorely-needed discussions around the female gaze, casting trans actors in trans roles, and adjusting cinemato-graphic practices to light actors with dark skin—the majority of work produced in Hollywood still lacks substantial diversity and inclusion in casting and creation. Visible on- and off-screen representation in the form of writers, directors, actors, and producers with traditionally marginalized identities, however, is only one part of the equation, and focusing too heavily on the quantity of visible representation creates additional issues. As Kristen J. Warner argues in relation to casting, when the focus is on the quantity of visual signifiers, "the degree of diversity [becomes] synonymous with the quantity of difference rather than with the dimensionality of those performances."[5] A focus on quantity thus yields what Warner terms "plastic representation," where "any representation that includes a person of color is auto-matically a sign of success and progress," which fosters a studio culture "whereby hiring racially diverse actors becomes an easy substitute for developing new com-plex characters."[6] Essentially Warner's argument exposes that a fixation on quantity short-changes a deeper look into the quality of representation. Quality, in this case, refers to the depth, complexity, and nuance afforded to a character in order to make that character feel genuine and coherent—as opposed to "plastic" or artificial—much of which is the purview of the screenwriter. Thus, missing from discussions of equity and inclusion in the industry is an engagement with how industry-wide acceptance of traditional screenwriting norms and story development creates bar-riers to telling nuanced and complex stories by and about marginalized people.

Favoring qualitative measures over quantitative measures, however, can yield equally fraught results. Too often, conversations about quality stop at identifying problematic stereotypes or tropes and categorizing various representations as either good or bad. When we focus solely on "positive" representation in the form of characters with marginalized identities holding significant if not lead roles in which they are shown as palatable and respectable (the Black doctor, the married gay person with children, the female CEO), we may chip away at long-standing problematic stereotypes perpetuating white supremacy, heteronormativity, misogyny, classism, and the like; but if we want to upend those systemic biases, we'd be wise to plumb deeper into the ways that storytelling paradigms perpetuate the dominant culture. As Jack Halberstam argues, "positive" representation is often assimilationist and, therefore, just as troubling as "negative" or stereotypical representation because the "positive" representation serves to mimic and reinforce the status quo by supporting its values.[7] This means that even when a media text depicts "positive" images of marginalized subjects, it may do so "without necessarily producing new ways of seeing or a new inscription of the social subject in representation."[8] Simply put, Halberstam acknowledges that queer people and others without dominant subject positions often think, behave, and live in vastly different ways, and when representation of those types of characters don't honor that, it erases alternative ways of living and being. Additionally, in relation to Black cultural production, Michelle Wallace contends that the fleetingness of "positive" depictions of Black characters in comparison to larger racist narratives that saturate the culture means that positive images of Black characters amount to "a temporary reversal of terms—like a media version of Sadie Hawkins Day—[and] not only [don't] challenge racism but may in fact corroborate it."[9] Too often "positive" representation disciplines and assimilates marginalized subjects to be in line with the status quo, which ultimately serves to make those characters palatable to white audiences and reinforce normativity. As Racquel J. Gates argues, media texts that are praised for presenting "positive" images

> are more likely to be those that bear resemblance to "proper" (e.g., white) films and television shows as far as the scenarios, characters, and behaviors that they portray, while "negative" texts are identifiable as such via their distance from those standards.[10]

While this is by no means a comprehensive look at the complexities and controversies of the "positive images debate," what Gates, Halberstam, and Wallace lay bare is the way qualitative approaches keep viewers, critics, and creators mired in a playground designed to favor the status quo. By moving away from the "positive images debate" that consumes so much of media studies and popular criticism, it becomes possible to enter a space more akin to transformative and healing justice. A transformative politics invested in healing and human dignity asks us to move beyond "strategies built upon the possibility of incorporation and assimilation" because they unjustly make the status quo accessible "for more privileged members of marginalized groups, while the most vulnerable in our communities continue to be stigmatized and oppressed."[11] Transformative and inclusive storytelling practices, therefore, must be suspicious of assimilating characters with marginalized identities into traditional screen narratives, lest they become normalized, disciplined, and more in line with cis, white, heterosexist, patriarchal values.

Privileging quantitative and qualitative analysis over structural analysis risks obscuring the foundational issues that undergird harmful representation. Put another way, the focus on the number of marginalized characters represented, alongside whether or not those representations are "positive," does not address important structural questions around who created those characters and how the paradigmatic requirements of screenplay structure shape character, world, and story in particular ways. When the creative process is left unexamined, we lose an opportunity to parse out the ideological investments of creators along with the ideological implications of their creative choices, not the least of which impacts how audiences and culture-makers perceive and understand screen stories, as well as what is recognized as a legitimate film or television series.

During the 2020 awards season, for example, some media critics lamented the lack of recognition for Greta Gerwig's lavish and clever adaptation of *Little Women*, Ava DuVernay's scathing and deeply moving series vindicating the Central Park Five *When They See Us*, and Lulu Wang's crowd-pleasing *The Farewell*, among many other critically acclaimed and financially successful films and series helmed by marginalized creators. Instead, the Academy of Motion Picture Arts and Sciences and the Hollywood Foreign Press Association—in a move that seemed oddly regressive considering prior recognition for films like *Moonlight* (2017) and *Get Out* (2018)—rewarded old standbys, exemplified by epically long and antiquated tales featuring white men brutalizing one another throughout history in films like *1917, The Irishman,* and *Once Upon a Time in Hollywood*. Progressive-minded critics scratched their heads in wonder: how could the Academy not see that *Hustlers* was as deserving as *The Irishman*? Though enigmatic, I argue that the question contains the answer: they can't see it because they can't see it. And they can't see it because—as I will demonstrate throughout this book—the signifying practices at the heart of screenwriting are designed to produce stories by, for, and about straight, white able-bodied men such that when films and series don't do that, they become at least somewhat illegible. In much the same way that heteronormativity thrives through the unspoken assumption that homosexuality is a poor imitation of heterosexuality, films made by women, Black people, folks of color, queer and trans people, and more are seen as "shadow[s] of the real."[12] Therefore, when a film is made by and about women—even if they're also white and straight—it's much harder for audiences to accept that it's a viable, serious, awardable screen story. Often films and series made by marginalized creators are glossed over, or, as Lili Loofbourow argues in relation to stories by and about women, they're dismissed by what she calls the "male glance." For Loofbourow, in a nod to Laura Mulvey's work around the "male gaze," the "male glance" results from the assumption that "we don't expect female [or other marginalized] texts to have universal things to say."[13] Therefore, we shrug them off, assuming that there is nothing to see, no deep insights into our collective humanity. This is how *Hustler's* becomes a "Chick Flick" and *The Irishman* gets nominated for ten Academy Awards. If we want to improve representation in both quantity and quality, therefore, we must engage in a sustained interrogation and upending of the hegemonic storytelling norms that perpetuate the idea that certain stories are originary, "proper," and "real" while others are derivative and/or too "niche."

One of the primary purposes of this book is to supplement quantitative and qualitative media analysis with structural analysis that examines the paradigmatic foundations of screenwriting, the identities of those writing film and television, as well as those holding the line on the rules that govern both. Thus, this book is, in part, about perspective and identity. As a queer filmmaker and professor of screen-writing, I'm often frustrated by the ways that narrative constraints like three-act structure and the hero's journey—with their lock-step patterning of plot points, midpoint reversals, and final resolutions—limit not only the types of stories that tend to be told, but the possibilities for representation within those stories. The standard screenwriting paradigms are not only inherently masculine—most obviously marked by Campbell's *Hero with a Thousand Faces*—but straight, in terms of linearity, causal reproductive logics, and structures of conflict that uphold binaries, which makes it difficult to create characters with distinctly queer subjectivities who embark on distinctly queer journeys. Additionally, common strategies for character-building such as psychological realism, individualized subjectivity, and transformative agency are based upon long-standing notions of the universal white male that do not easily map onto marginalized characters and, therefore, might not offer the best strategies for telling the stories of people who have long been stereotyped or erased for existing outside of the status quo.

To be clear, when I address identity, I am not referring to the individual properties of a person or character. Rather, in line with critiques of identity as too binaristic and tied to "forms of state-enforced identification and recognition" that "collapse, individualize, and homogenize both experience and meaning,"[14] I consider identity and affinity to refer to how one's gender, race, sexuality, ability, and more interact with the familial, social, economic, historical, and political context one lives in. Further, I consider that the relationship between one's identity and social context impacts how one moves in and is moved by the world. This is not identity as individuality, brand, or commodity, but as immensely complex, deeply personal, and irrevocably social.

This book grapples with the ways identity informs—but does not determine—one's material lived experience and worldview and how that manifests in and can be used to understand and challenge the storytelling paradigms we have come to rely on in terms of character-building, world-building, and narrative structure. Because much of this book focuses on under- and mis-represented characters, it's important to recognize that not all people who share facets of their identity are the same or experience the world in the same way. Since identity is relational, there are no monolithic examples that can account for the experiences of all people within an affinity group. This means that though I've chosen a range of intersectional examples to work from, they do not speak to or for all those who might share similar affinities, nor are my examples comprehensive. Notably missing from this book is a significant discussion of the representation of disabled people[15] in film and television, partly because there are still few strong examples of film and television work by and starring disabled people. One can look at the discourse around Sia's ill-conceived film *Music* to gain an understanding of what people with disabilities want in terms of presence and participation.[16] Similarly, while there is a vibrant and varied independent global Indigenous film community, there are very few people holding Indigenous identity on-screen or in writing and directing roles within mainstream Hollywood. At present, Taika Waititi is the most prominent Indigenous creator making his way around Hollywood, having recently directed high-budget Marvel films and the Oscar-nominated *Jojo Rabbit* (2019). His FX series *Reservation Dogs* (2021) with Sterlin Harjo might be the only television series with Indigenous people at every level of production unlike the Peacock series *Rutherford Falls* (2021), which left many Indigenous audiences disappointed in its focus on a central white male character despite an Indigenous-focused writers' room. Put simply, I have not included all identities equally in this book, partly due to the lack of good examples of inclusive and intersectional work and partly due to the lens of my own identities.

That said, from my experience as a white, non-binary lesbian, I can speak most thoughtfully on issues related to gender and sexuality. In laying the groundwork for how the cis, white, male perspective came to be embedded in screenwriting, one of my hopes is that new paths will emerge to explore how screenwriting norms impact people who sit at other intersections of identity. If not to tell truer stories about those with shared affinities, then at least less harmful ones. My hope is that a sustained focus on race, gender, sexuality, and more in the field of screenwriting opens a space for critical intervention in the ongoing systemic oppression and discrimination exacerbated by Hollywood narratives, and fosters new practices that center the life stories, experiences, and unique subjectivities of marginalized people. This moves us beyond "diverse" and "plastic" representation and allows us to imagine new possibilities for how identity, agency, and subjectivity are formulated and codified within film and television.

Methodology: Towards a Radically Equitable and Inclusive Cultural Imaginary

At the root of this book lies a fundamental conviction that all of life is deeply connected and relational, that to flourish along with the planet and one another, we must make profound shifts in how we relate to one another, the Earth, and ourselves. Our current cultural, economic, political, and social system—based on white supremacist, cis-sexist, heteronormative, predatory capitalist logics and marked by massive income inequality, perpetual war, rabid anti-intellectualism, assaults against reproductive rights, the erasure of disability and aging, climate catastrophe, pandemic-apathy, and an overall disregard for the suffering of others—is not sustainable. Activists from all disciplines are rightly calling for progressive economic and social change centered around principles of degrowth, decolonization, social justice, the value of Black lives, sustainable environmental policies, and the like. For some, concerns of this nature might be considered too political and thus outside the purview of the screenwriter. But as a queer, gender-variant filmmaker and educator who daily feels the pressing need for healing social transformation and who understands the unique power of storytelling, I disagree. We make the world through the stories we tell.

Due to their ubiquity and popular appeal, screen stories are central to how we understand ourselves—our agency, identity, and place in the world—as well as how we consider others with their unique identities, struggles, and humanity. As bell hooks writes in her inquiry into the possibilities of liberating Black representation from the disciplining mechanisms of white supremacist cultural production:

> [t]he emphasis on film is so central because it, more than any other media experience, determines how blackness and Black people are seen and how other groups will respond to us based on their relation to these constructed and consumed images.[17]

Because screen stories influence the cultural imaginary from which the symbolic order derives its strength, legitimacy, and power, ethical screenwriters are in a unique position to reshape how stories are told and contribute to more equitable futures. As I argue throughout this book, pursuing a generative and inclusive imaginary geared towards human dignity and flourishing must be rooted in a "radical equality" based in equity that fosters interdependent relationality over self-mastery and individualism. For queer and feminist theorists like Judith Butler and filmmakers like Céline Sciamma, radical equality can, among other things, manifest through embracing our fundamental vulnerability to reflect "social relations that depend for [their] articulation on an increasingly avowed interdependency."[18] An ethos rooted in radical equality shifts us away from the isolation of the bounded and individualized self and towards a relationality founded on connection and porousness. Too often, when we speak of the myriad ways we relate to one another, we do so within the confines of individualism and therefore reduce human connection to a series of transactions.

To reimagine our relationality through the lens of porousness allows for a recognition that in connecting we impact, influence, and alter one another irrevocably. We breathe one another's breath, a fact that has had devastating implications in the ongoing COVID-19 pandemic. We take on one another's turns of phrase, as evidenced by the proliferation of the Valley Girl attributed addition of "like" to American speech patterns in the 1980s. We leave imprints on one another's psyches. We don't exist by ourselves in a bounded way: we're part of an ocean rather than perpetually and individually formed raindrops. To accept this requires "letting go of the body as a 'unit' in order to understand one's boundaries as relational and social predicaments: including sources of joy, susceptibility to violence, sensitivity to heat and cold, tentacular yearnings for food, sociality, and sexuality,"[19] which we'll see play out beautifully via the interconnected characters of the Wachowskis' series *Sense8* in chapter 7. In pursuit of an imaginary grounded in radical equality, equity, and inclusiveness, I turn to the ruthlessly critical and creatively constructive work of queer, feminist, and anti-racist theory, as they are central to my analysis of how common narrative strategies reinforce and perpetuate the destructive imaginary underlying the status quo as well as my suggestions for how those narrative strategies can be adapted and innovated upon to alter screenwriting practice towards a more inclusive and equitable future.

From queer cultural theorists like Sara Ahmed, who reimagines phenomenology to accommodate queer bodies and queer orientations so that "[d]epending on which way one turns, different worlds might come into view;"[20] to José Esteban Muñoz, who challenges the negative turn in queer theory by envisioning queerness as "a structuring and educated mode of desiring that allows us to see and feel beyond the quagmire of the present;"[21] to critical race theorists like Kimberlé Crenshaw, whose work on intersectionality reminds us that when we fight discrimination by "addressing the needs and problems of those who are most disadvantaged . . . then others who are singularly disadvantaged would also benefit;"[22] to feminists philosophers like Adriana Cavarero, who "rescues" the maligned female figures of Western philosophy to inaugurate a uniquely female symbolic order:[23] the ongoing work in anti-racist, queer, and feminist thought aims to resist the violence of the status quo and imagine new, more equitable worlds for all people. Such utopian longings develop in response to a world that is "not enough" and yet is all we have, a world where you sense that so much more is possible just over the horizon.[24] Though not commonly used to think about screenwriting, threads from disparate scholarship in queer, feminist, and anti-racist theory can be woven together to create a new path forward, potentially jolting awake those either long-dulled into accepting the status quo or, hopefully, those who stand too much to gain from it to upend it. Through a blend of rigorous critique and a playful excavation of the non-normative, critical theory "offer[s] us one method for imagining not some fantasy of an elsewhere, but existing alternatives to hegemonic systems."[25]

It's one thing to imagine a more egalitarian future—one defined not by brutality and trauma but by cooperation and mutual flourishing—but liberation requires more than imagination. The transformation of the dominant economic, political, social, and cultural systems necessary to eliminate hierarchies of human value requires a framework that centers intersectionality and an awareness of the "interdependency among multiple systems of domination."[26] As Audre Lorde says, "I am not free while any woman is unfree, even when her shackles are very different from my own. And I am not free as long as one person of Color remains chained. Nor is anyone of you."[27] An intersectional framework articulates the distinct vectors of oppression while potentially building radically equal coalitions amongst groups that might not ordinarily see their causes linked.

In addition to building intersectional coalitions, an anti-racist, queer, feminist creative practice seeks transformation of oppressive systems over assimilation into those systems. Tweaks won't do. A transformative creative practice "does not search for opportunities to integrate into dominant institutions and normative social relationships, but instead pursues a political agenda that seeks to change values, definitions, and laws which make these institutions and relationships oppressive."[28] This anti-assimilationist agenda is central to the exploration of screenwriting paradigms and their relationship to media representation that follows. An assimilationist position within the field of screenwriting might understand that "depicting minority difference [is] necessary to combat phobic discrimination and violence," and, therefore, advocate for "the production of multiple and nuanced roles, narratives, and images" of minoritarian characters.[29] We see this happening in the standard practice of including characters of color and/or queer characters as side characters and in the way that most major studios have diversity initiatives seemingly meant to bring marginalized voices into the fold. However, in order to "pose critical alternatives, and transform our world views," screenwriters who want to challenge the status quo must find ways of "shifting paradigms [and] changing perspectives."[30] Without probing the normative values and assumptions undergirding storytelling structures, we risk lauding diverse casting and representation—paltry as those advances have been—while obscuring "the structural, material inequalities that produce and maintain minority difference in the first place."[31] It's more than just the presence of people or occasional switched out lenses that are necessary; we need to completely and permanently change the way in which we define and imagine what a world is. Not tourism into new worlds or lives, but honoring those worlds and lives on their own terms.

Put most simply, what I do in this book is the following: through an anti-racist, feminist, queer lens, I interweave analyses of screenwriting paradigms with analyses of screen texts in order to emerge on the other side with recommendations for how to approach future screenwriting in a way that has less potential to perpetuate the problems of the past. While neither screenwriters nor studios can control an audience's experience or interpretation of their work, or achieve what Stuart Hall refers to as "the ideal of 'perfectly transparent communication,'"[32] I contend that deliberate restructuring of screenwriting's encoding practices can result in markedly more inclusive storytelling. My goal is to begin lighting a path toward a transformative practice of screenwriting that uncouples success from harm, that releases us from what has been done and allows for new forms of creativity, and that appreciates the abundance of human experience rather than telling us all to get in line. I can't promise a revolution, nor do I expect to see one within my lifetime. But in my students' work and in much of the work I examine in my case studies, I see what's possible.

Overview

This book is divided into two parts. In part I of the book, I examine the most widely recognized screenwriting paradigms and the creators (or gurus) responsible for them to break down how the screenwriting rules became established and probe the inherent bias within them.

Chapter 1 describes the historical rise of—and inherent bias in—the standard screenwriting paradigms as exemplified by prominent screenplay manual writers like Syd Field, Robert McKee, Blake Snyder, Christoper Vogler, and others. The historic development and codification of standard screenwriting paradigms is linked to the symbiotic relationship between film production and film criticism within the Hollywood studio system and the entrenchment of normative character- and world-building practices that misrepresent the cis, heterosexual, white, male perspective as objective and universal. The rest of part I presents a series of chapters focused on specific elements of screenwriting craft from character-building through world-building. Chapters 2 through 4 focus primarily on issues related to character, with Chapter 2 covering agency, character versus characterization, as well as the ways that linear character arcs erase the multiplicity, fragmentation, and fluidity of many lives, particularly when viewed through queer and trans frameworks of thought. Chapter 3 extends the discussion on character to the mutually constitutive relationship between conflict and character. For the gurus, a character arc defined by conflict to produce essence discards "observable" characteristics like race, gender, and sexuality and therefore makes identity-centric stories structurally ineffective. Similarly, as the ultimate goal of screen conflict is resolution, narratives centered on institutionalized racism, coming out narratives, and widespread social antagonism are herded towards superficial redress without further exploration. Chapter 4 rounds out the focus on character by examining the ideological underpinnings of three-act screenplay structure, as contained in the transformation imperative of the hero's journey and its connection to white supremacy and masculinity. The perceived neutrality of structure is interrogated to refute the idea of form without meaning, which contributes to a paradigm of non-relational individualism, aspirational striving, and "mind over matter" at the expense of the body and the natural world. Chapter 5 focuses on world-building in screenwriting through the lens of feminist phenomenology to illuminate the ways in which location, as well as cultural, economic, historical, political, and social context impact how a character might live in and move through the story-world. Ultimately, I argue that embracing the interplay of character and setting captures a more equitable, inclusive, and holistic view of the world that accounts for the experiences of those with intersectional identities.

In part II, I provide four case studies from popular television that demonstrate how the paradigms can effectively be challenged, reworked, and re-imagined based on the paradigmatic analysis of part I. With the exception of the chapter focused on *Killing Eve*—which operates as a cautionary tale—the case studies are meant to provide generative, concrete examples of ways to reimagine screenwriting practice towards equitable and inclusive ends.

Chapter 6 focuses on how the series *Killing Eve's* adherence to traditional storytelling standards around character-building, narrative structure, and genre inhibit the liberatory potential of placing two female characters (an Asian-American, straight woman and a white, queer woman) at the center of the typically masculine spy thriller. Chapter 7 explores Lana and Lilly Wachowski's groundbreaking trans-genre series *Sense8*, an ensemble piece rooted in relationality, empathy, and liberation. By ignoring all of the standard screenwriting rules around efficiency, pacing, active characters, and transformative character arcs, the Wachowskis' *Sense8* is an example of what can be created when a writer is ready to break away from "the way it's always been done" to "how it could be." In Chapter 8 I examine Michaela Coel's limited series *I May Destroy You*. In rejecting the false binary of active agent versus passive victim, the use of normative structures to generate tension, and a reliance on redemption narratives for the abuser in cases of sexual assault, Coel's series pivots to a profound, empathetic focus on the survivor. Chapter 9 dives into Tanya Saracho's character-focused, half-hour drama *Vida* to highlight the importance of expanding screenwriting practice to include more culturally specific world-building and character design rooted in contradiction, multiplicity, relationality, and community. The first Hollywood series with an all-Latinx writer's room, *Vida* embodies an ethos of explicit political content specific to Latinx communities in the United States, and as a result, avoids generic conflict common to screenwriting practices that embrace an abstract universal neutral, instead centering specific issues like "gentefication" and the policing of identity within Mexican-American and queer communities.

Throughout the book, in centering films and series produced by major studios and networks or which have gained significant critical attention in the mainstream press or culturally resonant festivals like Sundance, my hope is to show that change is possible within the industry. This is not a book about counter-cinema, experimental cinema, or the avant-garde. Too often the onus of developing and implementing liberatory or innovative frameworks falls outside of mainstream systems, which ultimately allows the problematic aspects of those systems to remain intact. While the book as a whole looks at contemporary film and television, the case studies primarily focus on television as that is where the most significant progress is being made in terms of inclusive representation.

The interventions proposed throughout this book aim toward reclaiming the cultural imagination from the destructive forces of white supremacy, sexism, heteronormativity, ableism, xenophobia, and the like through screenwriting. Screen stories have a tremendous power to shape our sense of self, our identities, our sense of belonging, beliefs about what we think is possible for our lives, as well as how we see, understand, and interact with others. While much work has been done about the importance of representation within the fields of film and media studies, less focus has been placed on the role the screenwriter has in perpetuating the violences of the status quo. This book aims to change that.

Notes

1 Stacy L. Smith, et al., "Comprehensive Annenberg Report on Diversity in Entertainment," *USC Annenberg* (2016): 8–11.
2 "Where We Are on TV, 2020–2021," *GLAAD Media Institute*, 2021, 8–9.
3 "WGAW Inclusion Report 2020," *wga.org*, accessed October 17, 2021, www.wga.org/uploadedfiles/the-guild/inclusion-and-equity/2020_WGAW_Inclusion_Report.pdf, 5.

4 Ibid., 1.

5 Kristen J. Warner, "Plastic Representation," *Film Quarterly* 71, no. 2 (2017): 4.

6 Ibid.

7 Jack Halberstam, *Female Masculinity* (Durham, NC: Duke University Press, 2018), 185.

8 Teresa DeLauretis, "Film and the Visible," in *How Do I Look? Queer Film and Video*, ed. Bad Object Choices (Seattle: Bay Press, 1992), 224.

9 Michele Wallace, *Invisibility Blues* (London: Verso, 1990), 2.

10 Racquel J. Gates, *Double Negative: The Black Image and Popular Culture* (Durham, NC: Duke University Press, 2018), 18.

11 Cathy Cohen, "Punks, Bulldaggers, and Welfare Queens: The Radical Potential of Queer Politics?" *GLQ: A Journal of Lesbian and Gay Studies* 3, no. 4 (January 1997): 443.

12 Judith Butler and Sara Salih, *The Judith Butler Reader* (Malden, MA: Blackwell, 2004), 127.

13 Lili Loofbourow, "The Male Glance," *VQR Online*, March 5, 2018, www.vqronline. org/essays-articles/2018/03/male-glance.

14 Sam Spady, "Reflections on Late Identity: In Conversation with Melanie J. Newton, Nirmala Erevelles, Kim TallBear, Rinaldo Walcott, and Dean Itsuji Saranillio," *Critical Ethnic Studies* 3, no. 1 (2017): 90.

15 In line with the "Roadmap for Inclusion: Changing the Face of Disability in Media" report, I want to recognize that one of the debates within the disability community revolves around "people-first" or "identity-first" language. Because this book tends towards an identity-first position, I will be using identity-first language, while respecting the important perspectives contained within this ongoing discussion. See: Judith Heumann, Katherine Salinas, and Michellie Hess, "Road Map for Inclusion: Changing the Face of Disability in Media" (Ford Foundation, 2019).

16 Teo Bugbee, "'Music' Review: A Woefully Misguided View of Disability," *The New York Times*, February 11, 2021, www.nytimes.com/2021/02/11/movies/music-review. html.

17 bell hooks, *Black Looks: Race and Representation* (Boston: South End Press, 1992), 5.

18 Judith Butler, *The Force of Nonviolence: An Ethico-Political Bind* (London: Verso, 2020), 45.

19 Ibid., 45.

20 Sara Ahmed, *Queer Phenomenology: Orientations, Objects, Others* (Durham, NC: Duke University Press, 2007), 15.

21 José Esteban Muñoz, *Cruising Utopia: The Then and There of Queer Futurity* (New York: New York University Press, 2009), 1.

22 Kimberlé Crenshaw, "Demarginalizing the Intersection of Race and Sex: A Black Feminist Critique of Antidiscrimination Doctrine, Feminist Theory and Antiracist Politics," *University of Chicago Legal Forum*, no. 1 (1989): Article 8, 167.

23 Adriana Cavarero, *In Spite of Plato: A Feminist Rewriting of Ancient Philosophy* (New York: Routledge, 1995).

24 Muñoz, *Cruising Utopia*, 1.

25 J. Halberstam, *The Queer Art of Failure* (Duke University Press, 2011), 89.

26 Cohen, "Punks," 442.

27 A. Lorde, *Sister Outsider: Essays & Speeches* (Berkeley: Crossing Press, 2007), 132–33.

28 Cohen, "Punks," 445.

29 Summer Kim Lee, "Too Close, Too Compromised: Killing Eve and the Promise of Sandra Oh," *Los Angeles Review of Books*, December 4, 2018, https://lareviewofbooks. org/article/close-compromised-killing-eve-promise-sandra-oh/.

30 hooks, *Black Looks*, 4.

31 Lee, "Too Close."

32 Stuart Hall, "Encoding/Decoding," in *Culture, Media, Language*, eds. Dorothy Hobson et al. (London: Hutchinson, 1980), 51–61, 58.

PART I
Towards a Critique of Screenwriting

1

SCREENPLAY MANUALS AND THE HOMOGENIZATION OF THE IMAGINATION

At the root of Hollywood's representation crisis lies a failure of imagination. This failure is the result of over a century of severe constraints on who tells, sells, and green-lights screen stories. If imagination is, in part, the process whereby we "picture" or posit ideas, people, and worlds—in order to better understand our own—then considering the commonalities of who routinely writes, directs, stars in, and profits from the bulk of our culture's vast creative output becomes important. To be more specific: when "most working writers emerge from the middle and upper middle classes; most are white; and the majority, most strikingly from the 1930s through the 1970s, have been men,"[1] it invites questions about the investments and particularities of their perspective and how those commitments impact the output of their imaginations. How, for instance, might we be curtailing the cultural imaginary when such a limited segment of the population defines how stories are told, what characters are centered, who is deemed a villain, who a sidekick, and who a hero? And yet, too often, calls for diversity of perspective get sidelined by critiques rooted in the mire of "identity politics"[2] where identity is relegated to the realm of the personal and shunned from public discussion. True diversity of thought, it is argued, comes through transcendent differences in ideas, not differences in lived experience, as if lived experience, along with one's relationships to others, to history, and to place don't impact how one responds to, theorizes about, or imagines the world. One of the central tenets of this book is that such claims are a ruse: ignorant at best, disingenuous at worst. Simply put, point of view matters. A person's lived, material reality shapes their perceptions, perspectives, and imaginations in countless ways. When I argue that Hollywood suffers from a failure of imagination—in an industry that prides itself on superlative creativity, no less—I am not suggesting that there is no imagination, but rather that we've restricted the possibilities for storytelling by only allowing certain voices to speak on behalf of humanity. Confining storytelling in this way yields normative perspectives that

DOI: 10.4324/9781003170310-3

determine not only who populates screen stories, but the rules governing them, which, in turn, impacts our understandings of one another and the world. When we limit the storytellers, we limit the stories, and when we limit the stories, we limit the possibilities for life. Thus, to begin the investigation into how screenwriting paradigms perpetuate normative values, in this chapter I explore how a white male perspective came to inform the creative logic and ethos underlying screenwriting norms.

When analyzing practices that encode meaning into a film, perspective is most commonly situated in relation to how the screenwriter develops the worldview of the protagonist. Though the screenwriter imbues the characters within the screenplay text with particular backstories, identities, and perspectives, the point of view, life history, and historical context of the screenwriter is rarely examined in terms of how it impacts the story they are writing or how their attachments, investments, and ideological commitments are conveyed via the characters, themes, and worlds they create. Even more rare is an analysis of the perspectives and bias contained within the screenwriting paradigms or the people who most often promote them. Instead, the rules of screenwriting—like most elements of craft and aesthetics— tend to be seen as universal and point-of-viewless.

The penchant for universalizing and naturalizing the rules is not unique to screenwriting. The belief that the laws governing a system exist outside of the specific context and people who created those laws forms the basis of entrenched structural systems that range from economics and philosophy, to medicine and law. Within the field of legal studies, for example, Kimberlé Crenshaw's work establishing intersectionality as a framework for looking at how multiple vectors of marginalization work in concert to oppress different people in multiple and particular ways is grounded in one of critical race theory's central tenets: that institutions— despite claims to ultimate and universal authority—are not neutral. In fact, within legal analysis and practice, Crenshaw demonstrates that "what is understood as objective or neutral is often the embodiment of a white middle-class world view."[3] The consequences of this within the criminal justice system are as vast as they are damaging, as we see Black people and Latinos incarcerated at extremely high rates while their white counterparts often are exempt from the law altogether.[4] When we unquestioningly accept that the rules are objective and neutral—whether legal, economic, creative, or otherwise—we unwittingly support dominance hierarchies by glossing over the particular consciousnesses, perspectives, and lived histories of those making the rules and the way that the rules are designed to protect the rulemakers. In essence, we deny the fact that one's subjectivity is created within a particular context and is, in part, constructed through the very identities that notions of "objectivity" seek to conceal. As Crenshaw writes, people "view the world through a consciousness, constructed in part through race. The appearance of perspectivelessness is simply the illusion by which the dominant perspective is made to appear neutral, ordinary, and beyond question."[5] To expand on this claim through Crenshaw's intersectional framework, we can say that our consciousness is constructed through not only race, but gender, class, age, ability, sexuality, citizenship, and more,[6] and, in terms of consciousness-construction, this is just as true for those with dominant subject positions as for marginalized subjects. In effect, we elide the specificity of cis, white, able-bodied men under the rubric of the universal human, which erases the fact they, too, have particular consciousnesses, perspectives, and imaginations shaped by their identities, histories, and experiences. How, then, did screenwriting norms become universalized and entrenched, and what are the implications of obscuring the particularities of the men writing the rules?

The Development and Allure of the Screenwriting Manual

One way that the white male perspective came to inform the standard screenwriting norms that are widely accepted by professional screenwriters, networks, studio executives, screenwriting degree programs, and the WGA is through how-to manuals. Peddling universal and "perspectiveless" principles of "good" storytelling, how-to guides and advice for screenwriters in trade magazines have been an essential part of Hollywood screenwriting practices since the early days of film. Widely circulated and containing advice about how to write a script that sells, the original screenwriting manuals were largely—though not entirely—written by white men, which reflects the dominant demographic of screenwriters throughout Hollywood history. Like so many of Hollywood's creative practices, screenplay manuals straddle the line between the goals of the artist, with their concerns about craft, and the goals of business, with their concerns for efficiency and profit. In terms of craft, early guides like *How to Write Moving Picture Plays*, by William Lewis Gordon (1913) and *How to Write Photoplays*, by John Emerson and Anita Loos (1920) were often based on similar guides on playwriting. As screenwriting studies scholar Steven Maras writes on early how-to guides,

> [t]he handbook writers of the day thus found themselves drawing—with differing degrees of success and rigour—on classical notions of drama and rearticulating them in the context of the motion picture for an audience that may never have encountered them before.[7]

Though the focus on craft in the original manuals arose, in part, to help aspiring screenwriters understand a developing and changing medium, they also "serve[d] as a platform for the construction and teaching of scenario writing and [became] a zone of intelligibility and normativity."[8] While early films were short enough that scripts consisted of simple lists of scenarios, norming the screenplay became necessary as films grew from one-reel to multi-reel productions. Increases in film length led to increases in story complexity, which led to narrative and budgetary concerns as shooting days increased and production expanded. As film historian and theoretician Janet Staiger writes,

> with longer films, production times lengthened into weeks rather than days and the number of scenes multiplied per reel. The necessity to maintain

continuity, verisimilitude, and narrative dominance and clarity for the five- and six-reel film while keeping down costs and production time intensified the need for a more detailed script.[9]

This resulted in a kind of efficiency-model of screenwriting that favored specific formatting and structural requirements. In terms of formatting, precise rules formed about margins, spacing, font type, and size, as well as the way character names, sound effects, and slug lines are formatted. Courier 12, for example, became the only permissible font for a screenplay because—as a fixed-pitch font[10]—one page of text translates roughly into one minute of film, which makes things like scheduling and budgeting more manageable. Alongside formatting, rules about narrative economy and clarity developed in ways that made every scene count, essentially eliminating narrative excess as a cost-saving measure. While the history of screenwriting and its relationship with the screenplay manual is far more complex,[11] what is essential for the purposes of this study is to understand that the role of screenwriting manuals has been to codify and standardize screenwriting practices while promising access to a system whose gatekeepers are "interested in 'full profit maximization.'"[12]

Hollywood's capitalist inclinations are no secret. In fact, they are often a point of pride. Such self-mythologizing about the studio system's capitalist prowess, however, can obscure some of the underlying mechanisms that connect the profit motive with creative practices and how the desire for a "hit" movie or television series creates an environment that seeks to replicate and build upon prior successes, with success being narrowly defined as profitable and, secondarily, award-winning. Thus, to more fully understand the development and codification of standard screenwriting paradigms, an investigation of what media scholar John Caldwell calls Hollywood's "critical industrial practices" is in order. This approach acknowledges two essential points that will be fruitful in this inquiry: 1) as a cultural industry, Hollywood theorizes about itself, employing "interpretive schemes" about the work that it does, which makes it an incredibly self-reflexive industry, and 2) this self-reflexivity occurs in all aspects of production from the technical to "professional interactions" and includes, but is not limited to, "general framing paradigms that writers and producers use to conceptualize and develop screen content for film and television"[13] Caldwell's work asks those seeking to understand how studio practices produce culture to look more closely at "the culture of film/video production."[14] By way of example, genres developed through a system of trial and error in what Rick Altman calls the "Producer's Game," wherein producers and studio heads break down financially lucrative films into their component "successful" elements, study those elements, and then reproduce them in different arrangements in new films, all with the goal of replicating financial success. For Altman, this approach to filmmaking puts "studio personnel in the place of the critic,"[15] a highly analytical and theoretical mode that constrains the possibilities for production by locking it in a cycle of analysis, imitation, and replication. Subsequently, film genres "begin as reading positions established by studio personnel acting as critics, and are expressed through film-making conceived of as an act of applied criticism."[16] Altman's examination of the "critical industrial practices" at the root of Hollywood genre development lays bare the symbiotic relationship between film production, film reception, and film criticism within the Hollywood studio system, and perhaps most importantly connects those practices to the profit motive. Similar industrial impulses continue in the contemporary entertainment landscape through a recurrent interest in how algorithmic insight about audience behavior can help create shows that audiences are sure to love. In one high profile example, the Netflix Original *House of Cards* was considered pre-destined for success because "[s]ubscribers who watched the original series . . . were also likely to watch movies directed by David Fincher and enjoy ones that starred Kevin Spacey" which led executives to believe that "an audience was out there."[17] The quest for certainty through various iterations of the Producer's Game, in this case a "hit" guaranteed via algorithm, is not new. It's part of a long-standing set of critical industrial practices in Hollywood's profit-oriented, factory-model of storytelling, and screenwriting is not exempt from its allure.

The current rules of screenwriting, like their predecessors in the early days of film, developed following a similar set of impulses and practices. The most well-known authors of contemporary screenwriting manuals— Syd Field, Robert McKee, Blake Snyder, and Christopher Vogler, among others—were studio readers, development executives, or story analysts before formally systematizing their screenwriting paradigms in books and seminars. In the early 70s, for example, Field was a studio reader for Cinemobile Systems where he read hundreds of screenplays with an eye towards cost, quality, and budget. During that time, he began to formulate his ideas about what made some scripts worth passing on to studio heads and others worth tossing in the garbage. Through reading, studying, and green-lighting screenplays for now classic films like *The Godfather* (1972), *American Graffiti* (1973), and *Chinatown* (1974), Field gleaned the core tenets of screenwriting success that informed the courses he taught and the manuals he wrote, all of which eventually became "totally embraced by the film industry."[18] Likewise, in the 80s, while working at Disney as a story consultant, Christopher Volger wrote a legendary seven-page memo that took Hollywood by storm. Using the emblematic *Star Wars* as a guide, Vogler distilled Campbell's *Hero with a Thousand Faces*, most commonly referred to as the hero's journey, into a simpler set of steps for writing a successful film.

Other screenwriting experts, like McKee and Snyder, have established paradigms that they claim have raked in billions of dollars at the box office. According to Snyder, not only did he make millions as a screenwriter, but "taught [his] method and shortcuts to some of the most successful [screenwriters] in the business."[19] Because of this, studios send employees to seminars by these men in droves. McKee's seminars have been required for studio workers at Mirimax and Pixar, have been delivered to an "estimated forty thousand people," and draw some of the biggest celebrities, including "David Bowie, Ed Burns, Drew Carey (twice), John Cleese (three times), Kirk Douglas, Faye Dunaway, Emilio Estevez, Eddie Izzard,

Quincy Jones (three times), Diane Keaton, Barry Manilow, Joan Rivers, Julia Roberts, Meg Ryan, Joel Schumacher, Brooke Shields, and Gloria Steinem."[20] Movies are big business that attract big names, and the screenwriting gurus are not exempt from the gold-rush mentality and celebrity-making that undergirds so much of Hollywood culture. In playing the Producer's Game, the screenplay gurus perpetuate the system of studying movies to make movies in a cycle that replicates and repackages what is deemed successful (i.e., financially lucrative) and will be produced—at least by major studios.

While there are critiques to be made regarding the effectiveness of the Producer's Game in selecting and emulating successful tactics,[21] my analysis will move us in a different direction, one that uncovers the particular perspectives, and thus bias, at the root of this process and how that bias informs the conceptual foundations of the screenwriting paradigms. In distilling the elements of successful screenwriting into a set of coherent, enduring, and universal rules that can theoretically be replicated by anyone hoping to write a screenplay that sells, at least two pivotal and related problems emerge: 1) the sanctity of the paradigms glosses over their creators' identities by relying on a universal, mythical norm that does not account for difference; and 2) the biases and privileges of the people establishing the paradigms are rarely, if ever, acknowledged or interrogated. In the following paragraphs, I will draw out how a white male point of view dominates common screenwriting paradigms, which yields a mythical norm that leaves many stories unimagined and untellable.

Inherent Bias and the Universal Neutral in Screenwriting

Despite the fact that the most widely read and taught screenwriting tomes are written by white, cis, straight men,[22] the screenplay gurus rarely acknowledge how their gender, race, class, sexuality, lived experience, or point of view influence how they select, interpret, and evaluate films to theorize the paradigmatic patterns they espouse. Likewise, the fact that the successful films from which they've extracted the successful tenets of screenwriting share writers, directors, and stars from a similar demographic remains largely unexamined. Instead, there is an unspoken assumption that the qualities of a "good" and financially successful screenplay are universal and natural. In this way, the critical theorization at the heart of the Producer's Game creates a kind of critical distance that makes the rules seem objective, despite the limited commonalities of the subjectivities doing the theorizing. As Caldwell writes,

> [m]ost screenwriters will say that good screenplays aren't good because they illustrate Aristotle, Egri, or Campbell. Instead, working writers presuppose that Aristotle, Egri, Campbell, and successful contemporary screenwriters recognize and describe properties of narrative that are universal in nature. Theory (with a capital "T") gives way here to the assumption that writers are dealing with a kind of "natural law."[23]

In embracing the belief that the rules of screenwriting are distilled from "natural law," the paradigms operate through the unquestioned assumption of the naturalness of white, male-centric narrative practices as representative of all of humankind. Thus, it is essential to explore how these standard-bearers' identities—and the implicit and explicit commitments shaped by those identities—present themselves and influence the ethos upon which the manuals depend.

To begin at the level of gender, in Robert McKee's *Story: Substance, Structure, Style, and the Principles of Screenwriting*—in both the original printing in the late 90s and its most recent revision in 2006—he opens with a short "Notes on the Text," where he blanketly dismisses all but male pronouns. By way of justification, he explains that he's avoiding distracting constructions "such as the annoying alternation of 'she' and 'her' with 'he' and 'him,' the repetitious 'he and she' and 'him and her,' the awkward 's/he' and 'her/im,' and the ungrammatical 'they' and 'them' as neuter singulars," instead using "the nonexclusive 'he' and 'him' to mean 'writer.'"[24] Though framed as a minor housekeeping issue, in dispensing with the "annoying" task of recognizing gender difference, McKee centers the masculine and unwittingly suggests that men are writers while women (and non-binary "neuters") are not. The implications of this are deep and heavy, influencing the reader's perception of what a writer is in the same way that only seeing doctors, engineers, or world leaders as male on television (and in the world) influences who men, women, and gender non-conforming people think can hold those roles, and those who seek the education and certification to do those jobs. The very real effect of media on perceptions of who the public sees as qualified to hold certain jobs—as evidenced by the number of think pieces in recent U.S. election years on whether we, as a nation, are "ready" for a female president—plays out in every major industry: STEM, medicine, politics. And as we know from even the most cursory review of the history of Hollywood film and television, this tends to play out in much larger percentages of men being hired as screenwriters and, therefore, how men and women are depicted in screenplays.[25]

When it comes to screenplay manuals and the assumptive centering of masculinity, McKee is not the exception but the rule. In *Screenplay: The Foundations of Screenwriting*, Field links the development of his screenwriting principles to his rise from Hollywood tough guy (proudly claiming he inspired characters in *Rebel Without a Cause*) to screenplay guru. Field's privilege placed him in the position to find mentorship from filmmaking legends Jean Renoir (son of another legend, impressionist August Renoir) and Sam Peckinpah, who, in the 70s, modernized the Western, infusing it with his unique brand of rugged individualism and violent masculinity. As Field tells it, Peckinpah's script for *Major Dundee* led to his core insight that writing a good character requires establishing a "strong and defined dramatic need . . . an individual point of view, [and] some kind of change, or transformation."[26] Rooting his paradigm in *Major Dundee*—a film depicting Major Amos Dundee's (Charlton Heston) maniacal quest to avenge an Apache raid by slaughtering Indigenous people—is far from neutral, even as it is abstracted into general principles that posit that the central protagonist must have a "dramatic need" that fuels his racist vengeance. What so often gets lost is that Field's paradigmatic rules for character design originated with a particular film, one saturated with white supremacy, toxic masculinity, stark binary oppositions, and a linear (and genocidal) progress narrative that lays waste to the collective in favor of the individual. Seen in this way, we begin to understand how the presumed neutrality of archetypal abstraction masks particular identities and proclivities.

If one needs additional proof of the pervasiveness of the Producer's Game in Hollywood, Blake Snyder's *Save the Cat! The Last Book on Screenwriting You'll Ever Need* discusses the process directly in the chapter "Give Me the Same Thing . . . Only Different." For Snyder, one of the screenwriter's primary conundrums is "how to avoid cliché"[27] in a way that builds on the tradition of successful, box office hits recognizable to audiences while providing a new twist that makes the traditional story seem new and exciting. Towards this end, he takes the well-trodden path of his predecessor and idol Field and exhorts his audience to listen to master (i.e., male) storytellers like Scorsese and Spielberg while further reinforcing the importance of centering men in his seminal chapter on character, entitled "It's About a Guy Who . . ." He later doubles down on this impulse by renaming common Hollywood genres, coining his own versions with names like "Dude with a Problem" and "Buddy Love," the latter of which is Snyder's way of recalibrating the rom-com so that it doesn't get dismissed as a "Chick Flick" by virtue of centering female characters. Snyder thus erases one of the few genres that can be counted on to at least feature women. Even if those "Chick Flicks" still service heteronormative patriarchy by revolving the female protagonist's life around the pursuit of male mates and/or child-rearing, Snyder still felt it was important to more explicitly center men in the storytelling possibilities available to screenwriters.

In contrast with his peers, Vogler attempts to acknowledge the issue of perspective. In the preface to *The Writer's Journey*, though he claims that an essential humanity beyond gender difference lies at the heart of the hero's journey, he cites feminist criticism of the monomyth as a "masculine theory, cooked up by men to enforce their dominance."[28] He goes on to admit his own bias, stating that as a man he "can't help seeing the world through the filter of my gender."[29] To remedy the masculinist bent of his text, he includes a brief account of how the heroine's journey might differ from the hero's journey by virtue of being more cyclical and internal as opposed to linear and external, advising readers to seek out external texts like *The Heroine's Journey* and *Women Who Run With The Wolves* for alternative theories on the woman's journey. This brief concession, while refreshing in its acknowledgement of gender difference, simultaneously reifies existing stereotypes about femininity and masculinity and, in sending those interested in telling women's stories elsewhere, Vogler absconds responsibility and re-centers his paradigm as authoritative, placing the work of helping female screenwriters on other female writers, a time-tested "go talk to your mother" strategy that dumps the load off oppressors and onto the oppressed. Instead of allowing that the heroine's journey might be an equally viable paradigm, he concludes the preface stating, "I believe that much of the journey is the same for all humans, since we share many realities of birth, growth, and decay,"[30] basically negating anything he'd said previously about the possible value of a feminine version of his masculine-centered advice.

He was so close (on one tiny front), but in order for the center to hold, the center must be held.

From this brief sampling, which represents the general sentiments forming the cemented center of current screenplay orthodoxy, the masculine commitments of the screenplay gurus should be apparent. Though I have focused primarily on gender, in the following paragraphs I will demonstrate how masculinist commitments are connected to and provide support for other dominant normativities, such as whiteness and hetero- and cis-normativity. Further, I will explore how white male bias yields a commitment to universal, neutral norms for screenwriting that obscure how the daily conflicts that white men encounter and overcome are often quite different than the aggressive antagonism and violence faced by marginalized people. In short, I argue that universal story structures neglect structural racism, sexism, heteronormativity, ableism, xenophobia, and more; that they at once allow white, cis men to excel in stories predicated on paradigmatic models, while impeding such possibilities for stories grounded in marginalized perspectives and lives.

As I discussed earlier, through the "self-theorizing" inherent in the Producer's Game, films like *Star Wars*, *The Godfather*, and *Chinatown* became the prototypes for successful films and, thus, popular screenwriting paradigms. By examining this process of abstracting the rules for character and structure from films that follow male protagonists on paradigmatic journeys and claiming that those characters and journeys reflect universal archetypes, we can begin to flesh out how unchecked male bias assumes "the universal man as originary."[31] Whether it's Field claiming that "[a]ll stories . . . embody the same dramatic principles,"[32] McKee stating that "[t]he archetypal story unearths a universally human experience,"[33] or Vogler (parroting Campbell) insisting that "[t]he pattern of the hero's journey is universal, occurring in every culture, in every time,"[34] popular screenwriting paradigms advance what feminists in many disciplines have long critiqued as an abstract universalism that establishes the "founding figure of the human [as] masculine."[35] Masculinity, however, is not the only dominant trait hidden under "universalization of the finite."[36] Audre Lorde expands the concept of the universal human familiar to many white feminist scholars into what she terms the "mythical norm." Defined more expansively to include innumerable dominant identities that hold "the trappings of power" in society, Lorde defines the mythical norm as "white, thin, male, young, heterosexual, Christian, and financially secure."[37] Lorde's mythical norm addresses a larger cultural specter of interlocking identities, and it's not difficult to see that she essentially describes the primary protagonists and creators of most films and television series, as well as the writers of most screenwriting manuals.

In addition to consolidating power through an abstract neutrality, a paradigm that relies on the mythical norm runs the risk of eliding human variety, cultural difference, and historical change in favor of normalization and conformity. Put simply, in disregarding human plurality, we not only erase complexity, but shunt human experience into broad forms. This is not completely lost on the screenwriting gurus. To ward off critiques that screenwriting paradigms are too generic, McKee argues that a universal paradigm is essential because it is a value-free system that can accommodate an infinite variety of characters and stories. He writes, "[t]he archetypal story unearths a universally human experience, then wraps itself inside a unique, cultural-specific expression."[38] For McKee, there is a singular, prototypical human experience that exists outside of culture, and everything else is merely surface decoration. From this perspective, a writer could plug the culturally-specific expression of an Indigenous female character into a hero's journey story just as easily as a white male character with little, if any, alterations to the narrative required. While technically possible, such attempts are assimilationist and destructive in that there is no acknowledgement of how the life experiences or culturally-specific expressions of being female and Indigenous might impact the possibilities for one's narrative trajectory and, more importantly, what it might mean to try to fit all lives into the same, one-size-fits-all mold. For those immersed in a specific culture with a specific history, what McKee considers cultural window dressing is life itself. To render that history and culture inconsequential to fit a mold is a kind of violence via erasure. But that's not all. Writing an Indigenous female character in a hero's journey narrative that requires the hero to go on an adventure, conquer a decisive foe, and return home changed or transformed ignores the traumatic role that the myth of the white, male cowboy hero has had on Indigenous culture as a harbinger of genocide and obliteration. It ignores that a woman's journey might be different than a man's. And, finally, considering that many Indigenous cultures value tribal sovereignty and community over individual sovereignty, it ignores considerations around the role of the individual protagonist in relation to the collective tribe. In short, adherence to universal storytelling paradigms glosses over the need for important questions around how specific characters can be shaped by their environment, history, and culture. It is considerations like these that I will continue to explore in greater detail throughout this book.

Because most screenplay gurus disregard the role that the particularities of gender, sexuality, race, culture, and more play in shaping their perspectives, their paradigms tend to unwittingly perpetuate straightness, whiteness, masculinity, and more by virtue of their positioning as universal. Whether the issue is that of finding "a masculine subject which raises itself to the universal,"[39] unmarked whiteness perpetuating itself through "dailiness,"[40] or the unchallenged acceptance of "compulsive heterosexuality,"[41] what you end up with is a series of masks for maleness as a gender category, whiteness as a racial category, and heteronormativity as the default mode of sexuality and family-making. Put another way, the universal has a normativizing function that dilutes and erases particular identities, including—and perhaps especially—the particular identity of cis, white men. In reducing all ways of life and being into a singular prototype, we foreclose the possibilities for imagining other selves, other subjectivities, or other lives into existence. Instead we have the straight, white male hero who is at home everywhere, making history via narrative.[42] As Cavarero writes:

> And here lies the crux of the problem: I, like every woman, am now writing and thinking in the language of the other, which is simply the language,

nor could I do otherwise. This language, since I happen to be a woman, denies me as a subject, it stands on categories which compromise my self-identification. How, then, can I speak myself through that which, structurally, does not speak me?[43]

Cavarero illuminates the difficulty of narrating a subject *who has not been thought*, who has never been given a language—let alone a narrative paradigm—centered on the lived truth of one's specific, cultural, and socio-historical experience. In short, because the paradigms were created in white men's image, they tell white men's stories. This is true regardless of the race or gender of the characters on screen. Rather than reimagining the classic paradigms to accommodate different stories, audiences and creators with marginalized identities are expected again and again to contort ourselves into a template not designed to account for the paths and shapes our lives take. And as long as the paradigm doesn't change, neither does the world.

Notes

1 Miranda Banks, *The Writers: A History of American Screenwriters and Their Guild* (New Brunswick, NJ: Rutgers University Press, 2016), 7.
2 It's important to note that the term "identity politics" was originated by Black feminists and first articulated in the Combahee River Collective Statement (1977) as a way to capture the distinct lived experiences and needs of Black lesbians in relation to Black men seeking liberation and white feminists, both of whom derive power from Black women's oppression.
3 Kimberlé Crenshaw, "Toward a Race-Conscious Pedagogy in Legal Education," *National Black Law Journal* 11, no. 1 (1988): 3.
4 According to The Sentencing Project, "African Americans are incarcerated in state prisons at a rate that is 5.1 times the imprisonment of whites" and "Latinos are imprisoned at a rate that is 1.4 times the rate of whites." Ashley Nellis and Marcy Mistrett, "The Color of Justice: Racial and Ethnic Disparity in State Prisons," *The Sentencing Project*, January 10, 2019, www.sentencingproject.org/publications/color-of-justice-racial-and-ethnic-disparity-in-state-prisons/, 3.
5 Crenshaw, "Towards a Race Conscious Pedagogy," 6.
6 Kimberlé Crenshaw, "Mapping the Margins: Intersectionality, Identity Politics, and Violence Against Women of Color," *Stanford Law Review* 43, no. 6 (July 1991): 1241–99, https://doi.org/10.2307/1229039, 1244–45.
7 Steven Maras, *Screenwriting: History, Theory and Practice* (London: Wallflower, 2009), 160.
8 Bridget Conor, *Screenwriting: Creative Labor and Professional Practice* (London: Routledge, 2014), https://doi-org.ezproxy.depaul.edu/10.4324/9780203080771, 17.
9 Janet Staiger, "Blueprints for Feature Films: Hollywood's Continuity Scripts," in *The American Film Industry*, ed. Tino Balio (Madison, WI: University of Wisconsin Press, 1985), 189.
10 In a fixed-pitch font each character has the same width regardless of a letters actual width.
11 For more on the complicated and contested history of the screenplay and its cousin the how-to manual, see Conor, *Screenwriting*; Maras, *Screenwriting*; Staiger, "Blueprints for Feature Films."
12 Staiger, "Blueprints for Feature Films," 189.
13 John Thorton Caldwell, *Production Culture: Industrial Reflexivity and Critical Practice in Film and Television* (Durham, NC: Duke University Press, 2008), 5–6.
14 Ibid., 7.

15 Rick Altman, *Film / Genre* (London: BFI Publishing, 1999), 43.

16 Ibid., 44.

17 Kyle VanHemert, "The Secret Sauce Behind Netflix's Hit, 'House Of Cards': Big Data," *Fast Company*, July 9, 2018, www.fastcompany.com/1671893/the-secret-sauce-behind-netflixs-hit-house-of-cards-big-data.

18 Syd Field, *Screenplay: The Foundations of Screenwriting* (New York: Bantam Dell, 2005), 12.

19 Blake Snyder, *Save the Cat! The Last Book on Screenwriting You'll Ever Need* (Studio City, CA: Michael Wiese Productions, 2005), xii–xiii.

20 Ian Parker, "The Real McKee," *The New Yorker*, October 13, 2003, www.newyorker.com/magazine/2003/10/20/the-real-mckee.

21 For more on the effectiveness of the conservative tactics inherent in the Producer's Game, see: Thomas Schatz, "The New Hollywood," in *Film Theory Goes to the Movies*, eds. Jim Collins, Ava Preacher Collins, and Hilary Radner (New York: Routledge, 1992), 8–36.

22 While there are popular screenwriting manuals written by women, such as *The Nutshell Technique: Crack the Secret of Successful Screenwriting* by Jill Chamberlain, *Writing the Drama TV Series* by Pamela Davis, and *Making a Good Script Great* by Linda Seger, they tend to be by white women, have rarely achieved the notoriety of the work of their male counterparts, and tend to rely on the same male-centric paradigms. The primary challenger to these paradigms comes from *The Heroine's Journey* by Maureen Murdock, which is not a widely followed model for screenwriting and suffers from some of the same universalizing tendencies that I will go on to discuss throughout this book.

23 Caldwell, *Production Culture*, 18.

24 Robert McKee, *Story: Substance, Structure, Style, and the Principles of Screenwriting* (New York: Regan Books, 1997), xi.

25 According to the most recent Annenberg report: Of 1,518 individuals working as directors, writers, and producers across the 100 top films, 22.3% of the positions were filled by women. "Inequality in 1,300 Popular Films: Examining Portrayals of Gender, Race/Ethnicity, LGBTQ & Disability from 2007 to 2019." USC Annenberg Inclusion Initiative, 2020, 1–2.

26 Field, *Screenplay*, 63.

27 Blake Snyder, *Save the Cat! The Last Book on Screenwriting You'll Ever Need* (Studio City, CA: Michael Wiese Productions, 2005), 23.

28 Christopher Vogler, *The Writers Journey: Mythic Structure for Writers* (Studio City, CA: Michael Wiese Productions, 2007), xxi.

29 Ibid.

30 Ibid.

31 Adriana Cavarero, "Towards a Theory of Sexual Difference," in *The Lonely Mirror*, eds. Sandra Kemp and Paola Bono (London and New York: Routledge, 1993), 192.

32 Field, *Screenplay*, 3.

33 McKee, *Story*, 4.

34 Vogler, *Writer's Journey*, 10.

35 Butler, *Nonviolence*, 37.

36 Cavarero, "Sexual Difference," 192.

37 Lorde, *Sister Outsider*, 116.

38 McKee, *Story*, 4.

39 Cavarero, "Sexual Difference," 190.

40 Raka Shome, "Race and Popular Cinema: The Rhetorical Strategies of Whiteness in City of Joy," *Communication Quarterly* 44, no. 4 (Fall 1996): 503.

41 Adrienne Rich, "Compulsory Heterosexuality and Lesbian Existence," *Signs* 5, no. 4 (1980): 631.

42 Shome, "Race and Popular Cinema," 514.

43 Cavarero, "Sexual Difference," 194.

2

REIMAGINING CHARACTER

Now that we've examined some of the ways that screenwriting paradigms developed through a system predicated on universal and neutral storytelling principles, it is time to dissect how certain ideological attachments obscured by universalism manifest within the craft of screenwriting. Keeping in mind that the universal operates through a series of abstractions that blur the specifics of particular forms of embodiment while negating and excluding others, we can begin to examine the internal logics of character design, conflict, three-act structure, and world-building, and how those logics maintain the dominance hierarchies central to the status quo.

Character and Agency

One of the central tenets of screenwriting is that at the core of an effective screenplay one finds complex and nuanced characters who are actively trying to change the world or themselves. Even Snyder, whose paradigm is perhaps the least focused on character development, writes, "whenever I hear a screenwriter wind up to pitch his movie idea, somewhere in there I better hear some version of: '*It's about a guy who* . . . .'"[1] At first glance, this statement seems deceptively simple, perhaps even benign. The ellipsis, however, points to one of the primary requirements of a well-defined screenplay character: they must have agency. Agency refers to the character's ability to occupy their subjectivity in a manner that moves the plot through decisions or actions. The "guy" in Snyder's scenario is always already poised to do something. Reactive characters who merely respond to events in the narrative or passive characters who allow the story to happen to them are strongly discouraged, if not outlawed outright. As Lajos Ergi writes, "[y]ou cannot expect a rising conflict from a man who wants nothing or does not know what he wants."[2] In this conception, passivity—a trait often associated with the feminine in film, where women are the objects of the male gaze and/or the catalyst for male

DOI: 10.4324/9781003170310-4

protagonism—is the enemy of the screenwriter. Field captures this explicitly when he writes,

> it's important to remember that when you're writing a screenplay, the main character must be active; *she* must cause things to happen, not let things happen to *her*. It's okay to let *her* react to incidents or events some of the time, but if *she* is always reacting, *she* becomes passive, weak, and that's when the character seems to disappear off the page.[3]

It's notable that Field uses female pronouns in this section when the majority of his examples are male. The shift acknowledges that the world acts on the feminine—whether male or female—and suggests that to be acted upon is to be weak and, therefore, unfit for the role of the central character. Suddenly the ubiquity of the "strong female lead" category on various streaming platforms becomes clear: in order for female or feminized characters to qualify as the central protagonists in a film or series, they can't be ordinary (i.e., passive) women: they must be powerful agents of change like all of the white male protagonists who've preceded them, and with whom, presumably, they're fighting for the audience's attention. This is why many films and series featuring "strong female leads" could just as easily feature men. As screenwriter and actor Brit Marling writes, the "strong female lead" is "an assassin, a spy, a soldier, a superhero, a C.E.O. She can make a wound compress out of a maxi pad while on the lam. She's got MacGyver's resourcefulness but looks better in a tank top."[4]

To be clear, this is not an argument for passive central characters, but rather for an expansion of our understanding of what constitutes agency and a recognition that one's gender, race, sexuality, ability, social position, and more often constrain agency in such a way that it becomes unrecognizable to those with dominant subject positions. In traditional screenwriting, there is essentially nothing that differentiates a strong male from a strong female lead aside from physical appearance, which means that the unique ways that women across a range of intersectional identities seek and exercise power within the confines of patriarchy—often invisibly or in community—are left out of the equation. How, for example, can screenplay paradigms centered on individualistic, self-determined heroes accommodate the stories of women (or men or gender nonconforming folks) who work together in community in what scholars Jean-Anne Sutherland and Kathryn M. Feltey refer to as a "power-with" dynamic, which "hold[s] the promise and potential of communities forming in solidarity and working towards societal change."[5] Working in concert with others is a form of agency that does not fit easily into traditional notions of character design rooted in "hegemonic masculinity," which includes, but is not limited to, overt demonstrations of "physical strength, calculated decision-making, and dominance."[6] If there is not a genius, solitary, break-away thinker or innovator on which to pin the story and the medal of honor, how can you tell the story of the accomplishment? The existence of the "strong female lead" is just one example of how a limited understanding of agency in screenwriting impacts character design. The "power-over" dynamic displayed by "strong" female characters mimics masculinist concepts of subjectivity and agency, creating characters who "carry out his/her will over another" and are characterized by domination as the primary mechanism of empowerment.[7] The assumption of female passivity and male agency, which is directly related to the ways that women have been objectified by the male gaze and rendered objects in film as well as in life, is, thus, built into character design.

The "strong female lead" is not the only assimilative trope predicated on conceptions of agency that privilege the ability to act on one's intrinsic desires to overcome obstacles and/or alter reality. When characters with disabilities—whether cognitive, physical, sensory, or psychological—aren't sidelined, vilified, or left out of narratives altogether, they are often portrayed as "supercrip" characters, who overcome their disability in order to live "normal" lives. As scholar Alison Harnett writes, "the supercrip stereotype depicts a disabled person who, though astounding personal endeavor overcomes their disability—a cripple who learns to walk, a dyslexic person who becomes a writer."[8] In films like *My Left Foot* (1989) or television series like Netflix's *Daredevil* (2015–2018) or ABC's *The Good Doctor* (2014-present), "supercrip" characters betray the able-bodied bias underscoring heroic notions of agency within screenwriting. Each of these characters—whether in the form of the quadriplegic artist who conquers his disability to become a painter, the blind superhero, or the autistic-savant doctor—is made exceptional by overcoming or optimizing their disability to better fit into normative society. The trope of the "supercrip" centers a form of active agency that requires the disabled character to personally triumph over their disability and become an exception to the rule, which problematically assumes that "the ultimate goal of the disabled person is to be cured"[9] rather than to live happy lives as they are. Again, when agency is built on the ability to act on and alter one's circumstances—to perform the ultimate feat of mind over matter—stories about disabled people and/or women or other marginalized people become structurally difficult to organize a narrative around. The result, too often, is erasure or assimilation, neither of which serve those being erased or represented poorly.

Aside from whether the false dichotomy of active agent versus passive victim is a fruitful way to conceive of human capacity (it isn't), it's worth examining what additional assumptions undergird agency in screenwriting and how that influences the types of characters and stories that become possible in film and television. For a character to demonstrate autonomous agency, they must exhibit willfulness in the form of identifiable actions and decisions that steer the course of the narrative. They must "want something badly," have "difficulty getting it,"[10] and, ultimately, persevere. The fact that the object of their desire must be attainable means that their agency is determined, in part, by the ability to achieve their goals. This goes beyond simply not wanting anything or not knowing what one wants, forms of passivity that are routinely cited in screenplay manuals as death knells for the central protagonist. Such a narrow definition of agency limits what counts as agency, which eliminates any decisions, actions, or forms of resistance that don't achieve one's goals, or that are not recognizable to those in power, including those who green-light screenplays or have media buying power as an audience.

One notable implication of such a narrow conception of human agency is that characters who experience oppression are either not suited for central roles or must beat their oppressors in order to be centered in a narrative, perpetuating a false agent/survivor dichotomy. In reality, most people (especially those facing oppression and marginalization) enact innumerable strategies and forms of resistance that may or may not achieve their desired goals and must be undetectable to their oppressors or abusers lest they bring about further violence. Writing within the field of feminist legal studies, where scholars see similar concepts of agency harming women seeking redress within the U.S. legal system for domestic abuse, Martha Mahoney states, "[i]n this concept, agency does not mean acting for oneself under the conditions of oppression; it means being without oppression, either having ended oppression or never having experienced it at all."[11] This brings to mind the New Jersey Superior Court judge who asked a victim of sexual assault on the witness stand—after she described the harm she had been subjected to—whether she attempted to stop the harm by "closing her legs," insinuating that the victim had power over the outcome of the assault.[12] In Wisconsin, a felony rape case was overturned by the Minnesota Supreme Court because the victim had been intoxicated prior to her sexual assault.[13] Apparently by choosing to drink alcohol, she gave up any right to protest what happened to her body in the aftermath, which suggests that sometimes female agency is contingent on the assessments of those in authority. These instances of high judgment about inactive or, presumably, poorly acting victims from the bench aren't antiquated examples from yesteryear; the New Jersey comment happened in 2018; the Wisconsin ruling is from 2021. The legal system continues to judge those who, seemingly, do not act strongly enough to deflect the harmful actions of others, reflecting the attitude of wider culture, which then influences what we expect in our screen stories, where it is deeply ingrained that a strong central character "must cause things to happen, not let things happen to her."[14] The investment in masculine forms of agency that fail to recognize the experiences of non-male or non-power holding characters is deep.

When agency is limited to acting on the story world and, thus, driving the narrative, there is very little room to imagine characters who exhibit alternate forms of agency or willfulness. For people who experience domestic, social, or state violence, sometimes a smile, a prayer, or outright acquiescence might create a path towards survival where an act deemed too willful would get them killed or otherwise harmed. Consider, for example, the large number of women who live with their domestic abusers, who choose to stay and live instead of leaving and being murdered. To stay and to live is, in fact, an active choice, one that impacts and makes possible the continued material reality of their lives, but it is not a decision that is generally recognized as agency, neither within the legal system, nor in our storytelling practices. Because it is not oriented towards dominance or winning, the behavior is deemed passive and, therefore, unfit for attention.

Considered through this lens, it becomes clear why so many movies about domestic abuse and sexual violence feature female protagonists who must avenge their abusers. In films like *Enough* (2002), Jennifer Lopez plays a woman who takes revenge upon her violent and abusive husband after learning a self-defense regimen. Or going further back, I will never forget the animated conversations among the women in my neighborhood generated by the 1984 TV-movie *The Burning Bed*, wherein housewife Francine Hughes (Farah Fawcett) roasted her husband alive after surviving thirteen years of domestic abuse at his hands. Though the neighborhood women's fascination with the story focused on Francine's final straw moment of "empowered" and agential action, I've always been far more curious about the coping mechanisms and strategies she employed to endure thirteen years of ruthless domestic violence. When we hold limited views of how agency manifests for different people in different contexts, however, we eliminate the possibilities for telling vast numbers of stories. Perhaps more importantly, we lose the ability to imagine frameworks that would help us tell stories about characters who engage in what scholar Traci C. West calls "survival resistance work," where "rebellion against multiple forms of subjugation for the purposes of survival" might take the form of silence or acquiescence, or a "bond with a divine or spiritual presence,"[15] among other tactics of survival, while never manifesting in a final climactic battle.

Another example of the "let's get to the action" attitude toward the stories of survivors of abuse is the 2015 film *Room*, written by Emma Donaghue. The film is adapted from Donaghue's novel based on the real-life experience of survivor Elizabeth Fritzl. In the film, we meet the main character Ma (Brie Larson) after she has been kidnapped, repeatedly raped, and held hostage by her captor for years. In that span of time, she has been impregnated and given birth to a child. When we meet her, we see the life she has carved out within the horrors of her captivity, including the way in which she tells her son to occupy himself when their captor enters the room to violate her. Of course, the film *Room* isn't about any of the years prior to this when Ma has been held, assaulted, suspended from life by her captor, slowly and silently constructing her escape plan while literally growing her only ally. Instead, we meet Ma and her son, whom she's carefully and covertly been training for escape, right before that escape. The story, thus, skips the "boring" parts, focusing instead on the fruits of Ma's quiet, intense, years-long labor. Years-long trauma becomes backstory and fuel for the adrenaline-rush of flight and fireworks the audience gets to see on-screen.

In refusing to acknowledge alternative forms of agency—including those that recognize the necessity and power of survival over action—the tenets of character design reinforce white male dominance hierarchies that center masculine experience. An over-reliance on dominance as agency sidelines countless stories and lives. And though I've focused primarily on stories of domestic violence and abuse for my examples, an expansive concept of agency would help us tell stories of undocumented people from a range of countries who worry every day about discovery but evade surveillance without incident for decades; the single Latina who takes twelve years to earn her degree to make a mere four dollars more an hour to support her family, the disabled trans person who lives with substance abuse issues who never gets sober and also never overdoses, the average-sized white American male who gains five new pounds a year and slowly slides into a diabetes diagnosis without considering running a marathon, and others whose stories have never been told because they do not involve definitive "calls to action" or "all is lost moments," but instead the daily choice to put one step in front of the other before collapsing into bed.

Chloé Zhao's Academy Award-winning *Nomadland* (2020) is one example of a film centered around a character who does not seek domination or exercise traditional forms of agency. In the film, Fern (Frances McDormand) travels the country, taking seasonal jobs in remote places throughout the western United States as she grieves her husband and a life lost due to the excesses of capitalism and industrial collapse. There is no "call to action:" Fern is already on the road when the film begins. There is no "all is lost moment:" Fern already lost everything that ever mattered to her. Instead, like her grief, Fern wanders. She makes friends, sells things she doesn't need anymore, gets her van fixed, cooks meals on a tiny portable stove on a make-shift fold-out table in her van, and takes on odd jobs that one day might have her working in an Amazon warehouse scanning consumer goods and another day cleaning outhouses at a national park. Despite the open roads and vast landscapes of the film, Fern is not the active protagonist of so many road movies and Westerns. She does not seek redemption or revenge; she does not seek to change her own, nor anyone else's circumstances; she doesn't even have a map with a big red X marked over a final destination: instead, Fern is a woman content to indulge her own restlessness and grief towards no particular end. Late in the film, Fern is offered two opportunities to leave her precarious nomadic existence behind for a better, more aspirational lifestyle, one of comfort and means. In both cases, she refuses. Fern exercises a quiet agency. She's making a clear choice, but not one aimed towards altering mind, matter, or circumstance. There is no bargaining; no one need bend to Fern's will. Fern's choice: let things continue as they are, as they will. Why should such a quiet film feel so radical? In contrast to more paradigmatic films, where female characters are assimilated into masculinist and attention-worthy frameworks, Zhao provides an alternative to the "strong female lead." Zhao's depiction of Fern seems almost an answer to Marling's frustrations related to trying to find roles for women that capture alternate forms of subjectivity and agency in a system that offers very little to female characters: "I don't want to be the dead girl, or Dave's wife. But I don't want to be a strong female lead either, if my power is defined largely by violence and domination, conquest and colonization."[16]

Character vs. Characterization

In addition to reductive ideas of agency, the primary definition of character is conceptually bound by a binaristic distinction between character and characterization that positions character as superior to characterization. In film and television, a character is someone who "wants something badly and is having difficulty getting it."[17] Character is conceived as the end result of the tension between external wants and unresolved internal needs, and a character only comes alive on the page through the visible actions, reactions, and "creative choices" they make as they stumble through the obstacles placed in their path via the forces of antagonism.[18] Characterization, on the other hand, is defined as "the sum of all observable qualities of a human being, everything knowable through careful scrutiny: age and IQ; sex and sexuality; style of speech and gesture; choices of home, car, and dress; education and occupation."[19] Embedded in this dualism is a belief that a character's true essence emerges when put under pressure (an issue I will explore in greater depth in the following chapter on conflict) and that one's essence is neither related to the context of their lives nor intersections of their identity. Often this means that a character's essence boils down to abstract virtues or vices, such as courage or cowardice as opposed to specific aspects of one's history or identity and how those might shape the way a character experiences the pressures of living or the pressures of a particular situation within a particular context.

In a lengthy illustration of the difference between character and characterization from McKee, he describes a hypothetical film scenario in which an "illegal alien" who is a housekeeper and a white man who is a neurosurgeon happen upon a terrible school bus accident and rescue some children trapped inside. For McKee, these characters represent complete opposites in terms of characterization, but are identical in terms of character. Though they are "[t]wo people who have utterly different backgrounds, beliefs, personalities, languages," they demonstrate "an identical humanity" because they choose courage over self-interest.[20] Essentially, both are courageous heroes underneath their "observable qualities." Though the domestic worker and the neurosurgeon make the same choice in this hypothetical scenario, equating their essential humanity based on that choice is simplistic and highly questionable. The white male doctor, while putting himself at risk, is doing a job he's been trained for, whereas the domestic worker potentially has had no such training and—because of her status as an undocumented person—has far more to lose.[21] Thus, her ability to acquire hero status should not be based on how she behaves in this situation and is in no way comparable to the way the doctor behaves.

Let's make a quick list of what is at stake for each of these theoretical characters if they stop and help the hypothetical trapped children. For the doctor, he may lose a few minutes of his time, but ultimately he only stands to gain gratitude and admiration for attempting the heroic act of saving the children, even if he is unable to do so. While he could be injured and lose his livelihood, he is, presumably, trained to help the children, at least in terms of addressing their medical conditions, and because of his education and experience, he is ascribed a high level of trustability and respect. Again, if the children don't survive, few will question whether that is the fault of the doctor. The domestic worker, on the other hand, has much to lose, and those losses could be compounded based on her race and gender. She could lose her job for being late without an acceptable excuse. If she is questioned as a witness once emergency vehicles arrive, she could lose her ability to stay in the country, especially if she's not white or proficient in English. If she has children, she could lose them if she is deported. She could face imprisonment and legal bills as a result of her court case. She could also face intense scrutiny for trying to assist the children in ways that she is not trained to do. Rather than being seen as a good samaritan, she could be accused of causing more harm or even death. Further, if she's Filipina, Afro-Latina, or Haitian, for example, in addition to the perils afforded her due to her immigration status, she could also be told to "go back to her country" or endure a range of other racially and ethnically motivated abuses. Additionally, should the police be called, the domestic worker may experience a particular type of anxiety, as women—especially those who are undocumented and/or of color—are particularly vulnerable to sexual harassment and abuses by law enforcement in the United States, with certain officers preying on women who they know cannot report them without encountering other consequences; thus, she may want to stay away from contact with all law enforcement and first responders for her own personal safety. And on top of it all, because, presumably, she is not trained in medicine or emergency actions and does not have the self-care protocols of first responders, she would face her own personal trauma in the aftermath of the accident, especially if she is unable to save the trapped children. Because her agency is constrained, even if this woman "wins," she could lose. The doctor is in no such danger.

At the end of the day, heroism—if it exists at all—is relative to one's circumstances and privileges. It is not an inherent trait waiting for the right incident to reveal itself, as implied by McKee. Taking into account the domestic worker's circumstances, might the story not be more reflective of the difficult life choices inherent in the lives of those who are undocumented if she opts instead to make an anonymous call for help instead of martyring herself to play the role of the white male hero (a.k.a. "the strong female lead") in a Hollywood blockbuster? While according to traditional screenwriting norms such a move might be considered too passive, the domestic worker is simply exercising her agency in a less obtrusive manner than the doctor. In this way, we can see that attending to characterization is another way to draw out complex expressions of agency.

In not only separating character and characterization, but in placing more value on character, the screenwriting gurus return us once again to the false notion of a universal human who embodies universally recognized forms of heroic agency, while eliminating differences in history and identity as key factors that inform a person's ability to make choices under pressure within particular contexts. Having a speech impediment, being old, being queer, being Asian-American, being undocumented, or a whole host of other "observable qualities" inarguably shape how one moves in the world and how the world reacts in turn. In adhering to the idea of the universal human as a template for character, what is lost is an understanding that "[w]hat bodies 'tend to do' are effects of histories rather than being originary."[22] There simply is no such thing as a universal human prototype. As such, the reduction of character to a fundamental essential quality is a simplistic formulation of subjectivity that fails to acknowledge that we contain multitudes. Not only that, but there is no recognition that who we are in any given moment is dependent on the context we're currently in, as well as our unique histories and relationships, a topic I will explore more deeply in Chapter 5.

Though screenwriting manuals don't consider history or context essential to uncovering a character's essence, screenwriters are encouraged to heed characterization by writing detailed character biographies. These biographies are considered part of the character's interior life-world and serve to inform the character's actions while potentially remaining unknown to the audience.

> The *interior* life of your character takes place from birth up until the time your story begins. It is a process that *forms* character. The *exterior* life of your character takes place from the moment your film begins to the conclusion of the story. It is a process that *reveals* character.[23]

The biography is thus necessary to establish characterization and create an internal roadmap that might influence a character's outward behavior in terms of key decisions, actions, and reversals without overshadowing their essence. Toward this end, prompts like "is your character male or female," "is your character married, widowed, single, separated, divorced," and "[e]xamine his/her career, relationships, dreams, hopes, and aspirations"[24] guide the screenwriter in creating a legible and coherent backstory for their character. Grounded in linear chronologies of education, career, and marriage, or rigid gender binaries and biological family lineages, these prompts seem to actively court heteronormative and ableist assumptions in ways that uncritically emphasize normative modes of being and perpetuate what queer and feminist theorists refer to as the straight line of normative time.

Building a character who adheres to normative (i.e., straight, white, ableist) time supports capitalist, colonial, and patriarchal logics by way of emphasizing birth, gendered existence, maturing in accordance to one's assigned sex at birth, heterosexual mating rituals, reproduction, work, and inheritance,[25] as well as a "curative imaginary" that refuses to recognize life narratives not "deployed in the service of compulsory able-bodiedness and able-mindedness."[26] Left untroubled, writing prompts that revolve around these normative schedules seem natural and inevitable: as if one's life trajectory from birth to death operates according to natural laws like gravity or entropy. But all lives don't follow the same schedule, sometimes on account of cultural differences and histories, other times due to sickness and/or disability, and other times on account of the antagonisms wrought on non-normative bodies by normative systems. Thus, when faced with questions about a character's backstory, it's essential to remember that because all lives don't follow the same normative schedules, all characters' lives can't either. This is yet another way that characterization matters.

To illustrate how normative questions can be problematic, as well as how sidelining characterization denies important differences in lived experience, let's examine the assumptions inherent in biographical lines of questioning that ask for a coherent, chronological, and gendered trajectory from birth through death. Queer and trans theory challenge development narratives by questioning whether the achievement of maturity arrives with adult masculine or feminine "biological" gender, critiquing linear constructions that link subjectivity to a coherent connection between time and memory, and privileging fragmented and non-linear narratives that more accurately account for how gender and maturation might be lived, felt, and experienced across a range of gender identities and sexualities. Trans theory, in particular, is invested in expressing the open, variable, and expansive possibilities of trans-ness—in terms of embodiment, sensation, and ways of knowing—as a way to move beyond the normative effects of naming and classifying, which tend to collapse the complexity of life into precise definitions, medical pronouncements, and fixity in time/space.[27] As such, amongst other things, queer and trans temporality rejects cis-normative constructions of medicalized, trans histories that adhere to linear transitions from one gender to another because they preserve gender binaries and developmental notions of progress.

In "Revisitation: A Trans Phenomenology of the Media Image," scholar Cáel Keegan dissects how the gender dysphoria common to trans people creates altered internal histories, ones that don't jibe with normative straight time, nor normative modes of subjectivity. As a child in the 80s, the "Milk: It Does a Body Good" campaign transfixed him in a way that he didn't understand until he transitioned. In the ad, a young boy laments his scrawny body in a mirror, only to be reassured by the image of his future muscular, masculine self (made possible by milk). For Keegan, while this media text perpetuates normative constructions of masculinity, it unintentionally hailed his transgender self by calling attention to his obsession with mirrors and the dysphoric self-image that fed that obsession. In revisiting the text as an adult, he realized that "I now occupy both sides of the encounter, reaching across the distance of time to my younger self, insisting that becoming a certain type of man is, in fact, possible" and that "traversing this impossible leap between points, this circuit within myself, I never fully leave behind the dysphoric child, never fully arrive as the hegemonic ideal."[28] What Keegan describes is not a linear progression of development based on a chronology of gender. Instead it suggests an asynchronously gendered life narrative, marked by a rupture between past and present, one that yields a split subjectivity that exists in a sort of " 'pleated time' that mimics the folded-back temporality of gender transition, in which memory is experienced across differentially gendered versions of the self."[29] Cis white men may seamlessly occupy linear progress narratives where they triumph over adversity while maintaining a coherent sense of self and history, but for those on the margins, fragmentation and multiplicity are more common. To be clear, these are not just issues for queer and trans people: such multiplicity is common for those who survive by code-switching, those who thrive only when passing, and those who live within decolonial and Indigenous frameworks. Thus, if screenwriting is to make room for equitable and inclusive representation, instead of devaluing characterization and replicating normative chronologies and life histories, a conscious effort must be made to enable the creation of characters through non-dominant framings and alternative temporalities and subjectivities such that something like "[q]ueerness's ecstatic and horizontal temporality," which allows for more fluid subjectivity, could be used as "a path and a movement to a greater openness to the world."[30] Ultimately, when characterization is considered secondary to character, our media fails to reflect the wide range of ways one experiences self, which lends those with dominant subjectivities recognition and respect while marginalizing people who feel, sense, and think differently.

Short of creating new sets of questions that open up space to effectively characterize non-normative lives, it is also possible to eschew such exercises altogether, as French filmmaker Céline Sciamma suggests in a 2019 BAFTA screenwriting lecture titled "Ready for the Rising Tide." Sciamma claims that when writing a screenplay she doesn't think about her characters outside of the timeline and context of the scenes. She says, "I don't think about back-stories for them, I don't even give them surnames. When I'm asked about the future of my characters, I honestly answer that they don't exist."[31] While this may seem like some surly French posturing, it's worth noting that her film *Portrait of a Lady on Fire* won best screenplay at Cannes and, along with *Parasite*, was one of the most critically-acclaimed international releases of 2019. On the surface, Sciamma appears to be rejecting the way that screenwriting manuals conflate characters with real people, a tactic that harkens back to the New Critics of the 1920s, who "insisted that characters are textual constructs, and that no more can be known about them than what the text provides."[32] I argue, however, that Sciamma is doing something more radical. She rebukes traditional screenplay methodology precisely for the reasons I've outlined above: she writes about characters on the margins, those whose freedom, subjectivity, and agency are curtailed by and erased from the status quo. In her words, because women have been "objectified by fiction and by the patriarchal lore throughout history," in order to give them back their subjectivity, she allows them to exist only within the space of the narrative and world she creates. In the case of *Portrait of a Lady on Fire*, a film I will return to in subsequent chapters, the narrative space excluded heterosexist patriarchal characters for the majority of the film. In this way, Sciamma was able to give her main characters "back their desires,"[33] and agency, which, in turn, gave the audience access to the burgeoning of their unique subjectivity and consciousness.

Thought Exercises

1 What are some aspects of your own subjectivity, lived experience, consciousness, and/or expressions of agency that you've never encountered on screen? How might expressing those in a screenplay impact character design?

2 What might agency look like for a character who is not capable of and/or interested in dominance? How, specifically, do they enact their will? And how can you communicate that to a reader or audience?

3 How do your protagonist's unique intersections of identity impact plot, story, and narrative momentum? How does your character's identity impact their attitudes and behaviors towards self, friends, family, school, work, politics, history, time, place, etc.? Are there any particular aspects of identity that your character is invested in hiding or capitalizing on? In what contexts does this occur? How aware is your protagonist of the impact of their identity on their social interactions, and what are the implications?

Notes

1 Blake Snyder, *Save the Cat! The Last Book on Screenwriting You'll Ever Need* (Studio City, CA: Michael Wiese Productions, 2005), 47, italics in original.
2 Lajos Ergi, *The Art of Dramatic Writing* (Rockville, MD: Wildside Press, 1946), 136.
3 Syd Field, *Screenplay: The Foundations of Screenwriting* (New York: Bantam Dell, 2005), 69, emphasis added.
4 Brit Marling, "I Don't Want to Be the Strong Female Lead," *The New York Times*, February 7, 2020, www.nytimes.com/2020/02/07/opinion/sunday/brit-marling-women-movies.html.
5 Jean-Anne Sutherland and Kathryn M. Feltey, "Here's Looking at Her: An Intersectional Analysis of Women, Power and Feminism in Film," *Journal of Gender Studies* 26, no. 6 (2017): 618–31, 627.
6 Ibid., 623.
7 Ibid., 619.
8 Alison Hartnett, "Escaping the 'Evil Avenger' and the 'Supercrip': Images of Disability in Popular Television," *The Irish Communications Review* 8 (2000): 22.
9 Ibid.
10 David Howard and Edward Mabley, *The Tools of Screenwriting: A Writer's Guide to the Craft and Elements of a Screenplay* (New York: St. Martin's Press, 1996), xii.
11 qtd in: Traci C. West, *Wounds of the Spirit: Black Women, Violence, and Resistance Ethics* (New York: New York University Press, 1999), 161.
12 Taylor Romine and Evan Simko-Bednarski, "Judge in Rape Case Removed After Asking Accuser If She 'Closed Her Legs'," *CNN (Cable News Network)*, May 28, 2020, www.cnn.com/2020/05/28/us/nj-judge-removed-assault-trnd/index.html.
13 Konstantin Toropin and Hollie Silverman, "Minnesota Supreme Court Overturns a Felony Rape Conviction Because the Woman Voluntarily Got Intoxicated," *CNN (Cable News Network)*, March 31, 2021, www.cnn.com/2021/03/30/us/minnesota-rape-conviction-overturned/index.html.
14 Field, *Screenplay*, 69.
15 West, *Wounds*, 165.
16 Marling, "Strong Female Lead."
17 Howard and Mabley, *Tools of Screenwriting*, xii.
18 Field, *Screenplay*, 55.
19 Robert McKee, *Story: Substance, Structure, Style, and the Principles of Screenwriting* (New York: Regan Books, 1997), 100.
20 Ibid.
21 It's important to note that we cannot make the assumption that the domestic worker is not trained in medicine or emergency actions; many undocumented people outside of their home countries are highly trained individuals unable to work in their chosen profession.
22 Sara Ahmed, *Queer Phenomenology: Orientations, Objects, Others* (Durham, NC: Duke University Press, 2007), 56.
23 Field, *Screenplay*, 48 (emphasis added).
24 Ibid., 49–50.
25 Judith Halberstam, *In a Queer Time and Place: Transgender Bodies, Subcultural Lives* (New York: New York University Press, 2005), 5.
26 Alison Kafer, *Feminist, Queer, Crip* (Bloomington, IN: Indiana University Press, 2013), 27.
27 Jack Halberstam, *Trans*: A Quick and Quirky Account of Gender Variability* (Berkeley: University of California Press, 2018), 4–5: Cáel M. Keegan, *Lana and Lilly Wachowski* (Champaign, IL: University of Illinois Press, 2018), 5.
28 Cáel M. Keegan, "Revisitation: A Trans Phenomenology of the Media Image," *MedieKultur: Journal of Media and Communication Research* 32, no. 61 (2016): 34.
29 Keegan, *Lana and Lilly Wachowski*, 15.
30 Muñoz, *Cruising Utopia*, 25.

31 Céline Sciamma, "Ready for the Rising Tide," *BAFTA Screenwriters' Lecture Series*, February 4, 2020, www.bafta.org/media-centre/transcripts/screenwriters-lecture-series-2019-celine-sciamma.

32 Steven Price, "Character in the Screenplay Text," in *Analysing the Screenplay*, ed. Jill Nelmes (London: Routledge, 2011): 201–16, 202.

33 Sciamma, "Ready for the Rising Tide."

3

RETHINKING THE ROLE OF CONFLICT

Conflict and Character

Conflict, or the friction between opposing forces, serves two primary structural functions for the screenwriter: it defines the protagonist's singular essence, and it organizes and powers the narrative. Though there are arguments to be made regarding how using conflict as a narrative mechanism fosters a hostile and "predatory worldview"[1]—some of which I will elaborate on here—I want to shift the focus to the structural goals of conflict and their implications. By examining the structural function of conflict, we're better positioned to imagine other practices, or other engines, that might achieve similar ends in terms of establishing—and perhaps even complicating—character and generating narrative movement, thus expanding the toolbox available to screenwriters who'd like to write stories that expand the possibilities for what constitutes a screen story.

Conflict and character are intimately connected and mutually constitutive. As Field writes, "[a]ll drama is conflict. Without conflict, you have no action; without action, you have no character; without character, you have no story; and without story, you have no screenplay."[2] In this formulation, conflict and character are connected via action to reveal the story—defined as the character's inner journey—which is linked to the larger thematic concerns of a film. Conflict, then, is a tool that catalyzes a character's essence, which reinforces the character/characterization binary explored in the previous chapter. The process works as follows: 1) the screenwriter imagines and catalogues the character's physical characteristics, identity, backstory, and unique flaws; 2) the screenwriter establishes what the character wants via an external goal; 3) the screenwriter establishes what the character needs via an internal lack; and 4) the screenwriter invents a series of obstacles designed to prevent the character from fulfilling the external goal, which leads to a climactic battle that draws out the inner need and thus the true

DOI: 10.4324/9781003170310-5

self hidden beneath the "observable qualities" established in step one. Through this process, conflict serves as a sculpting device, chipping away at the outer layers of a character to reveal something akin to Michelangelo's *David* (sculpture's equivalent of Lorde's "mythical norm"), but for the psyche. Put another way, the external goal is a ruse exposed via the conflict. While that goal may guide the plot and reveal some surface truths about a character's values or interests, it does not hold the deeper story. Apprehending the inner journey happens as conflict—the screenwriter's pointed chisel—whittles away the surface of various aspects of characterization until we reach the essence, and this process establishes the inner journey or character arc. For this to be effective, however, some characters and conflicts are more suitable than others. According to this model, the most compelling narratives center protagonists who "offer the most conflict" and "have the longest way to go emotionally."[3] And while that could describe any number of human subjects, the relationship between character and conflict tends to favor characters who most closely align with the popularly thrust-forth universal human prototype. And ultimately, in an industry that strives for escapism and fantasy at the expense of social responsibility, the universal human prototype avoids certain forms of social conflict in favor of what's deemed more "essential" questions.

In order for a character to "offer the most conflict," they must be flawed and/or reluctant to change. Shortcomings in hand, the screenwriter is encouraged to pit the protagonist against a powerful antagonist and/or side characters that push them away from their primary goal while exposing their weaknesses. Again, the protagonist is defined and clarified through the forces of conflict. As Howard instructs,

> [a]n internal conflict in a story with an outside antagonist helps make the protagonist a more complex and interesting human being. An external source of conflict in a story where the main conflict is essentially internal helps make the two sides of the character visible, palpable; it gives them "lives of their own."[4]

McKee takes this notion of conflict as essence-defining even further, arguing that a "protagonist and his story can only be as intellectually fascinating and emotionally compelling as the forces of antagonism make them."[5] Like Snyder and Field, McKee doesn't only see conflict as central to the sculpting of character and story, but argues that it is this process of paring a character down to their essence that makes a screen story engaging. McKee contends that his theory of antagonism is corroborated by the fact that humans are fundamentally "conservative," by which he means something akin to passive. He claims that people always choose the "easy way," unless pressed to do otherwise. Therefore, to create fully realized characters the screenwriter is encouraged to enhance the "negative side of the story"[6]—the forces in opposition to the protagonist.

There are several issues with this line of thinking. For one, the claim that humans are fundamentally apathetic and need conflict in order to act or find meaning in their lives comes from a position of privilege, one that has rarely, if ever, had to contend with the ever-present specters of racism, sexism, ableism, and a wide range of antagonisms that plague the day-to-day lives of marginalized people. Of course, if characters are modeled on cis, straight, white males, manufacturing conflict follows a certain logic, in that a manufactured conflict designed to bring out their inner hero most likely won't compete with other forms of social violence faced by characters with marginalized identities. Through this logic, however, only certain kinds of characters will ever qualify as compelling or, rather, only certain kinds of characters will fit this generic mold. If a compelling character has the longest journey to travel, and that journey is defined by a set of obstacles designed to strip them of their external characteristics so they can become their true selves, we begin to see that it is very difficult for characters who are not cis, straight, white, and/or male to occupy the center of a narrative, or if they do, why they must emulate the universal neutral prototype. Because one's gender, sexuality, and/or race is not a personal shortcoming that can be done away with—without, of course, destroying the person entirely—if the primary conflict is related to a character's identity, the screenwriter can't use the conflict to strip them of that aspect of identity to reveal a generic and universally neutral essence underneath. Nor can they eliminate the surrounding culture that punishes them for possessing it. What we're left with is a dearth of options for characters on the margins and the kinds of conflicts they can be faced with inside of a screen story. Instead of finding ways to tell stories where marginalized characters encounter the social antagonisms reminiscent of our daily lives in addition to other non-identitarian conflicts, too often identity is sidelined and doesn't impact the narrative at all. This sort of storytelling is akin to race and gender-neutral casting, which white-washes, masculinizes, and otherwise assimilates characters with marginalized identities to be more in line with the default prototype. Because characters cannot ultimately directly address or change the ills of society, our stories ignore the problems of society entirely. Put simply, screenwriting paradigms encourage screenwriters to take the easy way out.

Not all stories featuring marginalized protagonists must focus on conflicts based on race, gender, ability, sexuality, and more. But when screenwriters do want to tell those stories, some rethinking is in order. First, the dictum that a conflict requires a resolution must be reconsidered, as none of the primary social antagonisms (racism, sexism, heteronormativity, ableism, and more) have been solved or are on the verge of being solved. This presents a problem for the screenwriter. As Howard writes, "the obstacle should not be so overwhelming that the protagonist has no chance of overcoming it. In other words, the objective must be possible, but very difficult, to accomplish."[7] Insisting that the central conflict be redressable forecloses the possibility for many types of stories. For example, in questioning whether or not Hollywood storytelling practices are capable of telling the stories of Black people in the United States, Afropessimist scholar Frank Wilderson argues that essentially they cannot on account of an important distinction between conflict and antagonism. Wilderson defines conflict as "a rubric of problems that can be posed and conceptually solved" and antagonism as "an irreconcilable struggle between entities, or positions, the resolution of which is not dialectical, but entails the obliteration of one of the positions."[8] This distinction between conflict and antagonism—one that is not made within traditional screenplay paradigms—draws into sharp relief the ways that for some, a conflict is something that can be faced and overcome, while for others there are antagonisms that seek the subject's total annihilation.[9] This is a conundrum for screenwriting pedagogy, as any force of antagonism that is too overwhelming is deemed unsuitable for a screenplay.

In consideration of Wilderson's distinction, while white supremacy, white writers (including the son of the protagonist), and a white director are certainly enough of an explanatory factor for white savior films like *Green Book* (2018), centering white people as the protagonists in films that explicitly try (and fail) to contend with racism also aligns with screenwriting paradigms that insist that the protagonist begin the narrative in a flawed and/or unaware state to then be reshaped by the conflict into a better, more enlightened version of themselves. Thus, a white character like Frank "Tony Lip" Vallelonga (Viggo Mortensen) in *Green Book* can begin the film as a curmudgeonly racist and end the film as a slightly less curmudgeonly racist due to his relationship with and '"protection" of world-class pianist, Dr. Don Shirley (Mahershala Ali). Further, because the conflict must be solvable, and racism has yet to find a solution, centering "a white character who saves a person of color from their troubles, troubles that the person of color can't save themselves from,"[10] fits the rules of screenwriting more seamlessly than centering a Black protagonist. When viewing screenwriting practices through the lens of social antagonism, we can see how screenwriting norms—with their demand for solvable conflict—foreclose the possibilities for certain stories. This isn't to say that one couldn't devise a screenplay—even a heroic one—about a queer Black pianist traveling around the country at the height of segregation, only that the rules around what a conflict must do to a character and the imminent solvability of that conflict leads the screenwriter's imagination in a different direction.

Further, while for Wilderson the distinction between conflict and antagonism is primarily relevant for thinking about stories featuring Black characters, it's not difficult to see how the insistence on conflict resolution prevents many stories that deal with social violence from being thought or developed adequately within screenplay paradigms. Discerning the difference between conflict and antagonism, it becomes clear why there are so many (of the so few) LGBTQ films focused on gay conversion therapy, as that is precisely the kind of narrative that lends itself to screenwriting paradigms where character and conflict are mutually constitutive. Even if the gay character survives, queerness intact, as in films like *But I'm a Cheerleader* (1999) and *The Miseducation of Cameron Post* (2018), conceptually the films follow traditional screenwriting norms in that because the protagonist is deemed insufficient by society due to their homosexuality, they are then sent to a camp where white Christians try to strip them of their queer attributes (because those are merely "observable qualities" after all and not at all foundational to one's sense of self and relationship to the world), all of which culminate in a final battle with the homophobic forces, where the true inner gay wins the day by avoiding obliteration.

This is a minor adjustment to paradigmatic requirements that insist that conflict reveal essence. In a simple reversal, these films argue that homosexuality, though initially deemed a surface defect by heteronormative culture, is, in fact, essence. As such, another path to homonormativity—or the alignment of LGBTQ lives with heteronormative values—is laid bare.[11] In striking contrast to the ecstatic, fluid, and often defiant possibility of queerness as liberation from prescriptive notions of gender, sexuality, and subjectivity, the protagonist assimilates the contradictions and boundary-crossing aspects of their queer subjectivity for a heteronormative one that holds singular essence over multifacetedness.

At the same time that screenplay manuals ignore the complexities of the various antagonisms built into the dominant culture, they fetishize conflict by suggesting that one's true character can only be found in hostile confrontation rather than moments of idleness, equilibrium, healing, pleasure, or many other states of being. Aside from the problem of reducing a person to a particular virtue, vice, or essential essence, this reeks of the Protestant work ethic and the way that "many 19th century Christians saw all forms of idle activity as evil, or at least a breeding ground for wrong-doing."[12] In much the same way that character ranks higher than characterization, conflict is prized over peace, which ignores the generative possibilities found in moments of solitude, contemplation, reverie, and other less obviously dramatic moments that are also valuable and formative. According to most screenwriting methodology, however, such moments do not contain enough visible action, which results in the injunction that action is exciting and passivity is boring. And yet, don't we miss so much of life—and thus the possibilities for dramatizing it—if we reject its less sensational moments? And if we're artists, shouldn't it be possible to render the "boring" moments of equilibrium or pleasure or idleness in ways that are engaging and provocative instead of eliminating them as narrative fluff? If we look to filmmakers outside the studio system, answers in the affirmative are more the norm. Chilean filmmaker Raúl Ruiz, for example, rejects Hollywood's reliance on what he calls "central conflict theory" because it reduces the possibilities for storytelling by expelling narrative excess. For Ruiz, when screenwriters learn that screenplays are like suspension bridges "with one end anchored in what the protagonist wants, and the other end anchored in the disclosure of whether or not he gets it,"[13] character-building ends up revolving entirely around conflict, which yields linear causal narratives that pit protagonist against antagonist in a series of battles that emphasize the role of dominance, violence, and ambition as the root of human existence. In contrast, Ruiz sees the "boring" moments as rife with life and possibility. Such moments offer opportunities for other kinds of character-building. Thus, when we eliminate them in favor of conflict and hostility, we lose opportunities for full artistic expression, and instead normalize a patriarchal and "predatory worldview."[14]

Conflict as Narrative Engine

In fixating on conflict as the primary mechanism for a character's development, conflict works to organize and power the narrative. As a general rule, conflict is "the very engine that propels a story forward; it provides the story's energy and movement."[15] Born out of an ever-present worry about stasis, boredom, and disorder, screenwriting orthodoxy argues that establishing conflict in the beginning and resolving it by the end gives the story a clear purpose and through-line that cohere and engage via steadily increasing tension. Because of this, screenwriters are cautioned against giving their characters what they want or, worse, allowing them to want nothing, lest the film lack tension. For without establishing what the protagonist wants, "there is no conflict," and the film "sags into a shapeless and ineffective mess."[16] Thus, scenes that lack conflict are few and far between in screenplays for fear that they don't sufficiently propel the narrative forward, which is presumed to create a droopy, lifeless arc that fails to cohere in the same way that a tight, conflict-oriented, and linear journey does. Screenwriters are therefore encouraged to employ a causal, problem-solution oriented logic fueled by conflict and its accompanying tension as a way to thrust a story forward towards the final climax and resolution. This is most frequently discussed in reference to the second act, which is the vehicle for the bulk of a film's conflict and rising tension, allowing the audience to engage in a process whereby they teeter between hope for a positive outcome and fear of a negative one.

In order to maintain narrative momentum, obstacles must increase in frequency and intensity. As Snyder writes,

> [t]he plot doesn't just move ahead, it spins and intensifies as it goes. It is the difference between velocity (a constant speed) and acceleration (an increasing speed). And the rule is: It's not enough for the plot to go forward, it must go forward faster, and with more complexity, to the climax.[17]

In this vein, a frequent refrain given to aspiring screenwriters is that they must "raise the stakes," which roughly translates to tormenting their protagonist or "making their lives hell," purportedly increasing tension and engagement, all in preparation for the final battle where the audience will finally get the big "pay-off." This fixation on conflict and tension is primarily about maintaining the audience's interest, as "[w]ithout conflict, there is no drama, and without drama, there is no interest in the reader. Conflict is crucial in maintaining the reader's interest in the story and in the characters."[18] Once again, this places an incredible onus on the work conflict must do. In addition to defining character, the rules of screenwriting presume that out of the myriad phenomena that occur within human society, only conflict and its resolution are capable of generating tension and sustained interest. One must wonder why we think so little of our audiences, that we must pull out firework after firework to keep them engaged.

This brings us to some important—and I hope generative—questions: what might happen if we released ourselves from our fixation on conflict as the sole driver of narrative storytelling? More pointedly, what other mechanisms might play the role of revealing character, and perhaps even a character's complexity and multiplicity instead of their "essence," while simultaneously powering the narrative engine? What might a narrative organized through a rubric of healing, desire, friendship, or pleasure look like? What might happen if we shifted our framework based on the identity of the character at the center of the narrative? And if opposition is to remain one of the building blocks of narrative, what new stories could be told if we simply expanded our ideas of what opposition looks like and how opposition is experienced by different people in different contexts? After all, I'm not arguing for a singular paradigm to replace the current paradigm; I'm arguing for a liberatory and intersectional approach to storytelling that honors the uniqueness of myriad and multi-faceted lives.

Céline Sciamma suggests one such a path towards decentering conflict, explaining that at the core of her screenwriting process is desire, both her own desire and that of her characters. To be clear, when Sciamma speaks about desire, she is not referring to the want related to an external goal, nor the need related to the internal journey at the center of screenwriting practices. Rather, Sciamma's focus on desire is akin to Audre Lorde's theorization of the erotic as a force "rooted in the power of unexpressed or unrecognized feeling."[19] In writing *Portrait of a Lady on Fire*—a film that depicts a brief love affair between a female painter and her female muse in the early nineteenth century—Sciamma refuses conflict in favor of "radical equality." To accomplish this, she set most of the film on a secluded island where the lovers live only amongst themselves and a female maid. In this way, Sciamma eliminates the pervasive pressures of patriarchy and heteronormativity, as they would be waiting for the lovers once they leave the island and return to society. Free from outside antagonism, the film focuses on the development of their relationship, on the ways the women recognize and act on their desires. They encounter no obstacles to their love affair, only the burgeoning of desire. Some of the most riveting scenes in the film are completely quotidian, such as a short scene where the muse cooks, the maid embroiders, and the painter serves wine. Even the social hierarchy is eliminated as the maid acts as artist and the women she ordinarily waits on act as servants. Contrary to the proclamations of the screenwriting paradigms, the scene is not boring, but rather crackling with possibility. Here Sciamma is worth quoting at length:

> Lack of conflict doesn't mean lack of tension; lack of conflict doesn't mean lack of eroticism; lack of conflict actually means new rhythm because of a dialogue not built on bargaining. Lack of conflict actually means new power dynamics that allow new surprises and suspense. That's what is at stake in a story with equality, actually. Equality brings unconventional power dynamics to the screen. So basically as a viewer you don't know what is going to happen, which is the base of being both entertained and committed to a story.[20]

There's no question that Sciamma understands the structural function of conflict in traditional narratives. This is why her intentional choice to center desire and equality as the primary interest-generating engine of the film, instead of conflict, is radical and notable. Her divergence from screenplay norms resulted in indisputable critical success, proving that audience curiosity and engagement can be piqued by something other than opposition, confrontation, or destruction.

Likewise, in two other queer films, *Carol* (Todd Haynes, 2015) and *Moonlight* (Barry Jenkins, 2016), a similar structural upheaval occurs. During the second act (the container for the bulk of a film's conflict within classical models of storytelling) of the film *Carol*, would-be lovers Carol (Cate Blanchett) and Therese (Rooney Mara) take a road trip through the Midwest, where the natural antagonisms of their daily lives within 1950s heterosexist patriarchy fall away and they are free to pursue their mutual desires without hindrance. In *Moonlight*, in all three sections of the film, the main character can only express himself—his quiet nature and/or his queer desires—when he is in a more safe environment, either with his chosen family of Juan (Mahershala Ali) and Teresa (Janelle Monáe) or with his would-be love interest, Kevin (André Holland). In the final scene of the film, an adult Chiron (Trevante Rhodes), now called "Black"—buff, gold-toothed, and emulating the toxic masculinity he grew up being bullied by and, thus, into—joins Kevin in his home after the two have shared a meal at the diner where Kevin works. Absent the outside world that has exacted untold punishments on the two men for being Black and queer, Chiron finds comfort in Kevin's arms. It is not sexual, but sweet: a moment of peace and vulnerability that highlights that Chiron's outer tough-guy stylings are a mask he wears to survive in an antagonistic world. In direct contrast to Hollywood's central conflict theory, queer/female/of color characters may need spaces free from conflict in order to become themselves, or enact specific aspects of their identities. Examples like these suggest that not only do we need a more nuanced understanding of how hostile forces may or may not shape and define character, we must also consider how multiple forms of conflict exist simultaneously for characters with marginalized identities. Employing a singular and resolvable conflict is a tactic that shrinks character to fit universal neutral conceptions of subjectivity and agency. For characters who are meant to speak to more complex experiences that fall outside of this realm, a much more robust mechanics of story and character development is required.

Thought Exercises

1   Outside of conflict, what other processes can serve as the primary narrative engine of a screenplay, generating tension and momentum?

2   If escalating conflict generates an arc that culminates in a final, explosive release, what shape might a narrative organized around healing, grief, care, friendship, or pleasure take? What are the implications of this new shape in terms of structure, rhythm, pacing, tone, etc.?

3   If conflict is replaced by another tension-generating mechanism—like grief or desire—how must your thinking shift about the role other characters play? Will there still be an antagonist or an antagonistic force? How might side characters behave if not in opposition to the protagonist?

Notes

1 Raúl Ruiz, *Poetics of Cinema: 1* (Paris: Editions Dis Voir, 1995), 11.
2 Syd Field, *Screenplay: The Foundations of Screenwriting* (New York: Bantam Dell, 2005), 25.
3 Blake Snyder, *Save the Cat! The Last Book on Screenwriting You'll Ever Need* (Studio City, CA: Michael Wiese Productions, 2005), 52.
4 David Howard and Edward Mabley, *The Tools of Screenwriting: A Writer's Guide to the Craft and Elements of a Screenplay* (New York: St. Martin's Press, 1996), 29.
5 Robert McKee, *Story: Substance, Structure, Style, and the Principles of Screenwriting* (New York: Regan Books, 1997), 317.
6 Ibid.
7 Howard and Edward Mabley, *The Tools of Screenwriting*, 49.
8 Frank B. Wilderson, *Red, White & Black: Cinema and the Structure of U.S. Antagonisms* (Durham, NC: Duke University Press, 2010), 5.
9 For Wilderson, once Africans were taken from their homeland and put onto slave ships, they became "socially dead" and, thus, incapable of being seen or treated as human. Further, the failure of the United States to adequately address and redress slavery, which has continued in the form of mass incarceration and gratuitous violence against Black people, has made it impossible to tell truthful Black stories within current narrative paradigms. He writes, "[t]he slave formation is a formation for which there cannot be an imagined resolution, which means that the structure of narrative, which demands a resolution is antithetical to explain the Black experience." Maria Berrios and Jakob Jakobsen, *Hospital Prison University Radio*, May 2018, https://soundcloud.com/hospitalprisonuniversityradio/conversation-with-frank-b-wilderson-on-fanon-etc.
10 Manny Fidel, "How White Savior Movies Hurt Hollywood," *YouTube*, Insider, March 5, 2019, www.youtube.com/watch?v=0sdC6RxaY-Q.
11 For more on homonormativity, see Lisa Duggan, "The New Homonormativity: The Sexual Politics of Neoliberalism," in *Materializing Democracy toward a Revitalized Cultural Politics*, eds. Russ Castronovo and Dana D. Nelson (Durham, NC: Duke University Press, 2002), 175–95; Jasbir K. Puar, *Terrorist Assemblages* (Durham, NC: Duke University Press, 2007).
12 bell hooks, *Black Looks: Race and Representation* (Boston: South End Press, 1992), 91.
13 Howard and Edward Mabley, *The Tools of Screenwriting*, 45.
14 Ruiz, *Poetics of Cinema*, 11.
15 Howard and Edward Mabley, *The Tools of Screenwriting*, 46.
16 Ibid.
17 Snyder, *Save the Cat*, 150.
18 Karl Iglesias, *Writing for Emotional Impact Advanced Dramatic Techniques to Attract, Engage, and Fascinate the Reader from Beginning to End* (Livermore, CA: WingSpan Press, 2010), 81.
19 A. Lorde, *Sister Outsider: Essays & Speeches* (Berkeley: Crossing Press, 2007), 53.
20 Céline Sciamma, "Ready for the Rising Tide," *BAFTA Screenwriters' Lecture Series*, February 4, 2020, www.bafta.org/media-centre/transcripts/screenwriters-lecture-series-2019-celine-sciamma.

4

CHANGING THE NARRATIVE (STRUCTURE)

Narrative structure is the organizational logic that shapes our emotional and intellectual experience of a screen story by providing a guide for how to arrange the narrative elements. In contrast to narrative elements like character, story world, and conflict—all of which are more readily recognized as potentially subjective because they draw more closely on a writer's personal experience for their creation—there is a tendency to see narrative structure as neutral and a non-factor in determining a story's meaning. As Field writes, "[t]he paradigm is a form, not a formula; it's what holds the story together. It is the spine, the skeleton. Story determines structure; structure doesn't determine story."[1] Field's claim that structure does not determine story is common among screenplay manuals. Similar to other frequent analogies comparing screenplay structure to a blueprint or scaffolding, the skeleton metaphor suggests that because skeletons support a diverse range of bodies and lives, they do not contain meaning by themselves. What Field fails to acknowledge is the way that the structure—or the organizational logic—governing a screenplay is inseparable from the narrative elements it arranges. Think about the way in which a skeleton determines the shape of a body, in what ways its limbs can be used, and how certain bones house and protect vital organs, as the skull does for our brains. Screenplay structure is similarly restrictive and deterministic when you think about acceptable pacing, ordering of significant events, and how particular story components—like set-up, rising tensions, and resolution—dwell within particular acts. Therefore, screenplay structure is not neutral but integrally connected to and imbued with meaning.

Returning to the common metaphor of screenplay as blueprint allows for a more in-depth examination of structure's supposed neutrality. In Patricia Highsmith's novel *Strangers on a Train*—unlike Hitchcock's adaptation of it—the protagonist is not a tennis player, but an architect. Early in the novel, Guy meets Bruno on a train. When Guy reveals his desire to leave his unfaithful wife to pursue his

DOI: 10.4324/9781003170310-6

girlfriend, Bruno—an eccentric with a queer interest in Guy—proposes that they trade murders, as Bruno is distressed by his overbearing father. Guy dismisses Bruno's proposal, but Bruno kills Guy's wife anyway and begins sending Guy drawings and maps of his father's house so that Guy can return the favor. The drawings provide make-shift blueprints of the home, including the furniture layout, the locations of windows and doors, and indications of steps and floorboards to avoid due to loud creaking. Guy resists at first, but Bruno is persistent and eventually coerces Guy to fulfill his end of the bargain.

As Guy traverses Bruno's father's house in the darkness of night, he counts his steps just as Bruno's instructions lay out. He knows which doors to enter, which doors to ignore, which flights of stairs to avoid. As he nears Bruno's father's room, he muses, "[a]s a house is built so the pattern of activity of those will be who live in it."[2] What Guy observes in this moment is the fact that the scaffolding of a home determines, in part, what happens inside it. There are rooms designated as bedrooms, kitchens, dining rooms, and the like. Architecture provides meaning: this is where we share food and conversation; this is where we sleep; this is where we store the wine. Windows determine where one can take in the view of the neighborhood. Doors determine where one enters and leaves. Stairwells provide the mechanism for moving among floors. Though houses can be constructed of different materials, painted different colors, and filled with different kinds of furniture to denote one's personal style, uniformity of blueprint—very common, for example, in suburban subdivisions—supports conformity and, to a certain extent, dictates what can and will happen inside of a house, and perhaps even a neighborhood made up of identical houses. It is only when an architect decides to challenge the standard blueprint as well as what that blueprint arranges that new forms and new ways of being become more likely. Consider, for example, Shusaku Arakawa and Madeline Gins, artists who re-imagined the architecture of the home to design the Bioscleave House, whose "architecture makes people use their bodies in unexpected ways to maintain equilibrium, and . . . stimulate their immune systems."[3] By rethinking architectural principles around floor design and replacing flat, rectilinear rooms with bumpy, textural, and uneven enclosures, the whole idea of what can happen in a room is transformed. With irregularly contoured walls and flooring, rooms shift from places where people sit idly, allowing body and mind to atrophy, and into spaces one must actively negotiate in new and life-affirming ways. To return to screenwriting, to suggest that story structure only provides form without impacting meaning erases the complex ways that the repetition of story forms embeds particular expectations into the structure while simultaneously ignoring the ways people throughout history and across cultures have organized their stories, minds, identities, languages, and communities in vastly different ways. To ignore this by insisting that form is neutral demonstrates, once again, the pervasiveness of perspectivelessness and the unquestioned commitment to an abstract unversalism that flattens difference.

If normativity thrives through repeated alignment with established blueprints, then examining the blueprints for whom and what they support—and whom and what they erase, malign, or contort—becomes important. By way of illustration, Sara Ahmed demonstrates how normative structures operate as "straightening device[s]" by describing a scenario where one uses tracing paper to replicate an existing design or blueprint. When the tracing paper and its markings are in alignment with the original design (in our case, screenwriting paradigms), the "lines of the tracing paper disappear" revealing one set of design-lines. She continues, "[i]f lines are traces of other times, then this alignment depends on straightening devices that keep things in line, in part by 'holding' things in place."[4] Thus, the structural, repeatable components of a paradigm hold some things in place and not others. It is with this in mind that I ask, what—and, more precisely, whom—is held in place by current screenwriting paradigms? Taking Field's metaphor to the extreme, we might rephrase the question: Whose stories—and what kinds of bodies—do traditional screenplay skeletons animate?

Three-Act Structure

Traditional screenplays typically abide three-act structure, with different paradigms providing varying degrees of additional support via specific beats that divvy up each act. The most straightforward of the paradigms is Field's Aristotelian three-act structure, which features—in addition to the act breaks between the set-up, confrontation, and resolution—two additional plot points at the ends of the first and second act that serve to "hold the paradigm in place," "anchor [the] storyline," and "hook into the action and spin it around in another direction."[5] Systems like Snyder's fifteen-beat *Save the Cat*, Paul Guilino's eight-part *Sequence Approach*, and Vogler's twelve-step *The Writer's Journey* may seem more complex on first glance, but are simply more detailed in their approach, breaking the three-act structure into smaller beats that more fully flesh out the particular functions of each act. Snyder, for example, developed his fifteen-beat *Save the Cat* structure after reading Field's *Screenplay* and finding that, despite Field's status as "the father of the modern movie template,"[6] he didn't provide enough structure. Snyder writes, "[l]ike a swimmer in a vast ocean, there was a lot of open water in between those two Act Breaks. And a lot of empty script space in which to get lost, panic and drown. I needed more islands, shorter swims."[7] Shorter swims for Snyder means that the dreaded Act Two, which is the longest of the acts and shoulders the weight of the rising tension, includes specifying options for how conflict might manifest, such as "fun and games," "the bad guys close in," "all is lost," and "dark night of the soul."[8] Providing screenwriters with particular goals and meaning for the various obstacles doesn't change the overall arc of a script, but goes a long way towards supporting screenwriters in plotting out the journey. This is all to say that despite how the various paradigms drill down into detail, the dramatic arc of three-act structure reigns supreme.

Part of the allure and staying power of three-act structure lies in its efficient and forward thrust. Whether the plot unfolds in a linear or non-linear fashion—in puzzle narratives like *Memento* (Christopher Nolan, 2000), for example—the plotting and its engagement with plot points must move the story forward towards resolution. As Field writes, "[y]our story always moves forward—it follows a path, a direction, a line of progression from beginning to end."[9] To flesh out this line of development, each act contains specific beats that support a specific purpose: Act One sets up the world and the protagonist, Act Two bombards the protagonist with escalating obstacles and conflict, and Act Three provides the climax and resolution to the problems of the prior two acts. Boiled down to its essence, "[t]he narrative progression of most films moves from equilibrium to disequilibrium to equilibrium."[10] Though there are variations on this structure, not only in terms of the ways the paradigms lay them out, but also between how television and film break up the acts, the fundamental building blocks of beginning, middle, end, and their accompanying ideological attachments remain the same regardless of medium or paradigm. Therefore, rather than critique the specific beats of particular templates or parse out the differences between a three-act film and a five-act dramatic television episode, I will examine the ideological underpinnings of screenplay structure, particularly as they relate to issues of climax, transformation, and resolution, as well as their connection to structures of whiteness and masculinity. To do this, I will focus primarily on Act Three—the container of the main character's transformation—as I've already explored the primary function of Act One through my analysis of character design and Act Two through my analysis of conflict in the previous two chapters.

The Transformation Imperative

In popular screenwriting methodology, the key to the third act is a stunning climax and satisfying solution to the narrative problem. While the climax and resolution can manifest in any number of possible scenarios, it's important to keep in mind that they work in tandem to support a larger goal, that of the protagonist's final transformation, which governs the meaning of a screen story. The climax achieves its definitive power in contrast to all of the ways that the protagonist failed to effectively dominate the obstacles presented in the second act. The climax is then the "do or die" moment where the main character must change in order to win, thereby linking success with transformation. It's where Neo in *The Matrix* finally accepts that he's "the One" and defeats Agent Smith, or when Max in *Collateral* takes on the hired assassin, Vincent, in a battle to the death after deciding to proactively pursue what he cares about instead of passively hoping it will one day come true. Despite the outsized importance of the climax in discussions about screenplay structure, it primarily exists to prop up the transformation imperative. Therefore, though there are critiques to be made around how the climax operates as a masculinist narrative beat rooted in the structure of cis, male sexual pleasure, in that the dramatic arc follows a pattern "that swells, and tautens until climax, then collapses,"[11] for the purposes of this book, it is perhaps more fruitful to uncouple climax and transformation. By decentering the climax, we may shift our thinking toward whether the final act must remain invested in transformation or the promise of transformation. If you take away the need to definitively transform from one state of being to another, then you potentially also remove the need for a singular, emphatic climax. This could make room for multiple climaxes—a series of becomings—or some other configuration of beats for act three, but most importantly, it makes room for new possibilities around what endings do and what kind of subjectivities and life experiences they support.

As I've argued, everything in the first two acts leads to the final, essence-confirming transformation of the central character or, short of that, the transformation of the world in relation to that character. As McKee writes, "[t]he finest writing not only reveals true character, but arcs or changes that inner nature, for better or worse, over the course of the telling."[12] Here, McKee is more flexible than others in making room for the negative trajectory of the anti-hero, a mode that is very common, especially in television. Most paradigms focus on the positive: "[i]n any good story the hero grows and changes, making a journey from one way of being to the next: from despair to hope, weakness to strength, folly to wisdom."[13] Thus, the climax of Act Three emblematizes the (usually aspirational) transformation of the central character so that the story can wrap itself up in the all-important resolution. Resolutions aren't simply conclusions, though. As Field writes, "it's important to remember that resolution does not mean ending; resolution means solution."[14] For Field, the transformation of the central character solves the narrative problem. Or inversely, the narrative problem exists to perturb the protagonist out of complacency, forcing them to change. Again we're back to McKee's "conservative" characters who, unless prodded by excessive antagonistic forces, would remain static. Hence, building on the previous chapters' exploration of character and conflict, three-act structure begins with a flawed character, tests that character through conflict, and, finally, transforms them to create a "new world order."[15]

Within the more mythologically oriented manuals influenced by Campbell's *The Hero's Journey*, the final transformation of the third act, called "The Road Back" or "The Return," is even more profound in its framing as an epic rebirth. As Vogler writes, "the hero who has been to the realm of the dead must be reborn and cleansed in one last Ordeal of death and Resurrection before returning to the Ordinary World of the living."[16] In the final moments of a film,[17] after many tests and trials, "[t]he godly powers sought and dangerously won are revealed to have been within the heart of the hero all the time. He is 'the king's son' who has come to know who he is" and "[f]rom this point of view the hero is symbolical of that divine creative and redemptive image which is hidden within us all, only waiting to be known and rendered into life."[18] Thus, the hero's journey presents a vision of transformation that arrives through a climax rooted in suffering and a resultant agency enacted to subdue that suffering. In overcoming the rising tension of Act Two, the hero cleanses their vulnerabilities and flaws to reveal an ultimate inner truth, which returns us once again to liberal humanism's idea of a bounded, self-determining self who engages personal agency to discover an ideal, essential self.

If we're inquiring into which selves are being held in place through classical three-act structure, an examination of the transformation imperative and its reliance on compounding conflict towards an ultimate climax to bring out a character's essence can help us understand how screenplay structure is steeped in and perpetuates hegemonic whiteness and masculinity. To begin, it is important to remember the ways in which whiteness and masculinity maintain their power through their "universality." or "dailiness,"[19] which render them invisible because of their position as default. Just as concepts of the universal male prototype hide the power of patriarchy, the invisibility of whiteness naturalizes white supremacy' while naming, classifying, corralling, and denigrating non-whites. For example, in her analysis of the American literary imagination, Toni Morrison argues that white masculinity operates as a double void (invisible in terms of masculinity and whiteness) and is thus reliant on the presence of Black people to form its subjectivity.[20] For Morrison, white writers use Black characters as surrogates for white identity; they are

> [t]he vehicle by which the [white] American self knows itself as not enslaved, but free; not repulsive, but desirable; not helpless, but licensed and powerful; not history-less, but historical; not damned, but innocent; not a blind accident of evolution, but a progressive fulfillment of destiny.[21]

Such projections are far beyond concepts of racism as a form of race-based and individual bias. Because white supremacy works not by defining itself, but its nebulous and ever-shifting boundaries: white people become everything that people of color are not. Morrison drills down into how the myths of white supremacy are initially formed and then gain traction and power. Within such narratives, Black and other non-white characters come to be seen as an antagonistic force, primitive and in need of discipline, which the white male hero must conquer and educate "for their own good."[22] Cinema and television are chock-full of white male (anti) heroes, from Ethan Edwards to Rambo to Walter White, who maintain superiority through progress narratives that entail individual white males conquering and disciplining marginalized people—usually people of color, but also non-Americans, women and gender nonconforming people, queer folks, and non-traditionally educated or poor people—who are depicted as amorphous, savage, and uncivilized.[23] This idealization of whiteness is deeply connected to what Richard Dyer terms "enterprise." According to Dyer, whiteness is not only connected to Christianity in the form of the mind-body split, but to colonial enterprise and its related concepts of the rugged individual, material achievement, order, extraction, progress, and self-transformation. He writes, "[t]he white spirit organises white flesh and in turn non-white flesh and other material matters: it has *enterprise*."[24] From the moment white folks arrived in the Americas, such "enterprise" has been the cornerstone of projects like Manifest Destiny, in which binaristic notions of European progress and civilization were contrasted with what was perceived as Indigenous peoples' backwardness and savagery, and used as a pretext to violently drive Indigenous people from their native lands, killing millions via genocide, and forcing those who survived onto reservations and into boarding schools, or the Industrial Revolution, which framed the need for efficiency, production, and "progress" in a way that "justified" the kidnapping, enslaving, and generations-long torturing of African people whose descendants on American soil continue to be stridently othered, excessively policed, and underestimated to this present day. Enterprise—and its deep connection to whiteness—has not only colonized the land we live on, but our imaginations as well.

Viewing whiteness through the lens of enterprise and its expression in settler-colonialism reveals that whiteness is deeply connected to the will, "the control of self and the control of others."[25] (What is the cowboy hero ideal of the Western if not willful?) To hold whiteness in place, then, is not simply a matter of centering white characters on screen: it is a structural, conceptual framework built around projections of the willful individual and linear progress. It is a way of seeing and being in the world, one that sees the self as something to work on and work out towards an idealized image in the same way that white settler colonialism sees the "other" and the environment as malleable, civilizable, and transformable. In short, at the heart of whiteness is a conflict-driven and transformational striving to control the self, others, and the natural world, such that they fit into an ordered and essential image. As Dyer writes,

> [t]he ideal of whiteness makes a strong appeal. It flatters white people by associating them with (what they define as) the best in human beauty and virtue. The very idea of the best and of striving towards it accords with the aspirational structure of whiteness.[26]

This "aspirational structure of whiteness" manifests within screenwriting through the transformation imperative, which places the lone central character in a position to endure multiple trials that invite a transformation of the self via the protagonist's increased ability to enact agency and shape their circumstances.

The transformation imperative also finds as one of its founding principles the mind-body split, which goes back to at least Plato and which lies at the center of Western culture and metaphysics. In transforming character into pure essence, the screenwriter elevates the inner workings of the mind or soul and its associations with rationality, enlightenment, and purity over the body with its associations of emotionality, impulsivity, and corporeal excess. In explaining the crux of the mind-body dualism, feminist theorist Elizabeth Grosz explains, "[d]ualism is the assumption that there are two distinct, mutually exclusive and mutually exhaustive substances, mind and body, each of which inhabits its own self-contained sphere. Taken together the two have incompatible characteristics."[27] These "incompatible characteristics" extend to the social order in ways that elevate the white, rational, civilized male as the ultimate subject whose agency can be activated towards self-transformation while denigrating women, Indigenous people, Black people, queer people, and more as irrational, uncivilized, savage, excessive, uncontrollable, and, thus, untransformable bodies. In essence, those associated with corporeal excess have no selves to transform. Once again, we are returned to the prototypical, abstract, universal human, in that the transformation imperative contains meta-physical assumptions about who counts as human and who a mere body. Because these notions are deeply embedded in Western philosophical, religious, political, and cultural traditions, they inform our storytelling practices such that we (often unconsciously) associate "mind with the sort of people who came to think of themselves as 'white men,' and body with the sorts of people they were oppressing around the world."[28] While the mind-body split is most often referenced in relation to philosophy and metaphysics, its influence on and manifestation in screen stories is deeply embedded in the Western through the Frontier Myth so central to Hollywood's myth-historiography. As Slotkin writes,

> The moral landscape of the Frontier Myth is divided by significant borders, of which the wilderness/civilization, Indian/White border is the most basic. The American must cross the border into "Indian country" and experience a "regression" to a more primitive and natural condition of life so that the false values of the "metropolis" can be purged and a new, purified social contract enacted. Although the Indian and the Wilderness are the settler's enemy, they also provide him with the new consciousness through which he will transform the world.[29]

From the mythic cowboy hero of the Western to his modern day corollary, the lone action hero or the rogue cop, the transformation imperative—fueled by conflict and solidified by climax—reveals a deep-seated assumption that the ultimate journey involves the white, "civilized" male encountering the "primitive other" in order to elevate his consciousness and transform the world. Consequently, while screenplay methodology doesn't explicitly call for the creation of white characters—as a matter of fact, because of its commitment to the universal neutral, there is little acknowledgement of race and how it relates to character or story at all—all characters are at risk for becoming "white" through the transformation imperative. Combined with mix and match or color-neutral casting, screenwriters who don't indicate race or other identity markers for characters (or simply don't write characters with race in mind at all), contribute to the casting of actors in roles that visually appear to hold difference but embody *structural whiteness*. This improves the quantifiable statistics on inclusion in the industry without actually exploring or acknowledging that one's race impacts one's ability to move in and be moved by the larger culture. This is cultural wallpaper of the worst order. Suddenly it becomes clear the way in which prescribing that all screen stories adhere to a "universal" and "standard" screenplay structure secures whiteness in an increasingly non-white world.

Chloé Zhao's 2018 film *The Rider* offers some initial clues as to how the transformation imperative and the whiteness that undergirds it can be challenged. In Zhao's reimagining of the classic Western, an Indigenous cowboy named Blackburn (Brady Jandreau) recovers from a rodeo accident that crushed his skull. The film opens with Blackburn cutting stitches out of his own head, then follows him as he hangs out with friends, takes care of his Autistic sister, visits another injured cowboy in an assisted living facility, and takes odd jobs breaking horses when he's not working at a small grocery in town. In a direct challenge to the typical "mind over matter" mentality at the heart of most hero's journey narratives—though Blackburn yearns to get back on the bronco—he does not overcome his newfound physical limitations, but instead comes to accept that mind is matter, that his injury is lifelong. Similar to *I May Destroy You*, which I explore in greater depth in Chapter 8, the inciting incident—a tragedy—has already occurred before the narrative begins. Blackburn does not need a wake-up call. Instead, "[l]ike a superhero who lost his power,"[30] Blackburn must learn to accept that his life has already irrevocably changed. He cannot play the cowboy hero and fight to make his newfound circumstances bend to his will unless he's willing to die. Zhao not only challenges deep-seated cowboy archetypes rooted in violent, white masculinity through her casting of Jandreau—a Lakota man—as the main character, but structural paradigms that insist that when the world is deemed out of order, the lone hero must set things right no matter what havoc that brings in order to achieve greatness via transformation.

At its root, the transformation imperative at the heart of three-act structure traffics in notions of non-relational individualism, aspirational striving, and mastery of mind and matter at the expense of the body and the natural world that lie at the heart of whiteness and toxic masculinity. The repetition of this paradigm in countless films and television series reifies and naturalizes not only white characters on screen, but holds in place the structures that perpetuate white, male supremacy. If screen stories are to become more inclusive and reflective of deep personal, social, and historical truths, examining the paradigms and the ways they replicate hegemonic systems of whiteness, masculinity, and more is imperative. As Ahmed reminds us, "[i]t is important that we think not only about what is repeated, but also about how the repetition of actions takes us in certain directions."[31] In the spirit of moving in a different direction, towards more liberatory frameworks, we must be open to unruliness, disorientation, and discomfort. For, "[t]he 'new' is what is possible when what is left behind us, our background, does not simply ground us or keep us in place, but allows us to move and allows us to follow something other than the lines we have already taken."[32]

Thought Exercises

1   Three-act structure is predicated on a causal, problem-solution oriented logic. What opportunities arise for storytelling when closure is not guaranteed or sought?

2   If you set aside the transformation imperative, which requires a whittling down of the central character to their essence, what other goals might a narrative have? Put another way, what are the other lines of life that can be followed?

3   How might the structure change to accommodate a narrative of integration, healing, relationality, or acceptance?

Notes

1 Syd Field, *Screenplay: The Foundations of Screenwriting* (New York: Bantam Dell, 2005), 29.

2 Patricia Highsmith, *Strangers on a Train* (New York: W. W. Norton, 2001), 150.

3 Fred A. Bernstein, "A House Not for Mere Mortals," *The New York Times*, April 3, 2008, www.nytimes.com/2008/04/03/garden/03destiny.html.

4 Sara Ahmed, *Queer Phenomenology: Orientations, Objects, Others* (Durham, NC: Duke University Press, 2007), 66.

5 Field, *Screenplay*, 143.

6 Blake Snyder, *Save the Cat! The Last Book on Screenwriting You'll Ever Need* (Studio City, CA: Michael Wiese Productions, 2005), 69.

7 Ibid.

8 Ibid., 70.

9 Field, *Screenplay*, 91.

10 Frank B. Wilderson, *Red, White & Black: Cinema and the Structure of U.S. Antagonisms* (Duke University Press, 2010), 26.

11 J. Alison, *Meander, Spiral, Explode: Design and Pattern in Narrative* (New York: Catapult, 2019), 6.

12 Robert McKee, *Story: Substance, Structure, Style, and the Principles of Screenwriting* (New York: Regan Books, 1997), 104.

13 Christopher Vogler, *The Writers Journey: Mythic Structure for Writers* (Studio City, CA: Michael Wiese Productions, 2007), 13.

14 Field, *Screenplay*, 26.

15 Snyder, *Save the Cat*, 90.

16 Vogler, *Writer's Journey*, 17.

17 In television, of course, transformation is somewhat more complicated in that decisive transformations are often denied on an episodic level due to the requirements of the serialized and seasonal format. Because television is segmented, each episode delays narrative closure and, instead, continuously returns the audience and characters to the initial moment of equilibrium rather than progressing toward a completed transformation in the way a singular film does. This allows each episode to start fresh as if the events of the previous episode have had no discernible effect on the characters. At the same time, however, series do follow at least one narrative line that unfolds over the course of an entire season, wherein the main character transforms to a degree, providing closure and, usually, a question or cliffhanger for the next season. Even though television frequently forgoes narrative closure and/or transformation from episode to episode, it is important to note is that the promise of transformation is always present, even if it is withdrawn by the episode's end. This is especially true in traditional sit-com structure where a status-quo perturbing problem is introduced, hilarity ensues as the ill-equipped protagonists try to fix it, and order is restored when the problem is finally solved in a way that makes it clear that the main character has somehow learned nothing from their travails, lest they become too equipped to handle such problems in the future and ruin our chances for more hilarity.

18 J. Campbell, *The Hero with a Thousand Faces* (Princeton, NJ: Princeton University Press, 2004), 36.

19 Raka Shome, "Race and Popular Cinema: The Rhetorical Strategies of Whiteness in City of Joy," *Communication Quarterly* 44, no. 4 (Fall 1996): 503.

20 Toni Morrison, *Playing in the Dark: Whiteness and the Literary Imagination* (New York: Vintage Books, a division of Random House, Inc., 1992), 5.

21 Ibid., 51.

22 Shome, "Race and Popular Cinema," 510.

23 Morrison, *Playing in the Dark*, 5; Shome, "Race and Popular Cinema," 510.

24 Richard Dyer, *White* (New York: Routledge, 1997), 15.

25 Ibid., 31.

26 Ibid., 80.

27 Elizabeth A. Grosz, *Volatile Bodies: Toward a Corporeal Feminism* (Bloomington, IN: Indiana University Press, 1994), 48.

28 Crispin Sartwell, "Western Philosophy as White Supremacism," *The Philosophical Salon*, May 27, 2019, https://thephilosophicalsalon.com/western-philosophy-as-white-supremacism/.

29 Richard Slotkin, *Gunfighter Nation* (New York: Atheneum, 1992), 14.

30 Chloé Zhao qtd in John Powers, "How Chloé Zhao Reinvented the Western," *Vogue*, March 22, 2018, www.vogue.com/article/chloe-zhao-the-rider-vogue-april-2018.

31 Ahmed, *Queer Phenomenology*, 56.

32 Ibid., 62.

5

ON WORLD-BUILDING

In previous chapters, I have argued that culturally specific and inclusive storytelling requires an embodied practice of screenwriting that reckons with the intersections of a character's identity. I now extend this line of thinking to argue that world-building practices within screenwriting must be equally attentive to the specificity of location, along with the social, political, and historical environment, especially in terms of how context impacts particular characters within the story world.

Towards a more robust world-building practice in screenwriting, Sara Ahmed's queer and feminist interventions in phenomenology offer a useful framework for elucidating the interdependent relationship between a character and the world they inhabit. While traditional phenomenology focuses on the self and the formation of consciousness, unlike ontology it does so through an understanding that humans are what Heidegger refers to as "beings-in-the-world." Where ontology is interested in a kind of disembodied consciousness (which supports notions of the abstract, universal human), phenomenology roots human consciousness in the body and its sensory interactions with the environment. Ahmed extends this interest in the interaction between people and the world through an attention to how the particular body one inhabits—in terms of gender, race, sexuality, ability, and more—orients one's experience in the world as well as one's consciousness of the world. For example, in "Phenomenology of Whiteness," Ahmed builds on the work of Franz Fanon through an examination of how whiteness manifests in people and places, how whiteness operates as the ability to move through the world without friction, that to be white is to be a "body-at-home" in the world. To do this, she relates an anecdote from *Black Skins, White Masks* in which Fanon—a Black man living in a white, French colony—thinks about reaching for a pack of cigarettes under a white man's gaze. The actions he describes—eyeing the cigarettes, reaching for the pack—would be casual and unremarkable if it weren't for the fact that they occur under a white gaze in a colonial context. For Fanon and

DOI: 10.4324/9781003170310-7

Ahmed, unlike white phenomenologists like Husserl, positing consciousness only through an attention to what the body does and the objects it encounters is insufficient. One needs an analysis of the social context in which one acts as well as the identity of the actors. As Ahmed writes, where

> phenomenology attends to the tactile, vestibular, kinaesthetic and visual character of embodied reality, Fanon asks us to think of the 'historic-racial' schema, which is 'below it'. In other words, the racial and historical dimensions [that] are beneath the surface of the body.[1]

In this way, Ahmed explores how Fanon's work connects lived experience to the socio-historical context of the world. When considered through this lens, it becomes clear that the world is not neutral: different places and contexts yield different results for different people.

In a similar vein, feminist disability scholar Rosemarie Garland-Thomson posits the "misfit" as a way to address the shifting terrain of the world and self for disabled people. Garland-Thompson explores the importance of the particularity of embodiment in relation to social and architectural barriers. Like Ahmed's "body-at-home," in which those who occupy dominant subjectivities move through the world without much friction,

> [f]itting occurs when a generic body enters a generic world, a world conceptualized, designed, and built in anticipation of bodies considered in the dominant perspective as uniform, standard, majority bodies.[2]

Thus, a person who "fits" within any given space finds congruity and flow, while a "misfit" finds incongruity and stoppage. Ahmed also addresses what it means to be stopped. She writes that for people who don't fit, who are not supported by social structures,

> bodily movement is not so easy. Such bodies are stopped, where the stopping is an action that creates its own impressions. Who are you? Why are you here? What are you doing? Each question, when asked, is a kind of stopping device.[3]

Framed through the rubric of fitting/not fitting or flowing versus being stopped, what emerges is that disability or race or gender or sexuality are not inherent. Marginalization is not something a body carries with it. Nor is marginalization purely reliant on infrastructure or location. Rather, what a body can do and how a person encounters the world and is responded to in turn results from the interaction between a particular body in a particular location at a particular time. As Garland-Thompson writes, "[w]hen the spatial and temporal context shifts, so does the fit, and with it meanings and consequences. The idea of the misfit emphasizes context over essence, relation over isolation, mediation over origination. Misfits are inherently unstable rather than fixed."[4] Thus, based on the specifics of one's iden-tity and location, certain objects, subjectivities, and experiences are in reach while others are not. In short, the relationship between a specific person and a specific environment impacts how one orients oneself in the world. An understanding of the relationship between people and the context in which they live has implications for engaging more creatively with place-based, material-reality-focused storytell-ing and world-building. For the purposes of this book, an understanding of the interdependent relationship between people and the world is crucial to deepening world-building practices, especially since, all too often, setting is relegated to the background and/or operates as universal and generic, and generic settings invite generic characters.

World-building Practices in Screenwriting

In screenwriting, world-building is often consigned to atmospheric backdrop, the-matic amplifier, iconographic genre marker, conflict-engine, or as a means toward lending a project historical context and accuracy. Perhaps most often, world-building is considered the domain of genre writers, particularly in science fiction, fantasy, horror, noir, and historical fiction. Within these genres, the worlds built are simultaneously meticulously detailed and abstractly symbolic, though not necessar-ily invested in the particularities of place. As communications scholar Jim Leach argues, genre films employ their locations "less [as] specific markers of place than [as] an iconography that locates them in relation to other films in the same genre."[5] Thus, though the neon hum of a futuristic city crowded with flying vehicles and overbearing advertisements signals to the viewer that they've entered the world of dystopian sci-fi, "it often matters little whether [those details] belong to a specific city."[6] Here, world-building operates as a testament to genre and provides detail without specificity. This is not to say that genre writers always leave the potential of world-building on the table. From *Blade Runner*'s (Ridley Scott, 1982) presen-tation of a dystopian future where corporations and governments have merged and humans and machines are virtually indistinguishable, to *Underground Railroad*'s (Barry Jenkins, 2021) fantastical and poignant engagement with the transatlan-tic slave trade and its impact on characters living in antebellum America, world-building within genre offers writers ample opportunity to engage audiences with setting in socially, culturally, and politically meaningful ways. That engagement, though, is a choice, an act, rather than a function of form.

Within screenwriting manuals, the gurus are largely silent on the issue of world-building. Neither Field's *Screenplay* nor Snyder's *Save the Cat* address setting or world-building beyond a few casual references. McKee and Vogler, on the other hand, both address setting, albeit briefly. In *The Writer's Journey*, setting is indirectly addressed through Vogler's engagement with Campbell's ordinary and special worlds within the hero's journey, which oddly yields worlds without world-ing. By this I mean that Vogler doesn't discuss worlds as specific locations with unique histories or rules. Instead, the worlds in question are functional in that they facilitate the narrative.

Cyclical in nature, act one of the hero's journey takes place in the ordinary world; act two takes place in the special world; and act three returns once again to the ordinary world. In distinguishing between two separate worlds, setting operates less as world-building in terms of establishing locality, time, atmosphere, character, theme, or genre (though it can do those things, too), and more as a container for specific narrative requirements and beats. First, the ordinary world operates as the situational context where the hero begins their journey and where the audience comes to understand the status quo. It's in the ordinary world where the audience learns about the protagonist's lack or wound, key information about their family, and, often, the specific stakes for the hero. The delivery of this introductory information is attached to specific beats. For instance, the protagonist encounters the "Call to Adventure," which is the catalyst that drives the protagonist out of complacency and catapults them out of the ordinary world and into the special world. Act two's special world performs as the unfamiliar terrain the hero traverses where they face increasingly difficult challenges suited to their unique wound that facilitates their ultimate transformation. In crossing from one world into another, the protagonist has access to new narrative beats. For example, crossing from the ordinary world into the special world, the hero encounters the "Tests, Allies, and Enemies" phase of the journey, where the hero's "manhood and determination are tested, and where friends and villains are introduced."[7] For Vogler, bars and saloons are great settings for this particular story beat because they are places where the hero can meet new people and obtain essential information while "learning the new rules that apply to the Special World."[8] In Vogler's formulation, setting is instrumental only so far as it aids the "universal" beats of the hero's journey. Place takes on a functional and somewhat symbolic purpose instead of a formative one that is deeply connected to story and the development of character. This isn't to say that arranging a narrative through the organizational logic of a journey from the ordinary world to the special world and back again can't be meaningful, only that within *The Writer's Journey*, world-building appears to be primarily utilitarian.

In contrast to other prominent manuals, in *Story* McKee devotes an entire chapter to setting and world-building. In the chapter "Structure and Setting" he argues that "[k]nowledge of and insight into the world of your story is fundamental to the achievement of originality and excellence."[9] For McKee, an understanding of the social, historical, political, and ideological context of the world is the key to avoiding cliché. Boredom—the cardinal sin of screenwriting—occurs when the "writer does not know the world of his story"[10] and instead turns to other films and series to flesh out familiar worlds. In McKee's words this amounts to "reheat[ing] literary leftovers,"[11] resulting in tired stories and disengaged audiences. Here, McKee articulates a fundamental issue in much novice screenwriting, which, ironically, is the result of the same Producer's Game that screenwriting is based on, where studios, directors, and screenwriters look to successful movies of the past to craft successful movies of the future. And while originality is a worthwhile goal, there is more to setting than establishing a new or highly specific story. In fact, an attention to a specific setting helps move screenwriters towards culturally specific storytelling, especially when done in conjunction with culturally specific characters.

According to McKee, setting has four primary components that impact the narrative possibilities in a screen story: period, which refers to time in history; duration, which addresses the span of time a narrative covers; location, which covers the physical and geographical dimensions of a story; and level of conflict, which covers the human or social dimension that results in social, ideological, and political tension. Most importantly, McKee acknowledges that a setting's specificity is essential, not only so that the audience understands the rules and possibilities of the world for the specific characters who reside within it, but because setting shapes story in significant ways. When discussing his irritation with aspiring screenwriters who argue that their screenplay could be set anywhere, he responds that a

> [b]reak up in the Bayou bears little resemblance to a multi-million dollar Park Avenue litigation, and neither looks like infidelity on a potato farm. There is no such thing as a portable story. An honest story is at home in one, and only one, place and time.[12]

In stark contrast to McKee's investment in universalist characters, McKee astutely argues that a neutral or fungible setting will not suffice because "[s]tories do not materialize from a void but grow out of materials already in history and human experience."[13] To take McKee's example further, just as there must be a stark contrast between a story set in the Bayou versus Park Avenue, when character design and a writer's unique perspective are taken into consideration no two screenplays set in the Bayou ought to be the same. As Howard contends,

> [w]ith the exception of some sequels, two movies usually don't inhabit exactly the same world. Instead, most films take place in a specially designed universe with its own rules, limits, and things that are important. This is true even if at first glance two films appear to take place in exactly the same world.[14]

If reimagining screenwriting norms requires a shift away from a reliance on universalist character construction, McKee's discussion of setting helps establish the importance of not treating setting as neutral either. When setting is understood as disconnected from material reality and history, inconsequential, utilitarian, or as a series of interchangeable backdrops, screenwriters lose the opportunity to not only tell unique stories, as McKee argues, but to tell stories that honor our connection to the world and the ways that our lives are impacted by the social, economic, political, and environmental contexts in which we live. The land we live on—whether urban or rural, mountainous or marsh-filled—impacts everything from the way people form community to the foods people eat to kinship bonds to social structures. The social, economic, and political environment—whether matriarchy or patriarchy, capitalist or democratic socialist—impacts how we live in relation to one another, the world, and ourselves. The setting of our lives and, thus, of the stories we tell are of consequence.

The Importance of Situated-ness in Screenwriting

Just as characters are representations of people with specific histories, family lineages, sexualities, genders, races, ability, and more, the setting of a screenplay represents an equally specific, material, and complex physical and socio-political environment. And just as specific identities inform character, specific environments impact how those characters are able to move in and relate to the world. To return to an example from previous chapters, *Portrait of a Lady on Fire* is set in eighteenth century France. Because Sciamma wanted to tell a lesbian love story in which both women are at liberty to explore their desires without impediment, she needed to attend to that particular social context. She needed a world without men, without patriarchy, without heteronormativity. Rather than defanging the oppressive historical realities women (especially ones who might desire other women) faced at the time, she created a world within a world. As a result, the majority of the film takes place on an isolated island off the northern coast of France. It wasn't that Heloise and Marianne didn't "fit" or find ways to be "at home" in other parts of France. As cis, white French women attached to wealth, both were adept at achieving a kind of flow within high French society. But they didn't have access to their entire selves there. As queer women living within strict heteronormative patriarchy, they were forced to "inhabit space tentatively, in a structure of self-contradiction that is inhibiting and self-distancing."[15] What the specific setting of the-island-without-men provides in the film is the ability for Marianne and Heloise to explore the parts of themselves that don't fit in hereto-patriarchal eighteenth century French society. Because of the attention to the ways social context orients people in particular directions, the film operates as a meditation on burgeoning lesbian desire, on what it feels like for a shadow part of the self to emerge—curiously, haltingly—into the light. In Sciamma's film, the interplay between particular characters with counter-hegemonic desires and a specific socio-historical context that impedes those desires operates to elucidate an experience of consciousness and subjectivity that many queer, trans, and non-binary people are intimately familiar with, especially for those of us who have lived at least part of our lives in the closet. This is where so much of the meaning and power of the film lies, and it could not have been accomplished in a generic setting. Part of what *Portrait of a Lady on Fire* demonstrates is how social and historical context impacts character and story. It doesn't matter what a character might think about themselves, or what the character's "essence" is, lived material reality has material consequences. This is what Vivian Sobchack refers to as "radical contingency," where

> as sensing and sensible objects, we are thrown into the material world and are a part of it—and, however much, as subjects who transcend our objective status through our consciousness and agency, we would like to further this fact of existence, we are always caught up short by it.[16]

In other words, no matter how much inner work you do, there is still an outer world to contend with, rife with sticks and stones and words that can indeed hurt no matter how at peace you are with your own identities.

This is all to say that setting and character are inextricably linked, and that social context—or the ecosystem that your character inhabits along with the role they play in that ecosystem—has intricate implications for how a character might behave or how their story might play out in any given situation. To further illuminate the link between character and setting, it's helpful to consider what goes into writing characters who code-switch—or purposefully alter their manner of speech or behavior depending on the environment in order to find a better "fit" or sense of belonging within that environment. From characters like Alike (Adepero Oduye) in Dee Rees' first feature *Pariah* (2011), who wears feminine clothes at home to please her conservative parents and masculine clothes at school to feel more like her butch lesbian self, to characters like Kumail (Kumail Nanjiani) in *The Big Sick* (Michael Showalter, 2017), who goes on dates with Pakistani women to avoid being disowned by his parents while secretly dating a white woman, characters who code-switch offer fertile ground towards understanding how entwined context and character truly are. In contrast to characters with clearly defined trajectories and little connection to place, characters who code-switch are often caught in a liminal space, traveling between multiple locations with different levels of safety, between multiple groups of people holding vastly different expectations, with few spaces where they can rest, exist, or be. The traveling amounts to a type of self-protective shapeshifting, for which there is little room within a paradigm that insists they boil themselves down to a core essence. Thus, reducing setting to a universally neutral place does not take into account lives that rarely alight in neutral territory, forced to dedicate significant time and energy to monitoring and adjusting outward presentation to avoid judgment, loss, and harm. At the same time, neutral settings potentially foreclose unique stories of lives in flux.[17]

One example of a film that overtly (and hilariously) features a character who code-switches is Boots Riley's *Sorry to Bother You* (2018), another film whose specific setting and social, economic, and political landscape is of consequence in multiple meaningful ways. *Sorry to Bother You* is an absurdist social satire and Sundance darling that takes on issues from capitalism to code-switching to the toxic media environment. The film follows Cassius "Cash" Green (LaKeith Stanfield) in his ascent to the prestigious position of "power caller" at RegalView, a telemarketing firm in the midst of a general strike. To climb the corporate ladder (a version of "fitting in"), Cassius betrays his artist and activist friends by first employing "white voice" and crossing the picket line to get ahead in the workplace before having his own awakening about class struggle.

The film is set in Riley's hometown of Oakland, California, or "the center of the known universe" as Black Lives Matter co-founder Alicia Garza is fond of calling it in her podcast *Lady Don't Take No*. And while there are aspects of the setting that lend the film a surface-level authenticity—such as the use of Bay Area hip-hop music by artists like Lyrics Brown and Mistah F.A.B. and jewelry designed by Oakland artist J. Otto Seibold—the essence of Riley's Oakland is as a hub of Black community organizing and activism in response to decades of racially motivated social and economic violence. In an essay for *Vanity Fair*, Riley—a veteran organizer—describes the history of Oakland from the 60s through the present as one where people of color were continuously antagonized by white, upwardly mobile people through gentrification, "development," and the criminalization of activities enjoyed by people of color. The film is, in many ways, a testament to his life, organizing, and his friends who—like the characters in the film—used to simply drive around Oakland as a form of entertainment because the city had shut down the skating rinks and pools halls where people of color liked to gather. For Riley, the relevance of setting to the film is vast and political. He writes,

> Production design courtesy of decades of city leaders kissing developers' asses. Like people of color who are often criminalized for simply being in plain sight, Cassius has to deal with notions of his existence and makes adjustments accordingly. Like the fight that generations have brought to the streets of Oakland, there is a struggle happening in my film. So much of Oakland shows up in *Sorry to Bother You*: bars, stores, streets, buildings, people, sideshows, fashion, slang. And the struggle. But the struggle is not unique. The setting of my film is Oakland, but the location is every city in the United States.[18]

The film's setting is not a replica of Oakland—no film's setting could be—but informed by a particular aspect of Oakland's unique history within the context of the United States. What Riley demonstrates here is an attention to worlds within worlds. Within the larger white supremacist, capitalist order, which is the macroworld, so to speak, we find Cassius and his friends in Oakland. But this is not a generic or white Oakland. It's not the developer's Oakland ripe for gentrification. Instead, Riley's Oakland is informed by a particular anti-capitalist perspective and built around those impacted (and angered) by racist, capitalist violence. It's an Oakland of artists, like Cassius's girlfriend, Detroit (Tessa Thompson), and activists, like his friend Squeeze (Steven Yuen), and ordinary people, like his uncle (Terry Crews), who are trying to survive while fighting against the dominance hierarchies that seek to displace or annihilate them.

As Riley admits, this isn't to say that a similar film couldn't have been set in a city like Chicago or Detroit, where artist and activist communities also exist in response to racist, capitalist violence. But that acknowledgment didn't push Riley towards setting the film in a generic leftist enclave. Instead, Riley honored the specific fashions, challenges, slang, and musical influences unique to Oakland. Further, Riley used Oakland's exclusive proximity to Silicon Valley to skewer tech billionaires via the primary antagonist, WorryFree's CEO Steve Lift (Arnie Hammer), the billionaire behind the human/horse hybrid, Equisapiens, a species designed for slavery. What Riley's film demonstrates is how a perspective-driven and culturally specific setting is instrumental to storytelling. It influences the types of characters who populate the film, the struggles the characters face, while also, potentially, providing thematic commentary, which in this case focuses on the still unfolding history of discriminatory practices in the region and around the country.

Though *Sorry to Bother You* is grounded in particular social, political, and economic realities, the film isn't interested in realism. The absurdist stylings of the film—an expression of Riley's worldview—allow the setting to take center stage instead of operating discreetly in the background. In the opening scene, for example, we're introduced to Cassius and Detroit in what seems to be an ordinary bedroom. Suddenly the scene, along with the audience's orientation, is upended when the walls begin to shift, revealing that it's not a bedroom but a converted garage owned by his uncle, who still holds the garage door opener, a surreal nod to the gentrification and the related real estate crisis in the area. Other elements of place are aptly and ridiculously named to highlight the violent and oppressive nature of living under capitalism. There is WorryFree, the omni-present mega-corporation that owns RegalView. In a searing example of Lauren Berlant's "cruel optimism," which describes how fantasies of the good life impede the very flourishing they guarantee,[19] WorryFree's billboards promise workers a lifetime of "worry free" food and lodging for the small price of their freedom and labor. The film doesn't stop there. The world-building is rich and complex. Riley skewers Reality TV through a game show that Cassius eventually becomes a contestant on called *I Got The Sh★t Kicked Out of Me*, where contestants get beat up and humiliated in front of millions of rabid viewers. The current social media landscape is also referenced. When a video of Cassius getting hit in the head with a can of soda by a white woman screaming "Have a cola and smile, bitch!" goes viral, merchandise, memes, and Cassius' further humiliation are soon to follow. This is all to say that just because a film is set within a world defined by race and class struggle with real-world corollaries, that doesn't mean that it can't also contain a distinct point-of-view and artistic sensibility.

Escape from Neutral-topia

Attention to specificity in world-building isn't only about communicating information or details about a world—a common rookie mistake. I've read far too many screenplays in which the screenwriter only wants to explain the intricacies and rules of the world without considering the impact those intricacies and rules might have on the characters inhabiting that world. What they fail to ponder is how the context—be it a suburb of Chicago, a small town in upstate New York, or a cosmopolitan metropolis like Toronto, Canada—contributes to the choices that a character does or doesn't have. It is the dynamic relationship between character and world that makes a story unique and powerful. This means that in addition to shifting away from a reliance on the universal neutral in terms of character design, screenwriters would do well to avoid generic settings. To return to the analytical frame I introduced at the beginning of the chapter, in "Notes Toward a Politics of Location," Adrienne Rich meditates on the relationship between her unique identity and her location in both space and time in a way that correlates to many of the ways setting can impact story and character. She writes,

> The body I was born into was not only female and white, but Jewish—enough for geographic location to have played, in those years, a determining part. I was a *Mischling*, four years old when the Third Reich began. Had it been not Baltimore, but Prague or Lódz or Amsterdam, the ten-year-old letter writer might have had no address. Had I survived Prague, Amsterdam or Lódz and the railway stations for which they were deportation points, I would be some body else. My center, perhaps, the Middle East or Latin America, my language itself another language. Or I might be no body at all.[20]

This acknowledgement—like Riley's attention to Oakland's vibrant activist history and Sciamma's awareness that her protagonists could not be the same people on the mainland as they could be on the isolated island—is further testament to the profound impact place and context can have on people with particular identities. Screenwriters looking to upend generic world-building practices that flatten reality into well-trod and clichéd settings like the gritty urban center, the sleepy suburb, or the dusty Old West would benefit from such reflections on the relationship between identity, place, and context. In order to tell stories that honor life in all its rich and vibrant messiness, we cannot continue to write stories that conform to abstract concepts of place any more than we can continue to write stories that rely on universal characters. Abstract ideals, in all their cold, notional fixity, not only extinguish human plurality, regional diversity, and the complexity of socio-political contexts, but the potential to breathe new life into the stories we tell ourselves, and, thus, the ways we conduct our lives. Embracing the nuances of life allows us to see and revel in the spontaneous, the generative, and wildly diverse and exciting aspects of what it can mean to be human.

Thought Exercises

1 How might incorporating a deep interdependence between place and character impact a narrative?
2 What is the relationship between your protagonist and the social, political, economic context in which they live? How has the environment shaped them?
3 Where does your protagonist feel the most "at home" in the world? Where do they not "fit"? How does their behavior change in these different contexts? How does their sense of belonging in different contexts impact the choices they make throughout the narrative?

Notes

1 Sara Ahmed, "A Phenomenology of Whiteness," *Feminist Theory* 8, no. 2 (2007): 149–68, https://doi.org/10.1177/1464700107078139, 153.
2 Rosemarie Garland-Thomson, "Misfits: A Feminist Materialist Disability Concept," *Hypatia* 26, no. 3 (2011): 591–609, https://doi.org/10.1111/j.1527-2001.2011.01206.x, 595.

3   Ahmed, "A Phenomenology of Whiteness," 161.
4   Rosemarie Garland-Thomson, "Misfits: A Feminist Materialist Disability Concept," *Hypatia* 26, no. 3 (2011): 591–609, https://doi.org/10.1111/j.1527-2001.2011.01206.x, 594.
5   Jim Leach, "The Landscapes of Canada's Features: Articulating Nation and Nature," in *Cinema and Landscape: Film, Nation and Cultural Geography,* eds. Graeme Harper and Jonathan Rayner (Bristol, UK: Intellect Books, 2010), 269–80, 267.
6   Ibid.
7   Christopher Vogler, *The Writers Journey: Mythic Structure for Writers* (Studio City, CA: Michael Wiese Productions, 2007), 13.
8   Ibid.
9   Robert McKee, *Story: Substance, Structure, Style, and the Principles of Screenwriting* (New York: Regan Books, 1997), 68.
10 Ibid., 67.
11 Ibid., 68.
12 Ibid., 70–71.
13 Ibid., 70.
14 David Howard and Edward Mabley, *The Tools of Screenwriting: A Writer's Guide to the Craft and Elements of a Screenplay* (New York: St. Martin's Press, 1996), 26.
15 Vivian Sobchack, *Carnal Thoughts Embodiment and Moving Image Culture* (Berkeley, CA: University of California Press, 2004), 33.
16 Ibid., 86.
17 I am indebted to and grateful for conversations with former students Dominique Prince-Points and Karan Sunil on the subject of code-switching as it relates to screenwriting.
18 Boots Riley, "*Sorry to Bother You* Director Boots Riley Takes a Ride Through Oakland's Changing Landscape," *Vanity Fair*, July 2, 2018, www.vanityfair.com/hollywood/2018/07/sorry-to-bother-you-boots-riley-oakland.
19 Lauren Berlant, *Cruel Optimism* (Durham, NC: Duke University Press, 2012).
20 Adrienne Rich, *Blood, Bread and Poetry: Selected Prose, 1979–1985* (London: Virago Press, 1987), 216.

PART II

Towards an Inclusive and Intersectional Practice of Screenwriting

6

FROM *KILLING EVE* TO AN EVE WHO KILLS

This section focuses on issues of progressive representation, particularly at the intersections of gender and sexuality, in the BBC series *Killing Eve* (2018–present) and how those representations are disciplined by generic and narrative conventions.

Critic and fan responses to *Killing Eve* are overwhelmingly positive. The show has been applauded for creating complex female characters who aren't defined by their relationships with men, who have "weird and wild inner lives," and who, unlike female characters whose complexity boils down to being acerbic, alcoholic, or both, are at once vulnerable, humorous, and deeply intelligent.[1] In addition, by centering women in the cat-and-mouse pursuit of the traditionally masculine spy thriller, the show has been praised for subverting tropes common to the genre, while maintaining its more traditional narrative schemes.[2] Thus, for the purposes of my argument, it is important to emphasize that although *Killing Eve* has been described as a show that does wonders for representation, it does so without challenging traditional narrative frameworks.

Before analyzing the disciplining mechanisms of screenplay structure in *Killing Eve*, I will first address one additional structural component: the generic conventions of the spy thriller/crime drama. Generically speaking, methods of detection within crime dramas are linked with specific narrative structures that carry ideological implications. Espionage stories—like their real-world counterparts—trade on information and, thus, the link between knowledge and power. In the cat-and-mouse pursuits between villain and hero, spy thrillers thrive on who has the most information, how that information is acquired, and how it is used to best one's opponent to either attain power or bring the world back into a stable order.[3] In terms of ideology, this usually happens by asking the audience to accept that the criminal must be brought to justice without addressing any of the underlying causes for their crime. Issues like capitalism, misogyny, systemic racism, state violence, globalization, wealth inequality and their relation to crime are never questioned

DOI: 10.4324/9781003170310-9

because of a rigid narrative structure that keeps us focused on the investigation and its ultimate goal: bringing the criminal to justice and restoring the (presumably peaceful) status quo, which, it must not go without saying, is also our larger society's goal. In ignoring the morally complicated reasons why one might become a "criminal" and in focusing on the pleasures of spectacle and heroism, crime dramas silence discourses that would enable an exploration of hegemonic power structures and ideologies.[4]

So, what happens when interesting and otherwise progressive, possibly feminist representations of women/of color/queer folks are placed within such a conservative, universal, generic structural frame? Between the relentless and efficient forward thrust of narrative structure, the paradigmatic tenets of character building, and the masculinist, hegemonic aspects of the spy thriller, it is my contention that potentially robust and complex female characters succumb to the masculinist bent of the universal neutral. For, when female characters chase masculine power (or are, in the case of media representation, squeezed into masculine molds) they become what Ariel Levy calls "loophole women." While attaining dominance seems empowering, Levy argues that "if you are the exception that proves the rule, and the rule is that women are inferior, you haven't made any progress."[5]

Representing Eve

Since the breakout success of her hit series *Fleabag*, Phoebe Waller-Bridge has been applauded as a fiercely feminist voice in television, creating (and playing) complex female characters who are flawed, funny, and deeply vulnerable. In relation to *Fleabag*, Waller-Bridge's brand of feminism has been compared to that of Roxane Gay in her seminal essay "Bad Feminist," marking Waller-Bridge as someone who rejects essential feminism "because it turns too intensely on misperceptions of what women should and can be, rather than the vast range of what their experiences are."[6] Waller-Bridge's characters aren't ideal or idealized women: they are broken women, funny women, violent women, women who disarm audiences with their razor-edged wit and all-knowing gazes.

If discussions of problematic gender representation for women revolve around the objectification of the female body, the over/under-sexualization of women through stereotypes like the vamp, the jezebel, and the spinster, the sidelining of female characters next to their fully fleshed-out male counterparts, or the reduction of women to wives, girlfriends, or mothers—the women at the center of *Killing Eve* can be seen as exemplars of complex, nuanced, and refreshing female representation as depicted through a female and feminist gaze. The protagonist, Eve Polastri (Sandra Oh), is a middle-aged British state security bureaucrat bored in her marriage and her job. From the moment we meet Eve—dressed in flimsy beige pajamas, hair a matted mess, drool at the corner of her mouth, screaming bloody murder because her hands have fallen asleep—we know that we will never see her jet-setting around the globe in fuck-me heels and a leather cat suit like her predecessors in series like *Alias* or *La Femme Nikita*. Eve is different and delightful, in part because she's painfully normal. And it is Eve's boredom with the agonizing normal-ity of her life that pushes her to take an interest in the antagonist/co-protagonist of the series, the prolific female assassin, Villanelle.

Villanelle (Jodie Comer) is a psychopathic, bisexual assassin whose kills are marked by equal measures of style, creativity, and relish, all of which fuel Eve's obsession. While Villanelle is attractive and feminine, she's much more likely to use her femininity as an invisibility cloak than a tool of seduction. We see this during her first assassination, where she sneaks into a party at an Italian country estate, slips on one of the hostess' dresses, and wanders the party, undetected, to identify her mark. When she finds him, she doesn't lure him away with her feminine wiles, but instead coaxes his grandson to call him upstairs to play so she can stab him in the eye with a poisoned hairpin. In many ways, Villanelle demonstrates what Joey Soloway—in their lecture on the Female Gaze—refers to as the "gazed gaze," which is a rebuke to the male gaze by way of an awareness that says "we see you seeing us," and now we're going to use the way you see us against you.[7] Through-out the series, Villanelle uses her understanding of the ways women are either objectified or glanced over by men to her advantage. So far, so good.

In terms of queer representation, Villanelle appears to be bisexual, and the bisexual representation is decidedly "good" in that Villanelle is seen being inti-mate with both men and women (sometimes simultaneously). While Villanelle leans lesbian—as evidenced by her multiple (and obsessive) past relationships with women—the show does not force her to choose, which allows her to defy the normalizing structures of both monogamy and monosexuality that usually result in bisexual erasure.[8] At the same time that her portrayal brings bisexual visibility, she also occupies a long-standing problematic trope for queer female characters: the lesbian psycho-killer. So much so, in fact, that after the season finale, New Yorker television critic Emily Nussbaum tweeted, "I enjoyed KILLING EVE. But I'm fascinated that it isn't getting any flack for suggesting—Basic Instinctishly—that lesbianism and murder are two great tastes that go great together."[9] In answer to Nussbaum's query, it's important to note that Villanelle is more refreshing than she is problematic, in part because there is more and (slightly) "better" representation of lesbian characters than there has been in the past, and in part because lesbian audiences enjoy their gay villains. Villanelle, like many "lesbian baddies" before her, gives lesbian-identified viewers the license to look, to desire. As Clare Whatling argues, "[a]s an audience or individual viewer, we can 'look around' the unpre-possessing figure of the evil lesbian (we can also love her for her sheer power and dynamism) . . ., channelling her transgressive ability to look (predicated upon her perverse and violent desire), into one's own voyeuristic pleasure in looking."[10] If anything, the mercurial Villanelle—who has a penchant for castration, threesomes, and masculine drag—is a destabilizing force in a genre known for enforcing the status quo. Thus, Villanelle's lesbian deviance, while foregrounding the "fatal link of sex and violence" that has so often plagued queer female characters, provides viewers an opportunity to "delight in deviance."[11] Based on Eve's obsession with Villanelle and the relish with which Villanelle's strangeness is foregrounded, queer deviance in *Killing Eve* is refigured as empowering rather than bringing erasure, punishment, and death.

With its distinctly female point of view and central female characters who are specific, highly capable, vulnerable, and funny, *Killing Eve* challenges heterosexist, patriarchal trends in the spy thriller. Seen in this way, the representation in *Killing Eve* is not only "better," it's refreshing and provocative. At the same time, however, the workings of genre and narrative structure discipline the representation in troubling ways.

Thrilling Eve: When the Spy Thriller Tops the Rom-Com

In addition to centering complex female protagonists in a cat-and-mouse scenario usually reserved for men, Waller-Bridge plays with other aspects of the genre in unexpected ways. The first time Eve and Villanelle meet, in a hospital bathroom as Eve is trying to protect a witness and Villanelle has come to kill that witness, the scene is played as a deranged "meet-cute" from a romantic comedy. As Eve futzes with her hair in front of the mirror, Villanelle stares, entranced. (We later learn she has a fetish for Eve's hair-type, making Eve "her type" via a clever bit of word play). Then, as she exits the bathroom she tells her to "wear it down." A few episodes later, after stealing Eve's suitcase in Berlin, Villanelle returns it full of new, form-fitting clothing and expensive perfume, a nod to every rom-com makeover scene in the history of film, where men like Richard Gere take their "pretty woman" on a shopping spree, making her, finally, just as beautiful on the outside as she is on the inside.

In *Killing Eve*, the tension created from the rom-com/spy thriller mash-up gives way to queer desire at the center of the series. When—in any given scene—the pursuit of justice/crime is subordinated to romance, Eve and Villanelle's mutual obsession becomes slippery. For example, in the third episode, as Eve describes Villanelle to a forensic artist, instead of providing the concrete details useful for a composite drawing, Eve grows wistful, lingering on the intangibles underpinning her desire such as, "she had a lost look in her eye." As Summer Kim Lee points out, "Eve's description is that of a crush seen in a fleeting moment, at the same time that it is a criminal profile. Eve's ability to identify Villanelle becomes Eve's desire to identify *with* Villanelle."[12] As the series continues, Eve's pursuit of Villanelle becomes increasingly questionable: does she want to be Villanelle, have sex with Villanelle, or bring Villanelle to justice? There is no doubt that Waller-Bridge's fluid genre-play is rife with potential; at the same time, however, there are other genre requirements that bring our characters back into line with normative discourses.

Unlike many spy thriller characters before her— Bond, Bourne, and Bristow— who offer a fantasy of internal agency (as secret agents no less) in an increasingly confusing world,[13] Eve occupies a much older thriller trope. If Sydney Bristow is a highly skilled killing-machine hiding behind an innocent, girl-next-door facade, Eve Polastri is a dowdy, middle-aged woman who wears her feelings on her fraying cardigan sleeves: she can't fight; she can't handle a gun; she can barely dodge a bullet.

And while this seems to make Eve a welcome reprieve from the ways that female characters in male genres are paradoxically masculinized and sexualized without care for the ways that men and women move in and are moved by the world differently, Eve occupies one of the most enduring tropes of the thriller genre: the Every Man (or in our case, the Every (Wo)man). The Every Man typifies McKee's "conservative" central character: an ordinary person brought into extraordinary circumstances and forced to fight a highly skilled villain—often a sociopath—who has shadowy, yet powerful institutional backing. From Hitchcock's *North By North-West*, where New York ad man, Roger Thornhill (Cary Grant), is mistaken for a CIA agent and forced to evade and outwit an international crime syndicate, to Michael Mann's *Collateral*, where Max (Jamie Foxx), a cab driver, is coerced into being an accomplice for a sociopathic hitman, the Every Man character is as pervasive as he is ordinary. Additionally, because of the deficit of power between the protagonist and the villain in the Every Man thriller, the optimal narrative for such a character is the hero's journey, which drives the transformation of the central character from someone who lacks the drive or skills to be effective in their lives to one who acquires the necessary skills to survive in a harsh world.

For Eve to be a true Every (Wo)man character, she must begin the series with a lack or inner need, which, Villanelle, as her antagonist, must address. This routinely plays out in scenarios where the protagonist takes on some aspects of the antagonist's persona. In *North By Northwest*, Roger Thornhill takes on the name and clothing of George Kaplan, the decoy secret agent he's mistaken for in the inciting incident of the film. In *Collateral*, Max enters a night club as mercenary Vincent (Tom Cruise) in order to acquire a flash-drive with a copy of Vincent's hit-list. In becoming Vincent, Max toughens his otherwise nervous persona: he deepens his voice, he mimics Vincent's words as if they are his own, all as a way to acquire the power the audience knows Max lacks. Likewise, Eve begins the series as an ineffectual mid-level bureaucrat. She's bored. She lacks agency. But as Eve pursues Villanelle, she changes—as she must: she starts dressing better, she gets more confident at wielding weapons, she slaps her husband when he accuses her of being turned on by a psychopath. Eve's identification with and desire for Villanelle bring her closer to being like Villanelle, to becoming someone who can kill with abandon and without remorse. In short, Eve is becoming the skilled "professional" at the core of most spy thrillers, who must be adept and aggressive "if the world is to be saved from the subversion of skilled conspirators."[14] The generic constraints of the thriller thus muddy the otherwise progressive female representation in the series and force Eve into a "power over dynamic," characterized by being in alignment "with elements of hegemonic masculinity, including physical strength, calculated decision-making, and dominance over subordinate[s]."[15] At this point, it should be apparent that in terms of hegemonic story structures, the hero's journey—as it has become entrenched in the Hollywood media-making machine—has become the ultimate narrative schema to represent and perpetuate an ethic rooted in the staunch individualism and self-transformation that defines white, heterosexual masculinity.

Characterizing Eve: The Universal Neutral Strikes Again

Though *Killing Eve* is purportedly a series focused on two female characters and their mutually obsessive relationship with one another, the machinations of the thriller genre and its related character requirements keep the series structurally in line with white masculinity. Particularly notable is the way Eve's ethnicity barely plays a role in her character or characterization, which further entrenches the structural whiteness of the series. Outside of the aspirational and transformational imperatives of whiteness embedded in the hero's journey and thriller genre, Eve's whiteness stems from two additional interlocking factors: the series is based on a book, *Codename Villanelle*, by a white man about white female characters and, over the course of four seasons, there was an all-white female writers' room.

In casting Sandra Oh as the lead, the show's creators, it seems, were quite comfortable cashing in on Oh's celebrity status and the "diverse" representation she brings to the series, without making inclusive adjustments to her character. Despite being the series' namesake and central protagonist, unlike the other characters—most of whom are white—we don't learn much about Eve outside of her central fixation on Villanelle. Does she have a family outside of her boring life with Nico? Did she grow up somewhere specific? Does she have siblings? A favorite cousin? Past love interests? We know many of these things about Villanelle, about Villanelle's handler Constantine, about Eve's boss Caroline, about Eve's husband Nico. Villanelle's past romantic, sexual, and family history are explored in great depth from season one through three. We learn about Caroline's family and past romantic liaisons. We spend several episodes with Constantine's unruly daughter during the first season. And despite his small role in the series as a whole, we meet Nico's relatives and learn the importance of his Polish heritage. Yet, somehow, Eve is never granted the same depth or complexity, so much so in fact that the series could easily be read as one deeply invested in white female psychopathy at the expense of its central character.

It isn't until season two that any reference to Eve's Korean heritage occurs. First, in an imitation of season one's conceit that as a woman Eve is uniquely suited to recognize that the elusive assassin everyone is looking for is female, Eve correctly deduces that the new evasive assassin is a woman of color, most likely someone working in the service industry because they're "the kind of wom[e]n who people look at every day and never see." "Ghost," Villanelle's early season two assassin-rival, turns out to be another woman of Korean descent living in Britain, whom Eve eventually captures and even speaks Korean with. The fact that Eve's highly attuned intuition is informed by her relationship with her own identity and cultural background is never addressed, as her discovery is merely a plot convenience designed to move the story forward and is quickly forgotten. In yet another cursory moment during season three, Eve visits New Malden, a predominantly Korean neighborhood just outside of London. This touch of non-neutral character design did not emerge from the writers' room, however, but was Oh's invention. In an interview for the *Los Angeles Times*, Oh states,

> I wanted it to be set in a place where Eve could try to disappear for a while. It was just a small bit of the show, but I wanted to bring the flavor of that

because we carry our culture, we carry our history. And typically, white Hollywood does not write it. Does not write our culture, does not write the depth of our culture.[16]

So much is packed into such a seemingly simple gesture of storytelling. In acknowledging that Eve might need someplace to disappear, it becomes clear that being an Asian woman in an almost exclusively white story world is wearing. It indicates that there might be places (or people) with whom Eve feels affinity, with whom she feels at home, who are not like any of the other characters in the series. It suggests that Eve has had a life, a family, a culture that has been formative, and, yet, doesn't inform the story of the series in any way. When screenwriters ignore a character's identity and the accompanying social context that helped shaped it in favor of universal neutral flaws and obsessions, we lose the depth and nuance that might allow for new stories, new directions, news ways of orienting in the world. In this way, *Killing Eve* is an example of a series that has somewhat diverse representation without thoughtful inclusion.

Eve's lack of specific character development demonstrates how character design rooted in notions of universally neutral human traits reduces the possibilities for storytelling. Where Eve's ability to speak Korean or disappear in New Malden or simply make more socially informed deductions to solve problems related to her job could have vastly transformed the trajectory of the series and enriched the audience's understanding of and relationship to Eve's character, instead the series operationalizes point-of-view and cultural context only when convenient for the plot's progression (or at the request of its most prominent star).

Structuring Eve: Narrative Machines as Killing Machines

Along with the genre and character-design conventions driving Eve's character arc, the structural constraints at the heart of classic screenplay paradigms corral Eve's trajectory even more precisely. Below I will analyze two key moments in the series: the first is a scene in episode five, which operates as the midpoint of the first season, where key expectations about Eve and her inability to use a knife are planted; and, the second, from episode eight, the climax/resolution of season one, where the midpoint moment is predictably reversed and the plant is paid off, as per every manual on screenwriting I've ever read.

At the season one midpoint, Eve returns home alone to find that her stolen suitcase has been returned after a forensic inspection. Inside she finds the gifts of clothing and perfume Villanelle bought her. Annoyance soon turns to curiosity— her Amy Schumer-sized wine glass full of Pinot Grigio might be partly to blame— and Eve tries on a tight black dress and heels, while dabbing the perfume (aptly named "Villanelle") on her wrists and neck. In the background, we hear what soon becomes Villanelle and Eve's anthem of queer desire, *Sigh* by Unloveable. A throaty female voice drones on about how "there's something about . . . the way you are" as Eve looks at and runs her hands over her ass in the mirror. There's an erotic quality to this moment, as this is perhaps the first time Eve sees herself through Villanelle's eyes, as someone desirable. Moments later, she hears a noise and discovers that Villanelle has broken into her home. Eve screams and runs towards the bathroom where she holds Villanelle off temporarily with a toilet brush before being tackled into the shower and doused with water by Villanelle who insists that she just wants to have dinner with Eve.

In the kitchen, soaking wet and sulking after being overpowered by Villanelle, Eve microwaves some shepherd's pie and sneaks a knife down her pants. Ever watchful, Villanelle smiles and warns her not to let it slip, and that she's welcome to hold on to it if it make her feel safe. The scene is at once awkward and tender, like a first date, and, eventually, hostile, as two women too smart to be outmaneuvered try to outmaneuver one another. As the scene wears on, it becomes clear how the two women operate as opposites of one another, with Villanelle being physically proficient while having no understanding of the nuances of human emotion (she is a psychopath after all) and Eve being emotionally astute, while having little physical prowess. This dialectic is an example of the conflict imperative central to screenwriting. Perhaps this is best captured in what Ruiz complains of as the "predatory worldview" espoused by Hollywood screenwriting techniques that makes a "flower . . . a battlefield where thesis and antithesis fight, looking for a common synthesis."[17] When Villanelle fakes an emotional break-down, Eve calls "bullshit," putting Villanelle on the defensive, at which point she becomes petulant, shifting to more aggressive tactics, telling Eve that she murdered her best friend Bill because he was "slowing [Eve] down." Eve, pushed to the edge and no longer in control of her emotional reactions, responds by trying to stab Villanelle, only to be quickly over-powered and pinned against the refrigerator with a knife at her throat.

While there is no doubt that the genre play within the scene wittily throws much into question, the scene is ultimately disciplined by the need for conflict, rising stakes, and by occupying the "midpoint" of the season, also known as "the ordeal." This is where the "fortunes of the hero hit bottom in direct confrontation with his greatest fear. . . . [where] the hero must die or appear to die so that she can be reborn again."[18] Further, it is the midpoint where we get a glimpse of how the hero will fare in the end, and it is often the "mirror opposite" of the final climax.[19] Read in this way, we can see that a part of Eve's innocence dies in this scene. Pinned to the fridge and forced to understand that she's not a physical threat to Villanelle, she promises that she's going to find the thing that Villanelle cares about and "kill it." Her failure to outmaneuver Villanelle births her desire to kill Villanelle, or at least a part of her. This, then, is a preview of the final solution, or resolution. We can now guess that the climax of the first season will find the women at odds once again, stakes raised to their highest level yet, with Eve finally using her superior emotional intelligence to outperform Villanelle. And if not only the rules of the midpoint are followed, but also the mandate that the "preparatory device" of the "plant" be followed during the resolution by a proper "payoff,"[20] we can (spoiler alert!) safely bet that a knife will be involved.

As I've discussed previously, the resolution—whether of a film, a series, or an episode—has major ideological implications. Resolutions require that the hero, no matter how grave the threat, "attain a solution that leaves the rest of the society untouched."[21] This is especially true in the spy thriller, a genre designed to tame the threats of an ever more confusing and globalized society. While many critics seemed excited by the possibilities offered by the finale of the inaugural season of *Killing Eve*, they also seemed to forget that narrative and genre constraints are autocratic in nature. For example, *New Yorker* critic Jia Tolentino wrote of the finale that "it seemed equally possible that Eve and Villanelle could team up, or try to kill each other, or fall into bed."[22] Because *Killing Eve* is such a fun and genre-bending show, Tolentino's high hopes are understandable. But, on account of the series' adherence to the tropes of the spy thriller, Eve's choice is almost predestined. As established in the midpoint, like all masculinist, professional secret agents before her, Eve must pursue a license to kill.

As the cat-and-mouse pursuit draws to a close at the end of season one's final episode, Villanelle has once again outplayed everyone—the organization she works for as well as the one Eve works for, which Villanelle believes "if you went high enough . . . are probably the same people." At this point Eve has lost her best friend, her job (twice), and is on her way to losing her husband, which means she's got nothing to lose. Instead of going home to nurse her losses, in an inverse of the midpoint episode, Eve breaks into Villanelle's home, where she is awed by the Euro-chic apartment and opulent wardrobe Villanelle's job affords her. Many reversals follow, none of which include a second round of shepherd's pie.

As Eve searches Villanelle's apartment, she becomes increasingly agitated at the decadence of Villanelle's lifestyle: designer dresses and sheets, chic wigs, drawers full of weapons. After pocketing a switchblade, a reminder of our midpoint plant (I sense a stabbing coming on), Eve opens the refrigerator to discover that it's full of expensive champagne. The decadence is too much for dowdy Eve with her boring cardigans, more boring state security job, and most boring husband, and by way of revolt she shakes up a bottle, uncorks it, and shoots champagne all over Villanelle's bedroom before taking a hearty swig. (Does she have a phallus now?) And when that's not cathartic enough, Eve smashes the bottles one by one in an envious rage just as Villanelle returns home.

Unfazed by Eve's outburst, Villanelle asks Eve if she's "having a party." Eve, exhausted or feigning exhaustion, sits on Villanelle's bed and confesses that she thinks about Villanelle all the time: what she eats for breakfast, what shampoo she uses, what she feels when she kills. And while this seems like an erotically charged moment, if we know how the midpoint operates in relation to the climax (which sadly we do), we know that just as Villanelle worked to emotionally manipulate Eve in the prior scene, Eve is now manipulating Villanelle, preying on Villanelle's queer desire, which, as fetishistic as it is, is very real, so that she can use the knife in her pocket to finally out-phallus Villanelle.

Eventually, the two lay down on Villanelle's bed. Villanelle sets her gun down and strokes Eve's hair. Eve—with an innocence that'd give *Alias'* Sidney Bristow a run for her money—tells Villanelle that she's "never done anything like this before," suggesting to Villanelle and the audience that a sex scene will follow.

Only, with Villanelle's defenses down, Eve doesn't get intimate with Villanelle; instead, in yet another undeniably phallic moment, she pulls out her knife, straddles Villanelle in missionary position, and jams the knife into her abdomen. In stabbing Villanelle, in claiming phallic power, in practicing the art of the kill, the title *Killing Eve* finally takes on a new meaning. This is no longer a show about the death of Eve: this is a show about how Eve becomes a killer, like Bond and Bourne and Bristow before her. To put it another way, the old Eve had to die to make room for a new Eve, an experienced Eve, a dominant Eve: an Eve-who-kills. And here we are once again with the predatory, hostile worldview endlessly reiterated on our television screens by "central conflict theory,"[23] brought to fruition through the relentlessly repeated narrative beats and techniques: midpoint and resolution, plant and payoff.

Rehabilitating Eve? Or How All Might Be Lost

What *Killing Eve* foregrounds is a tension between progressive, feminist, queer representation, and the corralling of those representations through narrative and generic constraints. This is what Gitlin refers to when he writes about how "[c]ommercial culture does not manufacture ideology; it relays and reproduces and processes and packages and focuses ideology that is constantly arising both from social elites [in this case classic generic and narrative constraints] and from active social groups and movements throughout the society [in this case feminism]."[24]

If, as Phoebe Waller-Bridge claims, *Killing Eve* is emblematic of social movements like #metoo, just as we're finally seeing more robust and exciting female representation, we're also seeing how long-standing generic and narrative codes discipline that same female empowerment.

After watching the first season, I'd originally hoped that the following seasons might shift in a new direction. I reasoned that because the arc of a series can extend over multiple seasons, if the series followed a heroine's journey instead of the classic hero's journey, season one could end up chronicling the phallic phase of the heroine's journey, where the female hero rejects the feminine and takes on masculine tools to navigate a patriarchal world. In this scenario, Eve, like many heroines before her, would learn that phallic power doesn't work for women the same way it does for men. With the advent of subsequent seasons, however, my hopes that Eve would give up on knives, guns, and other penetrative devices to embrace a different way of being were dashed. Instead of realizing, à la Maureen Murdock's heroine's journey that "[i]t's not the conquest of the other; it's coming face to face with myself"[25] that matters, the second and third season doubled-down on violence and bloodshed, forcing Eve and Villanelle to partake in increasingly deranged and psychopathic behavior, including Eve hiring Villanelle to torture another assassin, multiple scenes of castration, and the gutting of a man in front of a group of spectators.

By sending Eve down the well-trodden path of so many white, male protagonists and refusing to acknowledge the importance of Eve's cultural background, *Killing Eve* reminds us that assimilation is antithetical to transformation. Screenwriters cannot simply plug female/of color/queer characters into otherwise patriarchal, white supremacist, heteronormative narratives, and expect them not to be tamed into the shapes of their predecessors. This isn't to say that creators invested in equitable representation can't push back against or stretch the structures that seek to contain marginalized characters, only that it has to be done thoughtfully, purposefully, and inclusively. It is with this in mind that I turn to another contemporary television series noted for innovative storytelling: *Sense8*.

Notes

1 Stewart Clarke, "Phoebe Waller-Bridge Twists the Spy Genre with BBC America's Thriller 'Killing Eve'," *Variety*, April 13, 2018, https://variety.com/2018/tv/features/phoebe-waller-bridge-sandra-oh-killing-eve-1202742904/; Sophie Gilbert, "Killing Eve Is a Sign of TV to Come," *The Atlantic*, April 11, 2018, www.theatlantic.com/entertainment/archive/2018/04/killing-eve-review-bbc-america/557531/; Jia Tolentino, "The Pleasurable Patterns of the 'Killing Eve' Season Finale," *The New Yorker*, May 29, 2018, www.newyorker.com/culture/on-television/the-pleasurable-patterns-of-the-killing-eve-season-finale.
2 Summer Kim Lee, "Too Close, Too Compromised: Killing Eve and the Promise of Sandra Oh," *Los Angeles Review of Books*, December 4, 2018, https://lareviewofbooks.org/article/close-compromised-killing-eve-promise-sandra-oh/; Tolentino, "Pleasurable Patterns."
3 Mareike Jenner, "Telling Detection: The Narrative Structures of American TV Detective Dramas," *American TV Detective Dramas: Serial Investigations* (2016): 56; Rosie White, "Introduction," in *Violent Femmes: Women as Spies in Popular Culture* (London: Routledge, 2007), 2.
4 Jenner, "Telling Detection," 60.
5 Ariel Levy, "Female Chauvinist Pigs," in *Female Chauvinist Pigs: Women and the Rise of Raunch Culture* (Collingwood, VIC: Black, 2010), 112.
6 Hilarie Ashton, "In Defense of Fleabag Feminism," *Ms. Magazine Blog*, March 01, 2019, http://msmagazine.com/blog/2019/01/02/defense-fleabag-feminism/.
7 Joey Soloway, "Joey Soloway on The Female Gaze," *Lecture, Toronto International Film Festival*, Canada, Toronto, September 11, 2016, www.youtube.com/watch?v=pnBvppooD9I.
8 Maria San Filippo, *The B Word Bisexuality in Contemporary Film and Television* (Bloomington: Indiana University Press, 2013), 18.
9 Emily Nussbaum (@EmilyNussbaum), "I Enjoyed KILLING EVE. But I'm Fascinated That It Isn'T Getting Any Flack for Suggesting—Basic Instinctishly—That Lesbianism and Murder Are Two Great Tastes That Go Great Together," 28 May 2018, 10:05 a.m. Tweet.
10 Clare Whatling, "In the Good Old Days When Times Were Bad' The Nostalgia for Abjection in Lesbian Cinema Spectatorship," in *Screen Dreams: Fantasizing Lesbians in Film* (New York: Manchester University Press, 1997), 109–10.
11 Ibid., 92.
12 Lee, "Too Close."
13 White, *Violent Femmes*, 6.
14 Jerry Palmer, *Thrillers: Genesis and Structure of a Popular Genre* (New York: St. Martins Press, 1979), 14.
15 Jean-Anne Sutherland and Kathryn M. Feltey, "Here's Looking at Her: An Intersectional Analysis of Women, Power and Feminism in Film," *Journal of Gender Studies* 26, no. 6 (2017): 623.

16 Elena Nelson Howe, "Sandra Oh Layers in Her Ethnicity on 'Killing Eve' Because White Hollywood Does Not," *Los Angeles Times*, June 23, 2020, www.latimes.com/entertainment-arts/tv/story/2020-06-23/sandra-oh-layers-ethnicity-for-nuance-killing-eve.

17 Raúl Ruiz, *Poetics of Cinema: 1* (Paris: Editions Dis Voir, 1995), 15.

18 Christopher Vogler, *The Writers Journey: Mythic Structure for Writers* (Studio City, CA: Michael Wiese Productions, 2007), 15.

19 Paul Joseph Gulino, *Screenwriting: The Sequence Approach* (London: Bloomsbury, 2013), 16.

20 David Howard and Edward Mabley, *The Tools of Screenwriting: A Writer's Guide to the Craft and Elements of a Screenplay* (New York: St. Martin's Press, 1996), 72.

21 Todd Gitlin, "Prime Time Ideology: The Hegemonic Process in Television Entertainment," *Social Problems* 26, no. 3 (1979): 262.

22 Tolentino, "Pleasurable Patterns."

23 Ruiz, *Poetics*, 11.

24 Gitlin, "Prime Time Ideology," 253.

25 Maureen Murdock, *The Heroine's Journey* (Boston, MA: Shambhala, 1990), 9.

7

QUEER AND TRANS WORLD-BUILDING IN *SENSE8*

In contrast to the traditionally structured and normatively disciplined *Killing Eve*, this section focuses on queer and trans world-building in the Netflix series *Sense8* and how the Wachowskis radically reimagine paradigmatic conventions of genre, character, and narrative structure.

Lilly and Lana Wachowski began their careers as comic book writers who shifted into cinema when their script for *Carnivore* (a dystopian sci-fi horror about eating the rich) landed them an agent. They then made their first feature—the masterful neo-noir lesbian thriller *Bound* (1996)—on a shoe-string budget to prove they could helm a studio film. Following *Bound*, they made cinema history via the stylish, technologically innovative, and philosophically complex *The Matrix*, which ushered the blockbuster into the twenty first century. From the rehabilitation of the femme-fatale in *Bound*, to the invention of bullet-time in *The Matrix* (1999), to the inventive slide edits that elide time and space in *Speed Racer* (2008), the Wachowskis push the boundaries of what is cinematically possible with each project. It is thus no surprise that their first foray into television would mark one of the most ambitious televisual projects to date. Shot entirely on location, spanning sixteen cities in eleven different countries, *Sense8* challenges traditional televisual storytelling practice from script to screen.

As the first major studio project helmed by trans creators to feature a trans actor in a trans role, *Sense8* is the most explicitly queer project in the Wachowski oeuvre since *Bound*, that is if you measure queer content by the inclusion of identifiably LGBTQ characters. Including LGBTQ characters, however, is only part of queer and trans world-building, and the Wachowskis' work has always been more conceptually than concretely queer. As filmmakers deeply conversant with philosophy, literature, and film aesthetics, their work—even when focused on presumably straight characters like Neo and Trinity from *The Matrix*—operates queerly through rejecting binaries, blurring boundaries, blending genre, denaturalizing the natural, and,

DOI: 10.4324/9781003170310-10

ultimately, linking the transgressive and the transcendent. In an interview with Lilly Wachowski after coming out in 2016, for example, she stated she was glad that the "original intention" of *The Matrix* as trans allegory was finally being discussed in the mainstream, and that the film "was all about the desire for transformation, but . . . from a closeted point of view" because "the corporate world wasn't ready for it."[1] Although there are no explicitly trans characters in the film—despite the character of Switch initially being crafted as someone who appeared female in the matrix and male in the real world[2]—*The Matrix* is thematically trans in its exploration of transformation, the discrepancy between online and offline identities, and its overall utopian and anti-assimilationist bent. In the Wachowskis' hands, gender, genre, sexuality, race, ethnicity, time, and space—far from being distinct categories—intermix and overlap so that "queer" and "trans" no longer function merely as identity markers, but modes of sentience, consciousness, and relationality. For some, such narrative and conceptual experimentation reeks of a naive utopianism. But how else does the world change if we don't imagine it otherwise? There are few filmmakers who more clearly embody Muñoz's queer utopian ethos of "the rejection of a here and now and an insistence on potentiality for another world."[3] In this vein, as scholar Cáel Keegan argues, *Sense8* "seeks to aesthetically translate transgender as a form of consciousness—a way of perceiving or knowing that occurs between and across bodies, cultures, and geographies."[4]

If one of the purposes of creating utopian art is to query the possibility for positive futures, perhaps it's important to remember that within the work of queer theory, the negative—as embodied by a politics of refusal, the embrace of "bad feelings" and "bad subjects," and various forms of failure—is considered generative ground for queer world-building. The negative—because it acknowledges things like grief, failure, longing and, even, death, all of which are essential components of life—offers ways to creatively challenge "the cultural ethos of good performance and productivity, narcissistic models of self-actualization, the heteronormative family, and related reproductive lifestyles,"[5] all of which serve as fuel for life within a neoliberal capitalist order that puts profits over people. As trans cultural producers who've built their career inside the Hollywood studio system, the Wachowskis are no strangers to failure, for "failure . . . goes hand in hand with capitalism."[6] In fact, I'd argue that their career is best characterized by spectacular and generative failure. For many fans, *The Matrix*—with its bullet dodging, leather-clad, cyber punk heroes and complex philosophy about the nature of reality—marked the height of their filmmaking talents. This is no surprise. By all measures, from following the traditional hero's journey to delivering an action-packed techno-thriller to setting international box office records, *The Matrix* was everything a Hollywood studio executive dreams of. The sequels, however, did not live up to the promise of the original film and suffered major box office losses and fan attrition. Although *The Matrix* sequels featured the same leather-clad characters and continued to deliver technically-innovative fight sequences like the "Burly Brawl," which featured hundreds of Smith replications battling the singular Neo, they didn't *feel* the same. The narratives sprawled with a relentless, yet uneven momentum that threw off the balance between action sequences and expository scenes, leaving audiences as overwhelmed and confused as the characters themselves. Further, and this is what drove most fans of *The Matrix* away in droves: Neo wasn't "the one." He was one of many. Like every white(ish) male hero who had gone before him, he was a replication of a replication of a replication.[7] Put simply, the Wachowskis eschewed the traditional screenwriting paradigms that made the difficult philosophical premises central to their work easier to swallow. Moreover, not only did they use Neo's character to reject the hero's journey, they turned the paradigm inside out to expose the flawed patriarchal, individualist logic it relies on. Breaking the rules, however, meant they couldn't break the box office; and, therefore, they've had a somewhat rocky career ever since. And while they may have been nearly run out of town after the colossal box office failure of *Speed Racer*,[8] their career has not ended, but endured, and there are many lessons to be gleaned from their aesthetic and narrative experiments, as well as from the failure of those experiments to gain cultural traction. Failure to adhere to the status quo is often a sign of the radical work required for queer-feminist, anti-capitalist, and anti-colonialist struggle. This is a brand of failure I would call productive or instructive failure, and it is in line with what Halberstam refers to as "the queer art of failure." He writes,

> I tell it also as a narrative about anti-colonial struggle, the refusal of legibility, and an art of unbecoming. This is a story of art without markets, drama without a script, narrative without progress. The queer art of failure turns on the impossible, the improbable, and the unremarkable. It quietly loses, and in losing it imagines other goals for life, for love, for art, and for being.[9]

It is in this spirit that in the following sections I discuss some of the radical failures of *Sense8* and the radical possibilities those failures generate for screenwriters.

Representing an Eight-in-One: Characterization as Essential to Essence

As with much of the Wachowskis' work outside of *The Matrix*, critic and fan responses to *Sense8* have been ambivalent. Like *Killing Eve*, praise for the series as a "whacked-out masterpiece" tends to coalesce around the diversity of its central protagonists, which includes four men and four women: a transgender white lesbian, a gay Mexican man, and six other ethnically diverse characters from cities around the world, including Nairobi, Mumbai, and Seoul, Korea. In this vein, *Sense8* has been called "casually diverse"[10] while promoting intersectional feminist forms of solidarity that media scholars characterize as "the utopian notion that humans are connected across lines of nationality, race, gender, sexuality, and class."[11]

Sense8 follows the interconnected lives of eight co-protagonists who form an eight-fold psyche. In addition to living in different cities and countries, the characters occupy unique intersections of gender, sexuality, race, and ethnicity. Nomi (Jamie Clayton) is a white transgender "hacktivist" living in San Francisco with her biracial girlfriend Amanita (Freema Agyeman); Will (Brian J. Smith) is a white cop living in Chicago; Lito (Miguel Ángel Silvestre) is a famous (and closeted) action hero who lives with his boyfriend in Mexico; Sun (Doona Bae) is a business woman by day and underground martial arts fighter by night in Seoul, Korea; Capheus (Aml Ameen) drives a tourist bus called the "Van Damn" and cares for his sick mother in Nairobi, Kenya; Kala (Tina Desai) is a Hindu pharmacist in Mumbai, India struggling with whether she loves her fiancé; Wolfgang (Max Riemelt) is a safe cracker in Berlin, Germany; and Riley (Tuppence Middleton) is a depressed and drug-addled DJ from Iceland with a tragic secret. These simple character descriptions don't change over the course of the series, which consequently, is one of the show's most common mainstream criticisms. But we'll come back to that.

Over the course of the first season, the co-protagonists discover that they are part of a "cluster" of "sensates" born of the same mother on the same day and are telepathically and sensorially connected through their limbic system, the complex neural and nerve network responsible for instincts, moods, and basic emotions and drives. Through their connection they can appear in one another's minds/bodies at any moment to "share" emotions and experiences. In essence, they are empathy personified. Visually, this is depicted in a number of ways. Sometimes characters suddenly show up in the same spaces with other characters. This can happen with two or more sensates for something as simple as a conversation in a bar or as complex as a transnational orgy. Other times one character replaces another in order to share a particular skill like fighting or hacking a computer. In either case, all of the "visiting" scenes are filmed in and edited to include each of the locations unique to each character to emphasize the global, cross-spatial connection the characters experience. When Nomi is connecting with Lito, for instance, their scenes shift seamlessly between San Francisco and Mexico City. Similarly, scenes between Wolfgang and Kala cut back and forth between Berlin and Mumbai. Certainly the technically innovative Wachowskis—who filmed much of *The Matrix Trilogy* and all of *Speed Racer* with green-screen technology—could have used special effects to bridge the distance, but their insistence on in-person, on-site shooting for all scenes emphasizes the theme of connection across distance and division. While much of the series is focused on the interconnections between characters, eventually the antagonistic forces in the narrative compel them to work together to evade the evil Biologic Preservation Organization (BPO), which wants to capture and experiment on them. Simultaneously global and intimate, action-packed and quotidian, *Sense8* "appeals to audiences that have gravitated to it for its identity politics as well as its compelling characterization and themes."[12] With this brief introduction to what is sometimes a mind-bogglingly complicated series, I will now shift to an analysis of how *Sense8* defies and reimagines Hollywood storytelling structures related to character, genre, and narrative towards liberatory ends.

In terms of characterization, unlike *Killing Eve*, each *Sense8* characters' unique race, ethnicity, gender, and sexuality contributes to their specific problems. In *Killing Eve*, Sandra Oh plays a role originally written for a white protagonist, and, yet, at no point in season one is there a reference to her Korean-Canadian heritage, nor what it means to live as an Asian woman in a white world. In contrast, Sun, the South Korean co-protagonist of *Sense8*, deals with issues particular to her gender within Korean culture. Specifically, Sun faces forms of sexism unique to some Asian cultures, where long-standing patriarchal practices keep women from inheriting family businesses, with CEO fathers often marrying off their daughters to pass the business on to the husband if there is not a son available for the job. Within the world of *Sense8*, Sun's father hands their family business over to her corrupt brother when she's proven to be far more competent, ethical, and concerned about her family's legacy. By privileging what McKee would denigrate as Sun's "observable qualities" in the creation of her character, the Wachowskis upend the binaristic antagonism inherent in screenwriting paradigms that pit character against characterization. Sun's specific identity is not something to transform or overcome in a journey towards a universal and neutral form of virtue, but instead becomes the fuel that drives her in her quest for justice. Unlike Eve, who emulates masculinist violence to gain power and reinforce the status quo, Sun uses the violence of her martial arts practice to fight patriarchy and the other forces that oppress her and her fellow sensates.

In addition to racial, ethnic, and gender specificity, *Sense8* demonstrates a commitment to specific trans and queer representation. While the queer characters deal with trans-misogyny and homophobia, they are also given storylines and intimate partnerships that are celebratory and non-normative, which challenge dominant hetero- and homonormative paradigms of monogamous relationships and straight, reproductive time. Like heteronormativity, homonormativity espouses an assimilationist agenda, promising "the possibility of a privatized, depoliticized gay culture anchored in domesticity and consumption."[13] Put simply, the queer characters are not written to cater to a straight audiences by mimicking straight (universal and neutral) behavior. For instance, Lito and Hernando live with a straight woman named Daniela. While the three don't have sex together, Daniela often participates by filming the men during sex and masturbating. Daniela's spectatorship and arousal challenge negative and moralistic attitudes around gay male sex by making Daniela a fan of their love and love-making. Rather than relying on overused portrayals of queer love that employ straight-safe markers like coming out (to warn the cis-het people around them), queer marriage (to normalize non-normative relationships), or the time-tested "Bury Your Gays" trope (which makes queer characters nominal, expendable, and easy to kill off), *Sense8* depicts queer and trans characters doing things actual queer and trans people might do in real life: attend pride parades, participate in queer art performances, discuss queer politics, create chosen families, engage in vlogging and queer connection online, all of which are important cultural practices central to queer community.[14] Despite some critiques of "paper-thin" characterizations,[15] the *Sense8* cluster contains no bland, universal neutrals on which to project the straight audience's hopes and fears about queerness—instead the queer and trans characters start, live, and end immutably queer.

It is precisely this character specificity—established via a trust in the power of characterization and an accompanying awareness that identity influences (but doesn't not determine) how one moves in the world—that allows the sensates to demonstrate a deeply relational ethic that foregrounds the "the interdependency among multiple systems of domination"[16] and the solidarity required to upend those systems. Rather than acting as lone individual heroes pursuing their own wants and needs while encountering a series of conflicts designed to transform them into autonomous, "self-balanced" selves,[17] all eight characters act together as a slowly integrating and intersectional whole. As Elrod notes, "[a]s they advance into new, shared explorations of sexuality and interconnectedness they begin to transcend—or even negate—the limitations of separateness in a way that allows for shifting possibilities for new subjectivities."[18] Their empathic connection is predicated on a "vision of the self [that] acquires identity in relation to others"[19] and establishes a pluralism rooted in permeability, fluidity, and boundary-crossing. Unlike the bounded systems (border walls, prisons, etc.) manufactured by the state to corral human behavior and keep people apart, the sensates remain open to one another through free-flowing forms of exposure that "enable the characters to escape the 'trauma of enforced confines'" while becoming "part of a stronger collective."[20] This communal thrust is perhaps best captured by the character of Nomi, whose specific trans identity and way of experiencing the world informs her essential role in the cluster. Her name "Nomi Marks"

> can be translated as "one who is marked by knowledge" by possessing an organ of special insight. For Nomi, this organ is her sensate awareness, which is represented as a speculative extension of her trans★ sensorium—of *feeling something is there* that others cannot perceive. Nomi's central presence in the series is an initiatory lesson for how *Sense8* will require both its characters and audience to sense differently. The sensates are "marked" by a trans★ awareness that will move them into a pluralization of self, forcing them to abandon the feeling of autonomous personhood. In becoming sensate, Nomi and her cluster will become a "we"—in other words, a "no me." A sensate is therefore "one who knows they are not one."[21]

In this way, the highly specific nature of each character builds into a multidimensionality absent from the highly individualistic characters at the center of most screen narratives that follow a singular protagonist. Here we see reflections of Lana Wachowski's belief that "[s]overeignty is a particularly dangerous narrative—that we are alone, we are the one."[22] Instead, each character in *Sense8* is unique and not alone. Moreover, each character contributes to their cluster in ways that only they can (no color- or gender-neutral casting here). The identities so interchangeable to the gods of screenwriting like McKee or Vogler are immutable and essential to the characters, and, thus, to the story, forming what feminist philosophers like Cavarero call a relational ethic founded on vulnerability and radical equality.

For Cavarero, the individualistic, sovereignty-oriented framework at the heart of the Western tradition—and exemplified by characters like Eve who moves from a position of lack to a position of individuation, triumphant but alone—is best illustrated through the geometrical schematic of the singular vertical line, or the upright, air-tight individual. In her pursuit of a relational ethic founded on vulnerability, Cavarero critiques this vertical axis for being rooted in a convenient fiction most exemplified by Kant, whom Cavarero describes as someone fixated on a

> model of a self that legislates from itself upon itself—a straight and self-balanced self that takes its place in a straight line alongside every other self, over the earth's surface, all of which are likewise autarchic and at the same time replicas of one another.[23]

In contrast, the sensates are specific and pluralistic, not singular replications like the Wachowskis' most famous villain, Agent Smith (*The Matrix*) who, in trying to destroy the intersectional community of Zion, turns everyone he encounters into a "me" instead of a "we." Agent Smith's refrain of "me, me, me" is rebutted by *Sense8*'s Nomi—"no me." Thus, the ideology of individualism, which is foundational to screenwriting paradigms, elides the vulnerability, asymmetry, and dependence that are essential components of a relational ethic. *Sense8*, in opposition to individualistic narratives, asks us to "reorient our gaze" by centering unique and vulnerable members of society who, together, pursue a form of relational wholeness that relies on connection, mutual vulnerability, and uniqueness. For the screenwriter interested in rethinking how characters within an ensemble function in relation to one another, *Sense8* offers one possible alternative path with many generative possibilities.

Sensory Overload: Generic Excess

The only consistent consensus as to where *Sense8* fits genre-wise is that it has an "insatiable appetite for genre" so much so that it "def[ies] genre categorization itself."[24] Just as the sensate cluster seamlessly crosses geographical, gender, racial, and sexual boundaries to connect with one another inside their collective psyche, the series can be seen as a trans-genre project that whimsically, yet strategically, leaps between genres, from police procedural to Bollywood musical to maternal melodrama to martial arts to gangster noir. Where *Killing Eve*'s playful blending of the spy thriller and the rom-com gave in to the more conservative aspects of both genres, thus locking its characters into masculinist paradigms of individualism and domination, *Sense8* fluidly shifts between genres at such a fast clip that the boundaries themselves become blurred into more fluid forms that open new possibilities. In this way, *Sense8*'s queer and trans aesthetics harken back to the New Queer Cinema movement of the 1990s, where young queer filmmakers like Todd Haynes, Gregg Araki, and Cheryl Dunye broke new ground in queer representation by centering stories on queer characters while challenging the dominant modes of Hollywood storytelling through genre mash-ups (and send-ups) like *Poison* (1991), *Nowhere* (1997), and *The Watermelon Woman* (1996).

In accordance with my previous discussion about the ways genre works to discipline character and narrative, it's helpful to think of genre as a narrative cage or, more precisely, a cage inside of another cage, as narrative already operates via the particular limitations of three-act structure. With this in mind, *Sense8*'s wild romp across genre can be seen as a form of decarceration that sets its characters free. As Keegan notes, the series places each character inside a familiar genre representative of structural and cultural rules that might imprison them in real life, and, thus, functions as "an exploration of how static forms limit which stories can be told and which modes of life can thus become cognizable to others."[25]

Perhaps this is best exemplified in the way that the male characters in *Sense8* all coalesce around genre tropes founded on masculinist hero myths: Will is a cop and agent of state violence; Lito is a Mexican movie star and leading man; Wolfgang is an outlaw-hero and professional safe-cracker; and Capheus, arguably the gentlest of the main male characters, is the archetypal entrepreneurial underdog-hero who drives a bus called the "Van Damn" named after his favorite action star, Jean Claude Van Damme. Unlike other series rife with masculinist genre staples, in the Wachowskis' hands the archetypes are troubled and dismantled, revealing the heterosexism, misogyny, and destructive patriarchal power they're predicated upon, to the detriment not only of the ancillary characters but to the "main" characters themselves.

In the tenth episode Wolfgang, who lives inside a crime drama, runs into trouble when a rival gangster, Steiner, shakes him down for some diamonds he's stolen, demanding that Wolfgang explain how he got them. When Wolfgang tells the truth—that he cracked the safe—Steiner doesn't believe him because he'd failed to crack it himself. In order to protect his own masculinity, Steiner pushes Wolfgang for a different answer, threatening to kill him if he doesn't fess up. The only way for Wolfgang to save himself is to lie and downplay his ability, but because Steiner reminds him of his own abusive father, he freezes and cannot get the words out. Lito, who is in the midst of a personal crisis of telenovel-ic proportions, "visits" to counsel and then act for Wolfgang, which highlights a number of issues. First, Steiner calls Wolfgang every homophobic slur he can think of, which, once Lito arrives in Wolfgang's body, takes on new resonance.

Lito, unlike the movie-heroes he plays, is not a man for whom machismo comes naturally. When not on set or in public, he's often sensitive and sometimes silly. But because the world of macho action heroes is predicated on displays of violent heterosexual masculinity, Lito accepts a life in the closet in exchange for a career in the spotlight. At the point where Lito is visiting Wolfgang, the choice to live in the closet has decimated Lito's relationship with his long-time boyfriend Hernando, whom he loves deeply. When Lito arrives to help Wolfgang, he taps into his well-practiced ability to act—or, more specifically, to lie—a skill he learned not only through his chosen trade but by trying for his whole life to fit himself into the masculinist world represented by the homophobic and hyper-violent Steiner. In the case of Lito, in his life and now Lito-as-Wolfgang faced with Steiner, failing to lie could result in death. Such is the price of not passing. Masquerading as a tough guy has allowed Lito to save his own life in the deeply hetero-masculine culture he grew up in, afforded him a successful career pretending to be that tough guy on screen, and now gives him an opportunity to save Wolfgang's life. However, the experience of absorbing Steiner's homophobic insults is a turning point for Lito, contributing to his decision in a later episode to come clean about his identity and risk his career in order to be with Hernando. The action hero gives up his action-hero-ness for a different type of honor: authenticity and love. In this way, *Sense8* uses the trappings of genre against themselves to free its characters from their narrative confines.

If unthought adherence to the trappings of the spy thriller put Eve on the masculinist path of the Every (Wo)Man, *Sense8* strategically employs the genre tropes of the police procedural to comment on and dismantle its central hero Will, placing him on something we might call the un-hero's journey, which tracks with the "unbecoming" central to the "queer art of failure."[26] Will begins *Sense8* as the typical cop hero, meaning he pursues "bad guys," follows clues to solve crimes, and has access to information that other characters in other genres don't. As cop, he is an emblem of white male privilege and power who possesses "a heroic willingness to risk life and livelihood in pursuit of justice."[27] While many police procedurals rely on audiences to accept the "good guy" status of the show's central characters, Will's essential "goodness" is depicted as flawed and clueless. While the more marginalized characters like Nomi—locked in a techno-thriller and pestered by dead-naming and a medical industrial complex who wants to lobotomize her—are aware of the trappings of normative society as represented by genre, Will remains the most stubbornly attached to, and thus trapped by, the trope of the white-hero. From the moment we meet Will, we know he has a hero complex: he bends over backwards to take care of his abusive, alcoholic father, is obsessed with a childhood friend whom he failed to protect from a tragic fate, and, in what is widely considered the most problematic storyline in the series (for good reason), puts his job on the line to save a Black kid from Chicago's south side. To expose the trappings of genre, the Wachowski's lay them on thick, sometimes cringingly so; to sever the trappings of genre, they connect Will most intimately with Riley, the drug-addled and melancholic DJ from Iceland, who we eventually learn is living in the genre of a maternal melodrama from hell.

Over the course of the first season, as Will grows closer with Riley and consequently becomes incorporated within her genre, the liberatory potential inherent in melodrama shakes Will from the narrative cage of the masculinist police procedural. While melodramas are commonly associated with emotional excess, music, femininity, and social issues, they also "encompass a broad range of films marked by 'lapses' in realism, by 'excesses' of spectacle and displays of primal, even infantile emotions, and by narratives that seem circular and repetitive."[28] We see this most explicitly in episode ten, "What is Human?," when Riley and the cluster attend a symphony performance of Beethoven's "Piano Concerto No. 5." As the music swells, Riley—a motherless daughter and a daughterless mother—remembers her birth, which inspires an earnest, heartfelt, and bloody montage of birth-memories from each sensate culminating in Riley reliving the loss of her own child. The sequence is as long as it is emotionally wrenching, bounding across time and space from one simultaneous birth to another, some painful, some joyful, all of which link the past to the present, blurring the line between here and there, then and now in an explicit rendering of queer temporality.[29] Unlike the hyper-logical police procedural, which follows Field's problem-solution narrative paradigm through posing a seemingly unsolvable crime in the first act and solving that crime and serving justice by the final act, the melodrama foregoes solutions to ask "[w]hat would happen if this procedure were interrupted?"[30] Blending the stories of Will and Riley works to undercut Will's attachment to his genre and the heroic role he's required to play within it because melodramas simply don't believe in the certainty or the individual heroism at the root of the police procedural. Instead, "the desire for change is part of the appeal of the melodrama," and "[r]ecognizing that is a way to finding what is possible."[31]

Like Eve—who also loses a great deal on account of her romantic/obsessive attachment to Villanelle—Will loses his job, his status, and his access to power because of his connection to Riley. Unlike Eve—who claims power through seducing and stabbing Villanelle—in a reversal of common hero narratives, just as Will is poised to reclaim his power and prove he is the ultimate hero by saving his love from the evil clutches of the BPO, Will must give up his heroic, violent, masculinist, and white privilege in order to continue his narrative trajectory. In the final episode of the first season, Will encounters Whispers, a deranged sensate from a previous cluster, whose goal is to lock eyes with Will in order to gain access to the entire sensate clusters' collective consciousness. Will resists, but, unfortunately, as many women know only too well, when a man stares at you intently enough for long enough, it's hard to avoid their gaze. In a moment of weakness, Whispers catches Will's eyes long enough to get a glimpse of the access he needs to take the cluster down. Will is faced with a choice: he can either keep actively fighting, as is expected of a hero, or he can stand down and do the literal opposite: nothing. To save his fellow sensates—or, rather, to keep them whole—Will blocks Whispers' access to the cluster by giving up his own agency, willfullness, and consciousness, a feat made possible by Will's submission to a steady stream of heroin injections that keep him continually unconscious.

If passive characters are boring characters, a passive, perpetually passed out cop at the center of a police procedural is downright sacrilegious. The Wachowskis saddle Will with what is, for the white male hero archetype, perhaps the most radical challenge of all of his sensate-siblings, in that he has to do what no hero has ever chosen to do before: stop. Or, more precisely, he must, in the language of queer failure, "unbecome."[32] For Will, who has never experienced the brutal disciplining mechanisms of the status quo, this is the closest he's ever gotten to the ways many of his fellow sensates experience "the bodily and social experience of restriction."[33] Throughout Will's life, he played the part of Althusser's policeman; hailing the other, asking them questions, searching their bodies, each demand "a stopping device."[34] Thus, a reversal of the hero archetype and arc, the forced passivity over activity, contains liberatory potential in that "[a] phenomenology of being stopped might take us in a different direction than the one that begins with motility, with a body that 'can do' by flowing into space."[35] If Eve's narrative arc allows her to take up space through the mantle of masculinist violence, all to fill the void at the center of her life, Will's arc is to fail to play the hero, a radical and emblematic deconstruction of the Western male archetype through a return to the void.

Sensing Incoherence: Narrative Turbulence

The "queer failure" of the Wachowskis' work is most evident in reactions to how they remake structure. In the realm of popular media criticism, reviewers were perhaps most confounded by *Sense8's* narrative turbulence. When mild, critics muse that the series is "as meandering as it is masterful;"[36] when extreme, critics boil *Sense8's* failures down to "an utter lack of story structure and pacing" that "jump from moments of somber reflection, to high octane action, to plotting dribble, to mindless exposition and back again without any real pattern or logic."[37] When viewed through the lens of traditional screen story structure, such irritation is understandable. As viewers, we've been trained by media—and Field and his peers—to expect certain patterns, character types, and outcomes. When writers reject traditional models and embrace different organizational logics that are more in tune with other ways of being, it feels like something is amiss.

Sense8 "fails" narratively because it operates through digressive, excessive, and associative logics that fall outside traditional three-act structure with its causal, temporal narratives rooted in transformation arcs that redeem the central protagonist through a series of conflicts and rewards. Unlike traditional television series, *Sense8* digresses: it wanders from place to place and from storyline to storyline in a manner that often feels like a conversation, in part, because it is a conversation. As the sensates get to know one another, they "visit" with each other, taking time to relate to one another. In a visual medium primed for tension, however, this can feel like the show has taken an unnecessary detour. Additionally, because there are so many characters and so many narrative threads, it's difficult to know who or what is coming next at any given moment. In this way the audience is put into the same position as the characters, who can be visited randomly by anyone in their cluster. In contrast, *Killing Eve* has a taut, causal narrative trajectory—including a connected mid-point and final climax reversal—that functions as logical and redemptive. Once Eve plunges the knife into Villanelle's abdomen, central questions around Eve's agency and transformation are addressed while ending the season on a cliffhanger for future investment in the next season. *Sense8* paves no such trail.

Though co-creator J. Michael Straczynski claims that the series was designed to be watched in one sitting as a "twelve hour movie" broken up by "three-act structure,"[38] if we contrast *Sense8's* first season mid-point and final episodes, we're left with more questions than answers. Episode six, "Demons," balances its focus evenly across all characters except Riley and Will, who occupy little of the episode's narrative focus. Instead, Sun takes the fall for her corrupt brother and is sent to prison where she's brutally interrogated during her intake interview, which connects her to Lito, who faces an invasive "Access Hollywood"-style interview that forces him to lie about his love interest, thus putting pressure on the ways he's trapped in the closet. Kala encounters Wolfgang at her wedding and faints only to wake up and find him naked in her bed. Capheus agrees to use his tourist bus to help a wealthy man take his daughter to safety in exchange for money to buy medicine for this mother. Nomi and Amanita arrive at a safe house and have sex after Nomi escapes the BPO operatives that tried to have her lobotomized. During their love-making, they are connected to Wolfgang, Lito, and Will who all converge in Wolfgang's sauna for the first of the series' transnational, queer orgy sequences. While some of the scenes operate to advance individual plot lines, the bulk of the episode is thematically centered around the ways we become incarcerated by the status quo: Sun inside the cage of patriarchal misogyny; Lito and toxic masculinity and homo-phobia; Nomi and trans-misogyny; Capheus and cyclical poverty in the aftermath of colonialism. The orgy that marks the climax of the episode momentarily dis-solves these cages, as gender, race, and sexual norms are traversed through erotic excess and pleasure. Here we can see the way that *Sense8* enlists narrative to not only "operate outside or on the fringes of heteronormative spheres of contempo-rary capitalist society and conventional family life,"[39] but to rethink the narrative potential of the climax, ironically through a (pan)sexual climax. Leave it to the Wachowskis to pun their way to queer utopia.

In traditional narrative paradigms, the climax operates as the final solution to the narrative problem, which allows for a return to the status quo. The orgy sequence provides no such closure. In its digression from the plot, it "fails" to solve any of the narrative threads centered in the episode. As a matter of fact, Sun and Capheus don't join the orgy at all. Instead, it is a moment of intimate and ecstatic excess that marks "an exodus from the normative brutality of the available physical world" and a rejection of the normative boundaries that define the character's lives.[40] By stag-ing the "final solution" as a moment of narrative excess, the orgy–climax suggests that the solutions to our narrative and life problems lie not in logical, causal solu-tions, but through rapturous rupture and moments of intense intimacy. What other stories might be told (and what possible futures might unfold) if the function of the climax is continuously reimagined in other new and exciting ways? By positing climax as rapture over climax as solution, the Wachowskis prove that the paradigms don't have to be completely discarded (at least not entirely); only infused with new life, new meaning, new possibility.

In contrast to the unraveling and digressive, yet associated plot-lines of episode six, episode twelve centers Riley and Will almost exclusively in what amounts to a pulsating hour-long action sequence, complete with car and helicopter chases, in which Will flies to Iceland to save Riley from the grips of the evil BPO, doing so with the help of each sensate and their special skills. Instead of a clever plant to payoff, mid-point to climax reversal, what we have here is an eruption of a sto-ryline that was a blip in the mid-point episode: Riley and Will's initial meeting. If anything, the mid-point and final episodes work through thematic juxtaposition and association: episode six's climactic orgy announces the role of eros, connection, and love as the prime energies required to combat the divisive forces of thanatos, individualism, and hate exemplified by the over-long, *Matrix Reloaded*-esque chase sequence that consumes the bulk of episode twelve. Further, in contrast to *Killing Eve*'s final scene, which resurrects Eve through her act of masculinist violence making her into "the kind of [wo]man [s]he was before [s]he lost [her] will to live,"[41] the final scene of *Sense8* ends ambiguously with all eight sensates sitting together in the same boat at sunset. No one, not the sensates nor the audience, knows where they're headed, which draws attention to the way *Sense8* openly holds space for utopian queer futures. As Muñoz writes, "[q]ueerness is not yet here. Queerness is an ideality. Put another way, we are not yet queer. We may never touch queerness, but we can feel it as the warm illumination of a horizon imbued with potentiality."[42]

While the narrative inconsistency and ambiguity can leave audiences straining to make connections among the disparate narrative strands, the deviation from the norm is the point, and it doesn't prevent the series from progressing, as much as it challenges its viewers to reimagine possibilities for what progress means. So much of *Sense8* is comprised of what Ruiz refers to as moments of "narrative excess," where characters simply talk about their lives, their hopes, and their dreams. It's in these moments, such as in episode seven when Kala and Wolfgang have a conversation that spans stories from their pasts to the force of gravity to Kala's definition of the miraculous while shifting seamlessly from a Mumbai rooftop at magic hour to a Berlin cafe patio in a downpour that one understands that the mundane can be sublime, for the sensates' "[t]elepahtic empathy" emphasizes "the quotidian flow's extreme rupture."[43] Kala and Wolfgang's conversation adds nothing to the narrative thrust. But like a river, a "digressive narrative meanders; at times it flows quickly and at times barely at all, often loops back on itself, yet ultimately it moves onward."[44] The best way to describe the narrative structure of *Sense8* is undulating. It moves like waves that crest and ebb, like the waters on which the boat floats in the season one finale, but never culminates in a final tsunami climax that resolves the main tension or redeems the main characters. Instead, in contrast to most of televisual culture's preference for "completion and conflict resolution as accomplishment," *Sense8* "thrives when it indulges in building the interpersonal connections and metaphysical relationships among its sensates" and encourages "discovery, process, and patience instead."[45] In short, it allows us to live (and love) in time and across space in new and exciting ways.

For the screenwriter hoping to infuse new life into standard conventions, *Sense8*'s most oft-discussed weaknesses and "failures" come together to create its strength: it's an ensemble piece that's not an ensemble piece; it's a journey with no clear hero; it's full of "thin" characters woven together to create a sumptuous and layered beating heart, meant, possibly, to represent an ideal world or smaller community in which each participant truly sees, cares about, and empathizes with one another, sharing viscerally each person's pleasure and pain, showing up exactly when someone needs another, and joining together for both pathos and partying. No room for individual aims and singular accumulated wealth or successes in this world; they only survive if they all survive.

Notes

1 "Why The Matrix Is a Trans Story According to Lilly Wachowski | Netflix," *YouTube*, August 4, 2020, www.youtube.com/watch?v=adXm2sDzGkQ.
2 Ibid.
3 José Esteban Muñoz, *Cruising Utopia: The Then and There of Queer Futurity* (New York: New York University Press, 2009), 1.
4 Cáel M. Keegan, "Tongues Without Bodies," *TSQ: Transgender Studies Quarterly* 3, no. 3–4 (2016): 605–10, https://doi.org/10.1215/23289252-3545275, 606.
5 Mari Ruti, *The Ethics of Opting Out: Queer Theory's Defiant Subjects* (New York: Columbia University Press, 2017), 7.
6 Judith Halberstam, *The Queer Art of Failure* (Durham, NC: Duke University Press, 2011), 88.
7 The pain of this realization to the white male ego is most palpable with a cursory survey of the dozens of YouTube video essays, with legions of supportive comments, about "Why *The Matrix* Sequels Suck."
8 "Lilly Wachowski and Lana Wachowski," *YouTube*, uploaded by DePaul Visiting Artist Series, May 2, 2014, www.youtube.com/watch?v=ARoKJ00cEZ8.
9 Halberstam, *Queer Art of Failure*, 88.
10 Emily VanDerWerff, "I Watched Netflix's Sense8 and Don't Know If It's a Travesty or a Whacked-out Masterpiece," *Vox*, June 10, 2015, www.vox.com/2015/6/10/8756283/sense8-review-netflix.
11 Ava Laure Parsemain, "'I Am Also a We': The Pedagogy of Sense8," *The Pedagogy of Queer TV* (2019): 216.
12 James Elrod, "I Am Also a We': The Interconnected, Intersectional Superheroes of Netflix's Sense8," *Panic at the Discourse: An Interdisciplinary Journal*, www.academia.edu/39809616/_I_am_also_a_we_The_Interconnected_Intersectional_Superheroes_of_Netflixs_Sense8, 47.
13 Lisa Duggan, *Materializing Democracy Toward a Revitalized Cultural Politics*. Edited by Dana D. Nelson and Russ Castronovo (Durham, NC: Duke University Press, 2002), 179.
14 Parsemain, "Pedagogy of Sense8," 221.
15 Kevin Yeoman, "'Sense8' Series Premiere Review: Beautiful Nonsense," *ScreenRant*, June 5, 2015, screenrant.com/sense8-series-premiere-review/.
16 Cathy Cohen, "Punks, Bulldaggers, and Welfare Queens: The Radical Potential of Queer Politics?" *GLQ: A Journal of Lesbian and Gay Studies* 3, no. 4 (January 1997): 442.
17 Adriana Cavarero, *Inclinations: A Critique of Rectitude* (Stanford: Stanford University Press, 2016), 31.
18 Elrod, "Intersectional Superheroes," 52.
19 Sijia Li, "Netflix by Netflix: On 'Sense8," *Los Angeles Review of Books*, May 16, 2017, https://lareviewofbooks.org/article/netflix-by-netflix-on-sense8.
20 Elrod, "Intersectional Superheroes," 52.
21 Cáel M. Keegan, *Lana and Lilly Wachowski* (Champaign, IL: University of Illinois Press, 2018), 113.
22 Ibid., 134.
23 Cavarero, *Inclinations*, 31.
24 Li, "On Sense8."
25 Keegan, *Lana and Lilly*, 116.
26 Halberstam, *Queer Art of Failure*, 88.
27 Jonathan Nichols-Pethick, *TV Cops: The Contemporary American Television Police Drama* (New York: Routledge, 2012), 8.
28 Linda Williams, "Film Bodies: Gender, Genre, and Excess," *Film Quarterly* 44, no. 4 (1991): 3.
29 Judith Halberstam, *In a Queer Time and Place: Transgender Bodies, Subcultural Lives* (New York: New York University Press, 2005), 2.
30 Jonathan Goldberg, *Melodrama: An Aesthetics of Impossibility* (Durham, NC: Duke University Press, 2016), 33.
31 Ibid., 42.
32 Halberstam, *Queer Art of Failure*, 88.

33 Sara Ahmed, "A Phenomenology of Whiteness," *Feminist Theory* 8, no. 2 (January 2007): 149–68, https://doi.org/10.1177/1464700107078139, 161.

34 Ibid.

35 Ibid.

36 David Levesley, "Netflix's Sense8 Isn't Perfect, but It's the Best Queer Show on TV," *Slate Magazine*, June 22, 2015, slate.com/human-interest/2015/06/in-sense8-netflix-has-created-a-queer-masterpiece.html.

37 Merrill Barr, " 'Sense8' Failure in Structure Highlights the Biggest Problem with Netflix Programming," *Forbes*, June 10, 2015, www.forbes.com/sites/merrillbarr/2015/06/10/sense8-failure-netflix/.

38 Christina Radish, "J. Michael Straczynski Talks Collaborating with the Wachowskis on SENSE8," *Collider*, September 25, 2019, collider.com/sense8-j-michael-straczynski-talks-collaborating-with-the-wachowskis/.

39 Elrod, "Intersectional Superheroes," 52.

40 Kilyana Mincheva, "Sense 8 and the Praxis of Utopia," *Cinephile* 12, no. 1 (2018): 37.

41 Robert McKee, *Story: Substance, Structure, Style, and the Principles of Screenwriting* (New York: Regan Books, 1997), 104.

42 Muñoz, *Cruising Utopia*, 1.

43 Mincheva, "Praxis of Utopia," 37.

44 Jane Alison, *Meander, Spiral, Explode: Design and Pattern in Narrative* (New York: Catapult, 2019), 23.

45 Rox Samer, ed., "Sense8 Roundtable," *Spectator* 37, no. 2 (2017): 77.

8

THE GENERATIVE POWER OF PARADIGM DESTRUCTION IN *I MAY DESTROY YOU*

I May Destroy You (Michaela Coel, 2020) is a twelve-episode series that revolves around sexual assault, consent, trauma, and healing. Loosely based on Coel's sexual assault while writing the second season of *Chewing Gum*, *I May Destroy You* follows writer and Twitter phenom Arabella Essiedu (Coel) as she writes her second book for traditional publisher Henny House. The inciting incident occurs in the first episode during a frantic writing stint following a trip to Italy where Arabella put off completing her pages to have a fling with an Italian drug dealer. On her first day back in London, Arabella sequesters herself in the Henny House offices, but then takes what's meant to be a short a break from completing her pages and ventures out to a bar to meet some friends. While out, her drink is spiked, and she's sexually assaulted. The next morning, inexplicably back in the office with a bleeding forehead and smashed up phone, Arabella emerges into consciousness shortly before a meeting with her white editors—completely unaware of what happened the night before. In the following eleven episodes, the series follows Arabella's attempts to understand and process the trauma of what happened to her. She experiences violent flashbacks, pursues details about the night of her assault, and processes how the assault has reframed her self-understanding as a Black British woman living and moving in the world.

Coel May Destroy the Active/Passive Binary

I May Destroy You operates through an awareness that patriarchal culture impacts male and female agency in vastly different ways. Particularly, the series addresses how women's agency and subject-status are always already precarious within a world dominated by the male gaze. As Sobchack writes,

> [m]ore often than men, women are the objects of gazes that locate and invite their bodies to live as merely material 'things' immanently positioned in

DOI: 10.4324/9781003170310-11

space rather than as conscious subjects with the capacity to transcend their immanence and posit space.[1]

We see this explicitly in the spiking of Arabella's drink and subsequent sexual assault, where Arabella's ability to navigate, let alone posit, space is purposefully obliterated. As we learn more about the night of the assault through Arabella's recovered memories, we see how the two men scoped out the bar, honing their gaze on Arabella and her distracted friends. We watch them watch her slowly lose control of her body and senses as the drug takes effect. Their gaze, as well as their joint effort to carry Arabella around like a marionette—a mere thing—is a direct representation of the ways that the male gaze within patriarchal power structures has license to render women objects.

In Coel's hands, the ease with which a person can slip from subject to object is explored with great care. The drug-induced assault not only results in a loss of bodily autonomy, but of temporal and spatial awareness, memory, and sense of self. Arabella is, as her white friend Theo (Harriett Webb) remarks in reference to her own sexual exploitation, "turned . . . into something else," an object among objects. Coel's characters and storylines acknowledge that one's agency and subjectivity are radically contingent on things like gender and/or race, the social contexts we move in and out of, and the identities of the people we encounter in those spaces. Where traditional screenwriting posits characterization as secondary to character, in *I May Destroy You* the character's identities impact the narrative in essential ways, especially in regards to expressions of agency.

The characters in *I May Destroy You* exhibit many instances of traditional agency that are then contrasted with instances of what traditional screenwriting might deem passive behavior. Arabella, for her part, reports her rape, seeks counseling and support from her friends, writes as a way towards healing, publicly outs one of her abusers, and actively pursues clues to piece together her memories of the night of the assault. Additionally, as a way to explore society's complicity in rape culture, the characters in *I May Destroy You* often defy coherence through dualistic contradictions, as they fluidly shift positionalities depending on context. Whether it's Arabella's best friend Terry (Weruche Opia) giving Simon the go-ahead to leave Arabella alone on the night of her assault or Arabella abandoning Terry at a club while in Italy the night of Terry's assault, the

> [c]haracters are not always what they seem, and their arcs aren't straightforward; they twist, wind, and loop back in on themselves. The show is never prescriptive in its ethos; everyone, including Arabella's best friends Terry and Kwame (Paapa Essiedu), contains within themselves light and dark, victim and perpetrator.[2]

According to Coel, the mercurial nature of the central characters was deliberate and "crucial to how I crafted Arabella, how I crafted every single character in *I May Destroy You*."[3] Character duality and the inevitable betrayals it produces reflects

Coel's interest in recognizing that just as we've been wronged, we've wronged others, a sentiment she expresses in many interviews about *I May Destroy You*, but perhaps most saliently as "daring to find the brother in my enemy."[4]

As innovative as such duality is, in this section I want to draw attention to the ways that Coel allows her characters to slip into less recognizable, more traditionally "passive" behavior in order to explore options for complex character creation in screenwriting. In analyzing scenes where characters survive through "passive" resistance, I hope to build on the discussion in Chapter 2 about why it is important for screenwriters to expand their understanding of the myriad expressions of human agency, especially for those who live on the margins. Coel's embrace of complex subject formations challenges "overstated assertions and competing sets of claims classifying women as either victims or survivors [that] misrepresent the conditions of women's lives"[5] and forges a path for screenwriters who hope to create nuanced characters who can be understood as full agents even when not "mirror[ing] and perpetuat[ing] the white supremacist cultural fiction that assumes that every individual (woman) succeeds or fails solely on the basis of individual merit."[6] Coel does this by allowing Arabella and her friends moments of clear agency juxtaposed with moments of resistance and survival.

In episode four "That Was Fun," we witness two simultaneous sexual assaults, and in each case the assault isn't immediately recognized by the characters (and probably some members of the audience) as such. Kwame, when trying to leave at the end of a Grindr hook-up, is overpowered and assaulted by a man he has just had consensual sex with. At the same time, Arabella is assaulted by her publishing mentor Zain (Karan Gill) when he secretly removes a condom during sex. The episode begins with Arabella in therapy where she discusses her continued trauma, which includes difficulty focusing and flashbacks from the drug-facilitated sexual assault that opens the series. The therapist recommends several options for self-care, including creative activities like drawing, coloring, and painting. Arabella isn't initially thrilled with the suggestions, but later when flashbacks disrupt an awkward work meeting with Zain, she returns to her childhood home to pick up some colored pencils. Later, Zain comes to her apartment to read some pages from her book, and in the course of witty banter Zain reveals his Cambridge pedigree, thus exposing the reason for the awkwardness of their earlier meeting: he doesn't respect her as a writer because she has no classical training and because her first book was based on random thoughts she dashed off on Twitter. Arabella tries to laugh it off, but Zain's casually confident—and now sexually charged—gaze zeroes in on Arabella, freezing her in place. In less than a moment, Zain's gaze transforms Arabella into an object. In an attempt to protect herself and dissipate the sexual tension, she asks him if he likes colored pencils. He doesn't. And in this moment, which occupies the mid-point of the episode, we see Arabella make a profound shift, one I'd be willing to wager that every person who's ever been alone with a man in an unwanted and sexually charged situation is familiar with: Arabella recognizes that in this environment—patriarchy, not her apartment—his agency, subjectivity, and gaze carry more weight than anything she could possibly desire or need, more weight than even her trauma could possibly disarticulate her from. In this scenario, the world and the default scripts it has at the ready become the invisible hand guiding their interactions. She flashes back once more to the fragmented memory of her assault, smokes some weed, and proceeds to have sex with him. It's almost robotic, her response. In this way, the mid-point of the episode functions as a sort of fulcrum: once pressure is applied on Zain's side, Arabella slides from her presumed position of equality and subjective status toward Zain's end, where only his agency and desires matter. From subject to object, with one casual, but socially sanctioned and empowered stare.

Before moving on to the rest of the scene, it's worth exploring how Zain's gaze carries so much weight and why Arabella instinctively relinquishes her agency to accommodate it. Put another way: what are the conditions in which an active passivity might flourish? In philosopher Kate Manne's *Entitled: How Male Privilege Hurts Women*, Manne explores how patriarchy works to grant men explicit and implicit privileges to women's labour, consent, sex, and admiration. Early in the book, she reflects on Kristin Roupenian's "Cat Person," a short story printed in the *New Yorker* that went viral in 2017, as a launching pad for a discussion of how women's agency is curtailed by certain social scripts and expectations designed to protect men's feelings and power. The story follows a young woman, Margot, who has unwanted, but uncontested sex with an older man because she doesn't want to hurt his feelings. In going along with the sex despite not wanting it, Margot, like Arabella, is following what Manne refers to as "deeply ingrained social programming"[7] designed to make sure that men's feelings take precedence over women's actual desires. As many women and gender non-conforming people have no doubt experienced, to reject such social programming results in punishments that range from name-calling, to job loss or demotion, to violence and even death. Thus, though Zain does not physically force Arabella to comply with his wishes, because of "patriarchal social scripts" and his position as a mentor figure who could potentially mar Arabella's precarious publishing situation, the scene "raises the specter of sex that is unwanted, and even coerced, but not *by* any particular person."[8]

During sex, Zain asks Arabella to turn over so that he can take her from behind. As she turns her gaze away, he removes the condom behind her back. When she discovers his betrayal, he feigns innocence and gaslights her, claiming he thought she knew—despite being in a dark room, despite being turned in a different direction, despite him not telling her. In keeping with her now objectified status—no matter what we as an audience might want for Arabella—she laughs, shrugs it off, tells him that he has to pay for the morning after pill. Once again, we see Arabella taking care of his feelings at the expense of her agency, all so that she can survive now and in the future, as there is not only the immediate possible danger of dealing with an angry man, but her professional life and career are tied to how he thinks of her. Later they share a bag of crisps in what I can only read as a casual tactic designed to normalize and, thus, lessen the harm of their power/agency imbalance.

Later after spending the night at Zain's apartment, which is yet another way that Arabella extends the fiction of consent, Arabella learns from a podcast that secret condom removal is a form of sexual assault and that there are entire subreddits where men share their tactics and faux innocent apologies to help one another get away with it. This revelation startles Arabella, inciting a more immediately identifiable display of subjectivity and agency. Within moments, she's out on the street without having said good-bye, without bothering to put on pants. Agency restored, at least for now. In this sequence, Coel demonstrates that screenwriters can write characters who exhibit complicated forms of agency that exist outside of the victim/survivor dichotomy. *I May Destroy You* challenges creators to think about how gender and race impact the possibilities for agential expression. Arabella's decision to go along with the sex and with Zain's lie about the condom are only superficially passive. When grounded in Arabella's unique point of view as a woman living within rape culture, we can see that acquiescence—among other forms of resistance—is often a brave and deliberate act meant to ensure survival and reduce trauma. In short, resistance to recognizably agential acts of domination is also a legitimate expression of agency.

In episode six, "The Alliance," we see a similar portrayal of the ease with which women lose subject status within patriarchy. "The Alliance," an episode that Coel refers to as her "baby,"[9] marks the mid-point of the series, and the pivotal moment under analysis within this episode also occupies the mid-point: a double fulcrum. While mid-points typically spin a series or an episode in a new direction, "The Alliance" fully establishes one of the central themes of the series, marking Arabella's newfound awareness that while she's always understood what it's like to move through the world as a Black and poor person, she never considered how being a woman has also shaped that journey.

"The Alliance" is a flashback episode that takes us back to Arabella's school days and introduces us to Theo, who runs a support group for survivors of sexual exploitation. Though Arabella and Theo went to school together, they weren't friends. They were, however, linked through a complicated sexual assault. Through most of the episode, we follow young Theo as she navigates abusive and sexually charged situations at home and school. At school, Theo and Ryan—a Black student and friend of Arabella—sneak off to an unused room to have sex. During sex, while Theo's back is turned, Ryan snaps photos of her with his flip-phone. When she catches him and demands that he delete the photos, Ryan calls her a "psycho" and tells her that the other boys she's had sex with have all taken and shared similar photos of her. He then asks if she'll take money in exchange for allowing him to keep the photos and take more.

Damned either way, Theo agrees. In this moment, much like the moment where Arabella "agrees" to sleep with Zain, Theo's subject status hangs in the balance. Theo's ability to consent to the photos is long gone, as many boys before Ryan have taken and shared photos of her without her consent. In "consenting" to a violation that has already occurred, Theo grants herself the illusion of agency, which she then uses to punish Ryan by throwing his phone out a window, cutting herself between her legs to make it look like she was attacked, and claiming to school authorities that he raped her. As Ryan is interrogated by school officials,

Arabella and Terry discover the photos of Theo having sex via a male friend who has a collection of them on his phone, and Arabella reports this to school officials to clear Ryan's name. It is here that "The Alliance" of Black students is born. The alliance, of course, is warranted, especially when one considers the long history of white women lying about Black male violence, sexual or otherwise, so that white men can enact extrajudicial and gratuitous violence on Black people. At the same time, however, the situation contains additional, relevant layers, including Theo's repeated exploitation by multiple boys at the school, as well as the manipulation she experienced as a child when her mother coerced her into testifying that her father abused her so her mother could have custody. Once again, we see the blurring of binaries, as the complex intersections of race and gender coalesce to create scenarios where each character ends up playing both sides of the same abuser/abused coin.

For the screenwriter looking for ways to create complex characters whose agency isn't only expressed via acts of domination or redress, the characters in *I May Destroy You* offer a welcome respite as characters shift seamlessly from subject to object or agent to target in ways that mirror the intricacies of human relations.

Normative Culture as Tension Machine

Coel's Britain is not part of the homogenous continent of Neutraltopia in a number of ways. Where Sciamma creates tension in *Portrait of a Lady on Fire* by allowing her white female protagonists to follow their desires within an environment devoid of gendered or classed antagonisms, Coel explicitly creates tension and anticipation in *I May Destroy You* by situating her characters and their assaults within the normative order, with its gendered, raced, and classed antagonisms. This not only challenges common depictions of rape as something that happens to white women, but centers the role of cultural context. As critic Caetlin Benson-Allott writes,

> To witness so many separate incidents of sexual violence in one series is shocking, but their inclusion dramatizes rape culture in a way that no depiction of a single assault, survivor, or perpetrator ever could. Placing these incidents within a single community generates an accretive sense of rape culture as a systemic issue.[10]

Steeped within rape culture and set in a distinctly Black British milieu, *I May Destroy You* demonstrates the importance and generative power of specificity in relation to place, history, and social/political context for the screenwriter.

In rooting the series within the normative order, the core tensions central to the series are systemic and epistemic in addition to being personal and internal. By this I mean that the characters—like many people in real life—don't have a deep knowledge of rape culture and how it is supported by structures of power, and, yet, their lives are completely immersed within and are determined by it, which is precisely why they can't see it. As Hannah J. Davies writes of the series, "[i]ts quiet presence shows sexual abuse as something that exists inside our world rather than a threat from somewhere far away—something you or I or anyone else may have experienced without even realising it was happening."[11] Rape, unfortunately, is the default, and as I've discussed throughout this book, the danger of the default is that the social violence that maintains the status quo is so pervasive that it is difficult to see, name, or discuss. In positioning rape culture as room tone, many of the tensions between characters do not arise out of personal failings or internal needs, but are social failures that, by design, support the normative violence that maintains white male supremacy.

Despite notions of objectivity that would position knowledge as neutral, knowledge is socially and politically determined by relations of power in order to maintain the status quo. Our knowledge about the world we live in—the way it functions, its history, who matters within it—informs the world. Therefore, the discrepancy between what one understands about how the world works and the way the world actually works—in terms of patriarchy or white supremacy or heteronormativity, for example—generates tension. And in Coel's hands, this incongruity between the way the characters think the world works and the way it actually operates is put to narrative use.

Arabella, Kwame, and Terry each learn about the complexities of sexual assault at different rates and in differing degrees. Similar to Cameron Esposito's stand-up special *Rape Jokes* (2018), wherein Esposito underscores how she realized she'd been sexually assaulted only after telling the story as a funny joke and was pulled aside by a friend who told her that what she'd described was date rape, all three characters experience at least one sexual assault that they don't initially register as such. Arabella recognizes Zain's assault only after hearing other women talking about "stealthing" in a podcast; Kwame has to Google whether non-consensual humping is even a crime; and Terry initially brags about her threesome with the Italians. It is only near the end of the series, while on a date with a trans man, that she's encouraged to consider—through his gentle questioning—that she was the victim of a nefarious plot. Even if the audience is equally in the dark about the intricacies and pervasiveness of rape culture, because the audience knows more than the characters—we see, for example, that the two Italians Terry sleeps with are in cahoots—tension abounds because we see the characters unwittingly walk into socially brutal situations.

In keeping with the ignorance around rape culture, the characters not only lack awareness about what constitutes sexual assault, the conditions that allow it to flourish, and the omnipresence of sexual predators, but lack a co-extensive empathy that would have, for example, cued Arabella not to lock Kwame in a room with another man at a party shortly after his assault. In episode seven "Happy Animals," at Terry's birthday party, Kwame is distant and visibly distraught. After another party-goer, Jamal, flirts with him, he flees to the bedroom for respite. Not long after, Arabella shoos Jamal inside with Kwane and locks the door behind them to encourage a connection. While one might have expected that Arabella would be sensitive to or recognize Kwame's trauma on account of her own, the show refuses that kind of simplicity. Deep in her own trauma—which Arabella acts out by seeking validation and glorification via social media stardom—she can't always see the pain her friends are in, even when it mirrors her own. Further, as critic Caetlin Benson-Allot writes, Kwame's story is "central to the series' critique of heterocentrism in both rape television and survivor advocacy."[12] Neither Arabella, Terry, nor the police recognize Kwame's assault or lend it the same gravity on account of heteronormativity and the ways rape is conceptualized and depicted in film and television as a "women's problem." Thus, the complexity and inconsistency Coel allows the characters as a result of how they are oriented within heteronormative patriarchy creates tension and suspense without jigged up conflicts that are meant to exploit a character's inner flaws in a way that can eventually be resolved through a course of action that one might find in some pop-psychology, self-help manual.[13]

I May Destroy You is also situated within Black British culture. So much so in fact that in a talk with Coel for *British GQ*, Reggie Yates kicked off the interview by thanking Coel for creating a series that for the first time in "forever" depicted a Britain that he—as a fellow Black Britoner of Ghanaian descent—recognized, one where "white working class kids [are] side by side with children of immigrants, all using the same slang, all dancing to the same Afro-beat record."[14] Or as cultural critic Bolu Babalola writes, "[s]ophisticatedly woven themes of consent, sexual politics, and social media's power to amplify, soothe, and subsume are not presented within a neutral vacuum, but rather within a specifically Black British sphere. The story is told through our tongue, spliced from many."[15] Like *Vida*, which I discuss in Chapter 9, *I May Destroy You* firmly roots itself in place, culture, and time. This can be seen in something as simple as Arabella's Ghanaian last name, Essiedu, to the use of Black British dialect, with words like "rah," "ting," and "ova" peppering the dialogue, all of which capture the fact that "Black Brits are rooted from mostly the West Indies and Africa, and our cultural etymologies have melded throughout time to give us our own language, our own expressions."[16] Because the default world order thrives on assimilation and homogeneity, one might be tempted to reduce the cultural specificity here to observable, consumable, and interchangeable qualities—as if one can shop for culture or identity in the same way one customizes a latte at Starbucks—but the specificity in *I May Destroy You* proves how integral place and culture are to storytelling. Context not only deepens character, it fuels the narrative and generates the story. As Babalola writes,

> It would be easy to call this Black Britishness a "lens," but "lens" is clinical and anthropological—"lens" is external and removable. It is less of a lens and more of a feeling that coats the chords of the show. A culture rarely seen in mainstream television, it's not that Black Britishness (and the specificity of being a Black Londoner) assists in telling the story, nor is it that Black Britishness is its own character within the story. It is that it helps form the story. The rhythm and pulses chug narrative along, enriching the grain of the series.[17]

What Babalola touches on here is that culture impacts the way characters think, speak, and interact with one another and the world. It is just as much part of the story—influencing its cadence, pivots, and momentum—as any other aspect of story design.[18] Culture is not window dressing lending authenticity or local flavor; it is not secondary to character and narrative: it is the story. Rape culture and the way it manifests specifically in this world of Black British millennials makes the series what it is. A screenwriter could take this same scenario—a drug-facilitated sexual assault—and set it in the white BritPop scene of the 1990s, the Grime scene of the early aughts, or within a Southeast Asian British group of friends today, and the result would be a completely different narrative, despite the fact that only a few contextual variables have been altered. It would feel different, look different, sound different, contain different frictions. Within different contexts, cultures, and time periods, people interact with and understand one another differently, which impacts pacing, plotting, and how characters relate to one another.

The fact that the series focuses on Black British characters influences other aspects of the series as well. Though the series is not about race to the same degree that it is about sexual assault, the series acknowledges structures of racial and colonial violence as an equally essential part of the world. For example, in the ninth episode, after a routine medical examination, Arabella scolds her doctor when he assumes she is "Afro-Caribbean," effectively flattening the complexity of the Black diaspora and erasing the long-term ramifications of Britain's colonial conquests in Ghana and throughout Africa. While Arabella's justifiable and immediate response to her doctor's racist remark is one of many ways the series incorporates white supremacy as part of the world, the recognition of racism isn't always so decisive and direct, which works as a narrative tactic that not only mirrors the myriad ways people understand and respond to racism in reality, but also fuels narrative tension.

Just as the series explores the spectrum of knowledge on the sexual violence continuum, *I May Destroy You* centers a range of knowingness about the intricacies and manifestations of racism. As I discussed previously, race complicates Theo's response to her assault by Ryan in "The Alliance" episode and creates a years-long rift that causes Terry to—rightfully—distrust Theo when she re-enters their lives as Arabella's sexual violence support group leader. Arabella is more forgiving on account of being more recently attuned to the toll gendered violence takes. This trust, however, doesn't necessarily serve her as Theo proceeds to invite Arabella to work at Happy Animals, a white-owned environmental justice organization that pays Theo extra for bringing in "diverse" influencers to virtue-signal diversity on their social media feeds. While it is clear to Arabella's friends that she's being used by the company because she's a Black influencer, Arabella doesn't recognize it immediately, which creates tension as the audience is cued in to the ways she's being used (objectified once again) while remaining oblivious.

Finally, in a series so firmly rooted in a Black female point of view, often there is tension any time a white person appears on screen. Similar tensions exist in shows like Ava Duvernay's *Queen Sugar*, where the white characters tend to be written as antagonists. But Coel does something different. She does not write white villains; instead she posits the world as one where white supremacy is the norm. As such, when white people enter a scene—like Arabella's white literary agents, for example, or sometimes even Arabella's meek white male roommate—the tension is automatic. This works by virtue of *I May Destroy You* being rooted in a Black British world within a larger white supremacist Britain. Therefore, the possibility for racial violence, much like the ubiquity of sexual violence, is always already on the table. Sciamma achieves a similar tension in *Portrait of a Lady on Fire*, where after spending most of the film with the three women—the maid, the painter, and the muse—suddenly, in the final act of the film, there is a man sitting in the kitchen. The tension, which is startling, comes from the fact that we've been immersed in a particular world—a queer female utopia devoid of heteronormative, gendered, and classed antagonisms. The sudden presence of the man into that world operates like a breach, like a threat. Like the white characters in *I May Destroy You* whose presence always suggests and sometimes delivers on the possibility of racial violence, his presence calls attention to the different rhythms and freedom established in the absence of normative violence.

For the screenwriter looking for new ways to generate tension, *I May Destroy You* offers a masterclass in situating characters in clear relation to social, cultural, and political context, fueling engagement. This, however, is not the "feel good" tension arising from the typical hope versus fear dichotomy embedded in traditional conflict. It is instead a "feel bad" tension arising from concern for the well-being of the characters within the normative order: there will be no good ending here. As such, it fosters a different kind of engagement with character, a different kind of caring about them. The hope at the root of it is different, too. It's not a hope for triumph over adversity (though that may enter some minds); it's a hope for thriving despite the way the odds are stacked against them.

Coel Destroys the Redemption Narrative

Perhaps Coel's most radical challenge to traditional screenwriting practice is found in her declared and purposeful rejection of redemption narratives. Specifically, she defies common practices around how main characters must be pitted against a formidable opponent specifically suited to challenge their unique inner flaws in order to make them a more evolved person, worthy of redemption. In stories that feature rape or other forms of oppression as the primary force of antagonism, there's something deeply troubling about a notion of character development that insists that the screenwriter invent conflict and obstacles that prick at and improve some core personal failure. This sort of logic feeds narratives that blame the victim. We see this in cases of rape, where women are often asked what they were wearing or whether they were emphatic enough in their resistance, and in cases where Black people have been subjected to police brutality and murder, who are also blamed for the violence done to them—especially if they survive.

By interrogating the logic that links external obstacle to inner need, we may begin to understand why so many stories about sexual assault in media involve rape revenge fantasies. To get around implying that a character is personally responsible for the rape (despite, of course, the prevalence of such victim-blaming in the culture at large), the screenwriter constructs the survivor as ill-suited for vengeance, and the plot hangs on that. Coel, thankfully, rejects this logic, and thereby gives us a new model to think through how a series or film, particularly one centered on sexual assault, might end outside of the common redemption models we are taught to rely on.

The final episode of *I May Destroy You* explicitly rejects redress as a form of closure by first acknowledging what audiences have been taught to want, then quickly moving on to other possibilities that favor reclamation of self, radical empathy, and healing. In a *New Yorker Radio* podcast, Coel explains that while working on the end of the series, she stayed at an AirBnB in Michigan, where the woman who owned the property suggested she read Margaret Atwood's rape revenge story "The Stone Mattress" for inspiration.[19] Coel declined, asking instead "[m]ust there be bloodshed for there to be justice?"[20] In refusing to have Arabella pursue vengeance, Coel makes an important contribution to rethinking the logic of the final act. Arabella doesn't need to redeem or reclaim herself through an additional act of violence: she needs healing and solace. And not because she's a bad person, not because she has a nagging internal flaw that must be addressed by an external antagonistic force. Instead of looking for redress—especially in the form of vengeance which tends to rely on the binary of an external quest for revenge that belies an internal need for forgiveness—Coel rethinks and questions closure through the lens of her own experience, not "universal" storytelling structures. As Angelica Jade Bastién writes in *Vulture*,

> [u]ndergirding the finale's neon-lit escapades is a series of questions that don't have easy answers: Is closure a reality, or is it a lie that life can abide by neat narratives? Are we bound forever to our traumas, or is it possible to heal from them? And, if we can, how do we make that a reality?[21]

In lieu of a traditional ending, the series finale provides three somewhat surreal fantasy scenarios that contrast to a more mundane, realistic, and ambiguous ending. The final episode, "Ego Death," begins where the previous episode left off: with Arabella and Terry at the Ego Death bar where Arabella has returned once again to revisit the "scene of the crime." When Arabella spots her rapist, David, and his accomplice, she is immediately overcome with a series of detailed flashbacks that fill in the final puzzle pieces from the night of her rape, and she tells Terry. After calling Theo for back-up, the three stage a semi-elaborate sting operation where Arabella chats up her rapist, Terry distracts his accomplice, and Theo pickpockets David's roofies, mixes them with toilet water inside a syringe, and stabs him with it. Once he's out of it, the three women follow him from the bar, kill him, and hide him under Arabella's bed (where we've seen her hide other reminders of her assault throughout the series). We then travel back in time to the moment before Arabella ventured out to Ego Death and start the night over again.

In the second scenario, Terry insists that they lure the rapist into another assault so that the cops can catch him in the act. To pull this off, Arabella pre-games with loads of cocaine to mitigate the effects of the roofies. (Remember: This is a fantasy, not an effective tactic.) The moment her assailant tries to penetrate her, she turns around and confronts him. After the initial shock of Arabella's confrontation, he grabs her by the throat (a common and often unremarked upon form of misogynistic intimate partner violence that literally silences women, sometimes forever[22]) insults her, and, then, quickly shifts to play the victim, crying in Arabella's arms. Like the Iranian film *Circumstance* (Maryam Keshavarz, 2011), which likewise features a scene where a husband rapes his lesbian wife and afterwards cries in her arms, begging for comfort, this role reversal reminds us how often women and other marginalized people are not only victimized, but then asked to care for their abusers. Not only are men entitled to objectify and sexually assault women, but they are further entitled to ask for care in the aftermath, comfort that is often given and then eyed with suspicion and disdain if the women report their rapes. Towards the end of the second fantasy, we find ourselves back in Arabella's bedroom, presumably with Dead-David from the previous fantasy still stuffed under the bed, where New David chronicles the crimes he has served time for, including: date rape, spousal rape, corrective rape, and more. Arabella listens with compassion as victims are scripted to do. Eventually the police arrive. David cries some more, and they take him away.

In the third and most radically complicated scenario, Arabella approaches David at the bar, makes out with him, and takes him home to have consensual sex with him, which culminates in her topping him from behind. The next morning, she sends him away, at which point his corpse crawls out from under the bed and follows suit.

These fantasy scenarios are exactly that: fantasies of different paths towards closure, healing, and justice. The fantastic nature of the scenarios is emphasized by Arabella, in writer mode, writing a story card and posting it on the wall after each fantasy. In the first and second fantasies, we see two commonplace forms of retribution; in the third, we see Arabella attempt to reclaim her agency through a repetition of the initial scenario, but with difference. The difference, of course, is that she consents to the sex and dominates him in the end, effectively reversing their roles, reclaiming her sexual agency, and transforming sexual trauma into sexual pleasure (and—notably—not raping him as a form of retribution).

By positing multiple alternate endings, Coel is questioning the nature of closure itself. In the first two fantasies, a version of justice is served through retribution, first through vigilante violence, then through state violence, neither of which is very satisfying, effective, or feasible outside of fantasy. In particular, in relation to the efficacy of the state to provide any kind of satisfying conclusions for the victims of sexual violence, we need to look no further than the thousands of untested rape kits that sit in police precinct basements, the Supreme Court hearings for Brent Kavanaugh, or the Brock Turner case, all of which clearly document, at best, the disinterest in justice regarding sexual violence against women. And yet, these fantasies of closure are the ones we are most often sold by media narratives as a way to deal with trauma. In the third scenario, however, we witness less a form of revenge, and more of a power reversal through a reclamation of personal agency that reverses the slippages from subject to object earlier in the series. By including these fantasies, but not allowing any of them to provide the series' actual closure, Coel nods to the existence of such fantasies as part of sexual trauma, while also acknowledging how ineffective they'd be in actually solving Arabella's fundamental dilemma: how to heal? The different fantasies, taken as a whole, allow us to question the founding principles of three-act structure, with its fixation on redemption and solution. There simply is no solution to Arabella's injury: not now, not in the future. Rather than engage in false promises of redress and renewal, the final episode exposes the lie of closure, opting instead for "an evolution of the self that involves radical empathy for ourselves and others" while engaging fantasy to demonstrate how "creation is the antidote and antithesis to trauma's destruction of the self."[23] For those who insist that a proper character follows a transformation arc that hinges on the defeat of an explicit foe, the ending may feel more like a non-ending: if only they understood the demons that have to be slayed to create a completely self-possessed or self-forgiving woman.

Arabella is not designed with a particular flaw, or set of flaws, that must be prodded at and dislodged by antagonistic forces à la McKee so that she can learn about herself and become a better, more whole individual. Arabella is a whole and deeply flawed person from the start. When she's assaulted, it isn't a wake-up call to grow or change: it is a wake-up call to an awareness of the myriad forms of gendered violence in the world that create a constant sense of disequilibrium for those subject to sexual violence. The show doesn't focus on the neat, linear evolution of an individual, but instead on the messy, unpredictable, and erratic recovery of self after an act of unspeakable violation. While assault functions as a destabilizing force, once Arabella's world is thrown into disequilibrium, it cannot be re-stablized. There is no "back to normal," just as there is no "emerging on the other side stronger." The knowledge that she or her friends could (and will) be assaulted at any time, by any person, friend or foe, will never disappear, can never be set right; the additional expectation of outwardly expressed resilience (often code for resignation) is an insult. Thus, the series doesn't pursue that angle. Instead, in the final scenario, we see Arabella sometime later at a bookstore for the launch of her new book, which she's published independently, having lost her traditional publisher after missing her deadlines. As she cracks open the book to read aloud, there's a cut to Arabella on the beach in Italy, in her signature pink wig, just hours before she's assaulted. She looks into the camera and smiles enigmatically, recalling the final line from the script of the first episode: "confusion almost births a smile."[24] Only this time, her smile isn't confused: it knowingly holds the tension between "euphoria and pain"[25] that characterizes what it feels like to process trauma in a world designed to inflict countless wounds.

Notes

1 Vivian Sobchack, *Carnal Thoughts Embodiment and Moving Image Culture* (Berkeley, CA: University of California Press, 2011), 32.
2 E. Alex Jung, "Michaela the Destroyer," July 6, 2020, www.vulture.com/article/michaela-coel-i-may-destroy-you.html.

3 Eleanor Stanford, "How Michaela Coel Shaped 'I May Destroy You'," *The New York Times*, July 21, 2020, www.nytimes.com/2020/07/20/arts/television/i-may-destroy-you-influences.html.

4 Reggie Yates and Michaela Coel, "If You Don'T Show It, It Can Be Erased," Other. *British GQ*, October 26, 2020, www.youtube.com/watch?v=SZ_0_DEe_2A.

5 Traci C. West, *Wounds of the Spirit: Black Women, Violence, and Resistance Ethics* (New York: New York University Press, 1999), 160.

6 Ibid., 156.

7 Kate Manne, *Entitled: How Male Privilege Hurts Women* (New York: Crown, 2020), 58.

8 Ibid., 59.

9 Doreen St. Felix, "Michaela Coel on Making 'I May Destroy You'," in *The New Yorker Radio Hour* (New York: WNYC Studios, July 14, 2020).

10 Caetlin Benson-Allott, "How *I May Destroy You* Reinvents Rape Television," *Film Quarterly* 74, no. 2 (2020): 100–5, https://doi.org/10.1525/fq.2020.74.2.100, 102.

11 Hannah J. Davies, "*I May Destroy You*: Why Michaela Coel's Drama Is a True TV Gamechanger," *The Guardian, Guardian News and Media*, July 11, 2020, www.theguardian.com/tv-and-radio/2020/jul/11/i-may-destroy-you-why-michaela-coels-drama-is-a-true-tv-gamechanger.

12 Benson-Allott, "How *I May Destroy You* Reinvents Rape Television," 104.

13 It's worth noting that screenwriting manuals read very much like self-help manuals. See: Kathryn Millard, "Writing for the Screen: Beyond the Gospel of Story," *Scan: Journal of Media Arts Culture* 3, no. 2 (2006).

14 Yates and Coel, "If You Don'T Show It, It Can Be Erased."

15 Bolu Babalola, "The Innate Black Britishness of *I May Destroy You*," *Vulture*, August 4, 2020, www.vulture.com/article/i-may-destroy-you-black-britishness.html.

16 Ibid.

17 Ibid.

18 While I have pointed out a few ways that setting the series within a Black British milieu impacts the overall narrative, undoubtedly there are others that as a white American I'm not seeing.

19 St. Felix, "Michaela Coel on Making 'I May Destroy You'."

20 Jung, "Michaela the Destroyer."

21 Angelica Jade Bastién, "Let's Talk About That I May Destroy You Ending," *Vulture*, August 25, 2020, www.vulture.com/article/i-may-destroy-you-finale-ego-death-explained-analysis.html.

22 Kate Manne, *Down Girl: The Logic of Misogyny* (London: Penguin Books, 2019), 1–4.

23 Bastién, "Let's Talk About That I May Destroy You Ending."

24 Michaela Coel, *January 22nd*, "Am I Bleeding?" Unpublished manuscript (2019), 40.

25 Jung, "Michaela the Destroyer."

9
THE EXPLICIT AND SPECIFIC POLITICS OF *VIDA*

Vida (Starz, 2018–2020) is a half-hour, character-focused drama that tells the story of the Hernandez sisters, two Mexican-American women who return to east Los Angeles after a long absence to attend their mother's funeral. Over the course of three seasons, the sisters reckon with their grief, complicated and evolving family history, and identity as Latinas and members of the Boyle Heights community where they grew up. For eldest sister Emma (Mishel Prada), the return to her childhood home is complicated by the fact that her mother, the show's namesake Vidalia, sent her away as a teen to live with her grandmother in Texas for kissing a girl and writing about her queer desires in her diary. For Lyn (Melissa Barrera), returning home at first feels inviting on account of being able to reconnect with her childhood love, Johnny, but grows more complicated as Lyn confronts the ways she's spent her life diminishing herself to accommodate male fantasy and ego. To add fuel to both fires, the sisters are viewed as outsiders by their former Boyle Heights neighbors (they are frequently called "whitetinas" or, in an epithet reserved specifically for Lyn, "coconut Barbie") and struggle to re-incorporate themselves into—and find home within—their community.

The Cultural Specificity of Vida

One of the unique aspects of *Vida* is the way it employs a place-based, situated storytelling that honors and defends the setting of the series at a cultural and neighborhood level. Set in Boyle Heights, a historically Mexican-American neighborhood in close proximity to Silver Lake, Echo Park, and Los Feliz—three east Los Angeles neighborhoods that have been gentrified in recent decades—the series revels in the particularity of its setting and doesn't shy away from using the current socio-political dynamism of its community to fuel the story and build the world. As showrunner Tanya Saracho told me in an interview for this book, "It's a political

DOI: 10.4324/9781003170310-12

act to put a Brown body on screen."[1] More than that, it's a political act of reclamation to put an entire (misrepresented) Brown neighborhood on screen. Because Boyle Heights has often been portrayed by Hollywood through what Saracho calls "a safari eye,"[2] replete with harmful stereotypes focused on gangs and graffiti, Saracho and her team of creatives felt a responsibility to defend the neighborhood specifically and Mexican-American culture more generally. Outside of harmful media stereotypes, like many gentrifying Latine[3] neighborhoods around the United States, Boyle Heights faces rent hikes, white hipster colonialism, and loss of community as long-term residents are priced out of the neighborhood and forced to relocate while developers snap up property and upscale the neighborhood. These unique economic and cultural forces, along with the complex histories that produced them, are not glossed over as they might be in more culturally neutral series, but, rather, they generate the specific conflicts, tensions, plot points, and character contradictions that sustain the series.

This is by design. Originally pitched to Saracho by former Starz executive Marta Fernandez as a series premised on "gentefication," a term that captures the gentrification of Latine communities by wealthy Latine developers, the series is rooted in specific, place-based, classed, and contemporary frictions. Thus, the material living conditions of displacement, cultural loss, and capitalist extraction generate the primary plot lines and character arcs throughout the series. So much so, in fact, that the community's reaction to the series being shot in Boyle Heights became part of the story. According to Saracho, though she shares cultural commonalities with the residents of Boyle Heights, because she's not originally from the community, they saw her and the Hollywood production she brought to their neighborhood as gentefiers. Saracho explains, "And we are gentefiers. We come in with our big Hollywood trucks, and we take over blocks and blocks" including churches, parking lots, and people's homes. The epithets "whitetina" and "coconut Barbie" were originally leveled at Saracho and then incorporated into the series in a real-time, meta-commentary of the cultural conflicts that resonate in Boyle Heights.[4]

From the opening scene of the series, gentefication is marked as central when Mari (Chelsea Rendon)—a local activist "chingona"—performs an anti-gentefication manifesto for her vlog. In it, she rails against developers, calling them "occupiers" and denouncing them for re-colonizing and displacing the good working class people of Boyle Heights. By focusing specifically on gentefication over the catch-all gentrification, the series marks its specific cultural territory and recalls long-standing discussions by Chicana feminist theorists like Gloria Anzaldúa and Cherríe Moraga, whose work explores the ways that whiteness, Neo-colonialism, individualism, upward mobility, extraction, and patriarchy operate from without and from within Latine culture. *Vida*'s cultural heritage is vast, extending from present to past and back again.

To honor and deliver such place-based, culturally specific storytelling, Saracho created the first Hollywood series with an all-Latine and mostly queer writers' room, making it an example of what scholars Aymar Jean Christian and Khadija Costely White call "organic representation." Moving beyond "positive" on-screen representation that may lack connection to the communities represented, "[o]rganic representation begins when systems and institutions empower those who have been historically marginalized not only to appear in their stories but also to own and fine-tune narratives."[5] Having an all Latine and mostly queer writers' room allowed Saracho and her team to be "guardians of the characters" and the specificity of Mexican-American culture.[6] Historically speaking, when Latine people have appeared on screen, the majority of creators behind the scenes have not shared their identities, histories, or unique cultural positioning, and, as a result, stereotypical, universalist, and non-organic representation has been the norm. Without guardians for marginalized lives, experiences, and perspectives, it is difficult to create culturally brave spaces to tell stories that fall outside of or challenge the dominant culture. For example, in my interview with Saracho, she described working on a previous series as the "Latina ambassador" and how pitching something as simple as a Latino man working on a car can—when filtered through a white writers' room—be mis-translated as the stereotype of a Latino man in a "low rider." For Saracho, the cultural and ideological specificity of the writers' room is just as important as the cultural specificity of the story on screen. Too often, writers steeped in the dominant culture turn cultural specificity into the "Monsanto version of what you pitched: it's toxic."[7] In contrast to series reliant on the Anglocentric, male gaze, *Vida*, like Ava DuVernay's *Queen Sugar* and Issa Rae's *Insecure*, is part of a recent wave of "organic representation" that relies on a network of intersectional creators at all levels of production who share identities and ideologies with those at the center of the narratives they're in charge of stewarding. The fact that *Vida*'s writers share identities, histories, and, in some cases, even neighborhood affiliation[8] with the show's central characters influences the dynamism and specificity of theme and character, while also setting *Vida* apart in terms of its relationship with and honoring of the story world.

Firmly rooted in a Brown, queer point of view, *Vida* acknowledges that the communities we grow up in, the languages we speak, and the contexts through which we come to understand ourselves are consequential, formative, essential, and, thus, integral to storytelling. From the attention to the murals of the Virgin of Guadalupe to the boarded up storefronts to the sounds of "Suavecito" emanating from a random apartment, Boyle Heights is rendered with an attention to detail and awareness of cultural context from which the series derives the foundations of story and character. As with the gentefication theme, the social and cultural issues central to the neighborhood's inhabitants actively shape the story. For example, the mariachi mural on the side of the bar—which on most series would be relegated as a decorative, and perhaps authenticating, concern for the set designer—is integral to the plot. In season two, when the mural is painted over with a beer ad, it sends Eddy (Ser Anzoategui) into a panic and launches a season's long struggle with the sisters over how to run the bar without alienating the lesbian Latine customers who find refuge there. Eddy is not the only one upset by the mural: it becomes a site of contestation for local activists, as well. Over the course of the season, multiple protests occur at the mural because of the way it shifts the business and the corner it sits on towards a more hipster clientele, changing who traverses (and who will eventually take up residence in) the neighborhood. Through the mural's role as a site of contestation, Emma and Lyn must reckon with how the capitalistic practices required to keep the bar afloat alienate the community they claim to want to serve and be reintegrated into. In this way, the context and dynamic sociocultural history contributes to and shapes the story.

Vida not only creates a specific Latine world by Latine creators, it does so for a Latine audience. In contrast to the traditional ways that "[m]edia representation of marginalized people may function as the primary way that privileged people learn about them,"[9] *Vida* rejects the totalizing and assimilationist white gaze. Nothing is explained for a white audience: not the rituals, not the food, not the music, not even the language as there are no subtitles to help viewers as characters shift seamlessly between Spanish and English. In refusing the white gaze, the series creates a world with a specific cultural dynamic that is immediately recognizable to some viewers, particularly Latine and/or immigrant viewers, while not insulting those same viewers by taking the time to explain the culture it depicts to an assumed white audience. This model of world-building centers the perspectives, knowledge, and material reality of members of the represented community, which creates what Saracho calls an "alchemy of recognition that the dominant culture does not have."[10] From simple household items like a can of "Bustelo or [the] margarine container that has beans in it"[11] to how Emma eats her tacos "like a sandwich, like a white girl"[12] to Lyn's connection to brujeria via the building's señora, Doña Lupe (Elena Campbell-Martinez), this "alchemy of recognition" is necessary to honor and affirm characters and audiences who have been traditionally erased or misrepresented by the mainstream media.

In the script for the first episode, for example, Vidalia's funeral is described with an explicit rejection of default cultural norms as "[t]he second thing we see is the CROWD OF BAWLING MOURNERS around the CASKET—this is no WASPy funeral choking suppressed emotions, no, at this Mexican entierro the tears and the mocos freely flow."[13] Saracho cues the reader as to how *Vida* sets itself apart through the unapologetic embrace of and attention to Mexican-American culture and community. Just as there is no universal human prototype to base a character on, there is no universal way that humans conduct themselves at funerals. We mourn and love and express ourselves in ways shaped by particular cultural norms rooted in history, community, and place. Cultural rituals bond communities in meaningful ways, and to erase those rituals in favor of ones more easily digestible to the dominant culture is not only an act of violence, it's dishonest storytelling. To over-explain those rituals to make the show more inviting to a white audience would be to add insult to injury. And for the purposes of storytelling, it is through the specificity of the social rituals within the series that we understand that Emma and Lyn don't always fit into the community to which they have returned: they've left and come back strangers. Unlike the bawling mourners, neither Emma nor Lyn cry at the funeral, marking them as outsiders. This cultural tension runs through *Vida* like a current, with Lyn and Emma's lack of emotionality resurfacing in episode five as Vidalia's grief-stricken wife, Eddy, challenges the sisters about their stoicism surrounding their mother's death. Lyn then joins Eddy and her friends in a drunken "Salúd! to "after-Vida," while Emma storms upstairs to cry alone after trying (and failing) to masturbate her grief into submission, yet another way the series marks Emma's estrangement from the culture she feels rejected by but wants to be a part of.

The cultural specificity of *Vida* doesn't only exist on a micro-cultural level: it extends to larger social forces shaping Anglo- and Mexican-American culture. Like *Sense8* and *I May Destroy You*, the series acknowledges the forces of racism, sexism, and homophobia, then situates the characters in relation to those forces without making them the primary conflict for the characters. In the same way that the sun rises and sets each day without many of us giving it much thought, these characters can count on various forms of social violence to operate in the background at all times. For Emma, the fact that her mother sent her away for being queer drives many of her decisions, contradictions, and behaviors. And while we eventually learn that Vidalia did it to protect Emma from her abusive (and homophobic) father, the homophobia itself is never the focus. There is no "very special" homophobia episode with spelled out lessons on the importance of empathy. Instead, homophobia is ever present, the water in which the sisters swim, and Emma's wounds are the oars she paddles her raft with and sometimes hits people with. For example, in the final episode of the first season, Emma aims her grief and rage at her mother toward the partner who survived her, Eddy. Claiming that the bar started failing once Eddy entered Vidalia's life, Emma insults Eddy and her friends, forcing them to go drink elsewhere. While at another neighborhood bar, one filled with primarily straight men, Eddy is beaten within an inch of her life for trying to defend one of the lesbian friends from unwanted male advances, ending up in the ICU.

And yet, the episode isn't about the dangers that queer people face in a heteronormative world: *Vida* is merely situated in a world where that happens. Just because Emma inflicts harm on Eddy does not mean she understands what she's doing.

For Saracho, the way that Emma repeats a form of the actions her mother took against her reflects the understanding that we are all steeped in the normative order. In Saracho's own words,

> [e]ven though the show is not about immigration, you see everyone's point of view about it. You see a piñata of Trump. You see that Mari wears a "FuckTrump" pin. You don't have to telegraph it. You just have to wear it, be steeped in it.

Sometimes the social violence rises to the fore, other times it fades from view. From Emma's childhood exile, to Lyn's struggles to please men, to Eddy's beating, all the characters experience different kinds of patriarchal and/or heteronormative violence because these forces are the very threads of the fabric of the world they live in. And while each character responds to these forces in a different way, at no point do these social antagonisms define them, nor their journeys.

Characters from the Borderlands

As I explored in Chapter 2, popular screenwriting paradigms rely on a reductive notion of character-as-essence while diminishing the role of characterization as superficial. As a result, in traditional film and television identity rarely serves to define characters in any meaningful way. Instead, a binaristic approach that roots identity in opposition to the status quo or erases identity is the norm. If identity is brought to the forefront in a screen story, it is only done for characters with marginalized identities and, even then, the act of naming identity quickly devolves into a narrative about a defining moment of social antagonism, including misogynistic, racist, or homophobic violence. This short-sightedness about how identity might impact one's life in myriad ways—positive, neutral, and negative—ends up centering the often violent response to difference by the dominant culture. On the opposite end of the spectrum, many writers avoid naming identity altogether, instead drawing characters defined by internal struggles that are in no way related to the particular community the character inhabits or the identities the character holds. If we return to our example of *Killing Eve*, we could say that Eve's character is based on just that type of struggle with little acknowledgement—except at convenient plot points—of the fact that she's a woman. Further, there is no acknowledgement of how being a person of Korean descent might factor into how Eve moves in the world. Instead, the story centers a fundamentally neutral struggle contained in how beneath Eve's normalcy as a dowdy, state bureaucrat with a husband, friends, a job, and a quirky interest in female violence belies an equal and opposite shadow-self that harbors deranged and psychopathic tendencies that are initially expressed via her queer desire for Villanelle.

Binary oppositions like the one in *Killing Eve* are the lifeblood of Hollywood character creation. In series like *Dexter*, we get the serial killer with the heart of gold; in *Breaking Bad*, we get Walter White, the ineffectual high school chemistry teacher turned cold-blooded, drug-lord; in *Homeland*, we get Carrie, the assumedly stable CIA agent fighting terrorism, who is actually a person with a severe mood disorder also sympathizing with possible terrorists; in *Nurse Jackie*, our heroine cares for others while harboring a secret drug addiction that sometimes puts her patients in danger.

This isn't to say that these inherent contradictions don't fuel conflict and tension: they most certainly do. But the conflicts they produce are reductive by virtue of being manufactured out of a simplistic and unrealistic conception of human complexity and the way that complexity is shaped by our histories, identities, and the cultural context in which we live. While Walter White's inner sadist could very well be linked to his identity as a cis, straight, white man, who—for the first time in his life—is forced to reckon with his utter incompetence in a culture designed to ensure his success, the show never frames it that way. Instead, it is posited via traditional notions of screenwriting that insist that the true essence of one's character is related to deep-seated truths about a person that only emerge when in tension with an external antagonistic force. If it weren't for the cancer, Walter may have never discovered his inner ruthlessness and power. Finally, because his identity is not central to the creation of his character, violence is never addressed as a sociopolitical issue or manifestation of white male rage.[14]

Vida moves us in a significantly different direction, rooting its characters firmly in their intersectional identities as queer and/or Latine, with all of the contradictions, tensions, joys, and community-affiliations those identities entail. Further, it does so without making these same characters emblematic representations of those identities, which is to say that at no point does *Vida* reduce its characters to their identities. Instead of archetypes, *Vida's* characters are rich, complicated, and contradictory, which is, in part, due to the way they navigate the complex intersections of identity. To return to our discussion of place-based storytelling, just as Gloria Anzaldúa's concept of "the borderlands" can mark the liminal, transitory space where multiple cultures and histories converge, conflict, or influence one another in physical space, the borderlands also impacts the landscape of the psyche. As scholar Carmen Quiñones writes of *Vida's* connection to the borderlands ethos of Anzaldúa's work,

> the show meditates on the highly unstable, messy convergence of different cultures and classes in the Southwestern US. Like Anzaldúa, Vida focuses on the particular wounds borne by Mexican and Chicana/x women and queer people of color who inhabit these cultural quicksands.[15]

Anzaldúa's borderlands isn't only a place in the world but a consciousness born of that world, a "*mestiza* consciousness." In Anzaldúa's theorizations on what it means to inhabit multiple homelands that often feel at odds with one another, she writes that Chicanas must move beyond the dual consciousness that captures the contradictions and ambiguities arising from life as Mexican-Americans within Anglo-American supremacy towards a multifaceted consciousness that embraces one's indigenous identity and other identities as well. For Anzaldúa, binaristic dualisms—which within the context of screenwriting form the central mechanism of character creation—lead to violence through a war of opposites. She writes,

> [b]ut it is not enough to stand on the opposite river bank, shouting questions, challenging patriarchal, white conventions. A counterstance locks one into a duel of oppressor and oppressed; locked in mortal combat, like the cop and the criminal, both are reduced to a common denominator of violence.[16]

Anzaldúa teaches that while such a "counterstance" marks territory outside of the beliefs and practices of the dominant culture, it is still dependent on that culture to define the terms of the argument. This is not liberation. For a liberated consciousness, Anzaldúa suggests that

> on our way to a new consciousness, we will have to leave the opposite bank, the split between the two mortal combatants somehow healed so that we are on both shores at once and, at once, see through serpent and eagle eyes.[17]

The new mestiza cannot destroy one part of herself and allow the victor to dominate the psyche, or be reduced to a singular identity or expression of subjectivity. Instead, the way towards wholeness lies in existing on multiple shores at once, where one's multifaceted self is honored and celebrated. Similarly, rather than posit characters through a binaristic either/or logic of opposition, *Vida* embraces an intersectional logic of character design that establishes characters with multiple identities and their concurrent interfacings, longings, contradictions, and convergences.

Emma and Lyn grapple with their complex identities in different ways. Emma, the eldest of the Hernandez sisters, is a no-nonsense, queer Latina with a head for business. Initially introduced as someone who passes as white, but who, if you know where to look, is "true rice and beans,"[18] Saracho marks Emma as a character who lives in the borderlands between Mexican-American and Anglo-American culture. Throughout the series, Emma, whose corporate job in Chicago puts her in a different class than her Boyle Heights neighbors—many of whom have never left the neighborhood and/or are undocumented—is viewed with suspicion for her proximity to whiteness and the way it manifests in her overall prissiness, hyper-rationality, and aloofness. Despite how others see and define her, Emma doesn't identify as white, and whenever she's confronted with her white-seeming behaviors, she reacts with a hostility that we eventually learn is a protective mechanism. As Carmen Phillips writes,

> [b]eing a queer upper middle class Chicana raised by your working class Mamí under a veil of her own self-hatred and homophobia is more than just a mouthful to say out loud; it's a network of familial hurt, pain and systematic oppression that can't be unraveled into neat, separate boxes.[19]

The first of many identity-laden confrontations for Emma occurs towards the end of the first episode. As Emma and Lyn leave a local taqueria, Emma explains how—despite Lyn's protestations—she's going to sell their mother's building, leaving Eddy and the other residents in a bad way. Just outside Mari is scolding a white woman (a "Warby Parker bitch") for recording a vlog about the taqueria so that white hipsters can earn Neo-colonial social capital in Brown neighborhoods. When Emma scoffs at the scene outside the taqueria, Mari turns her ire on the sisters, calling them, "pinches gringas aguadas," which loosely translates to "watered down foreigners:" a challenge to their place in the community. For Emma and Lyn, the question of what it means to be a "real" Mexican is as fraught as it is common, even—and perhaps especially—from those within their community. Emma responds to Mari's challenge with equal vitriol, telling Mari that she can't tell her what borders she can or cannot cross. As the argument escalates to its breaking point, Emma calls Mari a "cholo" (a masculinizing epithet) and accuses her of trying to kiss her. There is much to unpack in Emma's defensiveness, all of which stem from the complexity of her characterization, which, in *Vida*, is not secondary to nor separate from her character, but, rather, forms character.

Emma's aggression betrays her discomfort in being called to account about where her loyalty and sense of community lie, while also challenging the fact that Mari is policing what it means to be Latina. Echoes of Anzaldúa ring out: "[l]ike others having or living in more than one culture, we get multiple, often opposing messages. The coming together of two self-content but habitually incompatible frames of reference cause *un chocque*, a cultural collision."[20] The external tension between Mari and Emma in this moment mirrors the irreconcilable struggle in Emma's head. Who is she? Is she the person she believes herself to be: a queer Latina who lives life on her own terms; who speaks Spanish fluently, but who passes as white; who was exiled from the community, but still holds that community as foundational to her sense of self and belonging? Or is she a traitor and a tourist, someone who discarded her community in favor of whiteness and has only returned to extract value from that community? In grappling with and refusing to answer these questions, *Vida* forces the audience to reckon with a larger question: what does it mean to be all these things at once? How do we navigate our highly specific contradictions, especially when they are also the contradictions of the culture at large?

In contrast to Emma's complex and contradictory characterization in this scene, Mari appears to exist as someone who is more whole, more singular. She is firmly and somehow more "authentically" Latina. Her anti-gentrification activism lends her a kind of credibility as someone who cares deeply for her community, so much so that she proudly calls out random white women on the street. It isn't until later in the series that the lie of this wholeness begins to unravel, as different external conflicts force her to reckon with the complexities of being not just Latina, but Latina within patriarchal culture. For Emma, these same external forces have already made her life and identity more fraught. In masculinizing and queering Mari, Emma acts out the ways her community has betrayed her, foreshadowing how the community will eventually do the same to Mari. More to the point, when Emma insinuates that Mari is hitting on her, Emma calls up yet another complicated aspect of her identity: her queerness and its connection to whiteness. The reason for her flight away from the neighborhood (and towards whiteness) in the first place was not by choice: her mother exiled her because of (and perhaps to protect Emma from) the traditional, heteronormative, and patriarchal values of the community. Once again, place and culture situate and create character: there is no essential Emma. She is a myriad of contradictions and collisions stemming from being a queer Latina with a strong-willed personality that masks a deep vulnerability, who was exiled from her community and is now being scolded for surviving by embracing her white-passing privilege.

Emma's queerness adds additional complexity to the many "chocques" or cultural collisions that expand our understanding of her character throughout the series. First, it's worth noting that Emma is not an *L-Word* lesbian, by which I mean she doesn't refer to herself as a lesbian, align herself or surround herself with lesbians, dress like someone concerned with accumulating social capital in West Hollywood, or center that part of her identity. By some standards, she might not be a lesbian at all. It might be more accurate to say she's bisexual or, perhaps, pansexual in that over the course of the series she has sex with cis men, non-binary people, and butch lesbians. In allowing for Emma's complex, queer sexuality, *Vida* challenges the penchant for classification and labeling that even people within the queer community succumb to and insist on, instead asking "[w]hat might it mean for a queer femme to claim sexual attachments to masculinities that traverse a range of queer, butch, and trans-male bodies as well as cis-male bodies that become queer through our erotic attachment?"[21] There is no easy answer, and *Vida* seems comfortable with that lack of clarity. Emma, for her part, refuses labels altogether. And while she's confident with her lack of adherence to any particular label, that doesn't mean that other characters are at ease with that refusal. As such, in the same way that she's not Mexican enough for Mari, Emma's queerness becomes a point of contestation for other queer characters who insist that she identify herself, as happens in season two, episode three when Emma attends a queer wedding and gets scrutinized by her recent female hook-up's friends. After the table comments on everything from Emma's squirming away from public displays of affection to the lack of queer signaling in her fashion choices, Emma erupts: "I'm sorry that I don't abide by your dated categories of queerness. I'm sorry that you think I'm confused or indecisive because I have a wide range of what I can get off to." As Carmen Phillips writes, "that's a dynamic that's rarely talked about on lesbian television with as much bell-ringing clarity as it is right here."[22] In refusing labels, Emma simultaneously refuses to bow to an identitarian landscape while engaging deeply with identity and self via being true to her own complexity and fluidity. The innumerable incongruities inherent in Emma's character stem from internal and external pressures that are explicitly tied to Emma's identity and upbringing. In positioning characterization as central to depth of character, the writer's of *Vida* eschew an imagined secret essence in favor of multiplicity and contradiction.

In contrast to the high-strung and head-strong Emma, Lyn is free-spirited and malleable, which sometimes appears as flakey and other times as over-accommodating. Lyn, with her conventional good looks, penchant for shopping, and tendency to allow herself to get lost in a man, is the kind of female character who is often dismissed as the "girly-girl." When we first meet Lyn, she's dating a man-bunned, white hipster named Juniper, who breaks up with Lyn only two days after Vidalia's funeral and only moments after she's eaten his ass. At the same time, she's still hung up on Johnny—her neighborhood sweetheart—whom she has sex with at Vidalia's funeral despite his pregnant fiancé being just upstairs. Lyn—like many straight women deemed conventionally attractive—often trades on her looks, downplays her intelligence, and survives, in part, by being a "good girl:" pliable, obedient, catering to male pleasure and ego. Unlike Emma, who refuses to abide other people's assumptions or labels, Lyn has spent her life contorting herself into molds defined by her male partners and the misogynistic culture that shaped them.

If we whittled down Lyn's character with conflict, as McKee and the other screenplay gurus would insist we do, what do you think we would find? How could a woman like Lyn know who she is when all she knows is being who other people (and the whole culture around her) insists that she be? The closest you can get to the "essence" of Lyn is that she wants to be exactly what the world around her wants her to be, so that they will like her and keep her around. A character like Lyn doesn't have a chance as a central character under the scrutiny of the screenwriting gurus, who prize brazen heroes, rugged individuals, and mavericks. Luckily, in the world of *Vida*, there is space for Lyn.

Within the first season, for example, we find out that Lyn's breast implants were an unwanted but nevertheless accepted gift from a boyfriend, and over the course of three seasons, we witness a character arc that is neither progressive nor linear, one that acknowledges that change, if it happens at all, comes in fits and starts. Case in point: Lyn's season three relationship with local politician Rudy (Adrian Gonzalez), who shares her enthusiasm for fitness, likes to have non-vanilla sex (but refuses to talk about it), and for whom Lyn once again regresses into old patterns, such as attempting to transform herself into the woman that Rudy wants her to be. Lyn's desire to please Rudy extends to pleasing his traditional (and wealthy) Mexican mother, who disapproves of Lyn's inability to speak Spanish, the way she dresses, and the fact that she's co-owner of a neighborhood bar. Ultimately, Lyn's doomed quest to win the approval of Rudy's mother leaves her spinning like a top amidst the glass shards of a precious, borrowed, and inevitably dropped family heirloom mixed with the equally shattered remains of her seemingly perfect relationship. Lyn tries so hard and so earnestly that half the time it feels like she doesn't even know what she's trying at or who she's trying to be. The only thing we know is that she so strenuously strives to be liked, loved, accepted, and forgiven that we are left wondering whether she has energy left to like, love, accept, or forgive herself.

Like Emma, Lyn has a complicated relationship with her community. In the script for the pilot, she's introduced as "27, indigenous features made of cinnamon, calls herself Chicana but it's doubtful if she knows what that even means."[23] In addition to learning that she doesn't pass as white like her sister, we learn that Lyn is not in touch with her heritage, even when telling Emma that she's starting a line of "Aztec-inspired jewelry." Though Lyn doesn't pass as white, throughout the series we see that she often (perhaps unconsciously) embraces the ease that comes when putting herself in proximity to whiteness, often through white or white-adjacent men. At the same time, her beauty and recognizably Indigenous features lead to particular forms of fetishization within white culture that force her to reckon with her values and her identity.

This all comes to a head in the fourth episode of season one when Lyn steals a bunch of Vidalia's credit cards and goes on a shopping spree in a wealthy, white part of Los Angeles. Bags in hand, she stops at a restaurant where she meets a rich Australian who invites her to a house party in the Hills. At the party, the white partygoers engage in multiple racist behaviors from eroticizing the way Spanish speakers roll their Rs to fetishizing Lyn's eyebrows, which a drunk white girl swooningly refers to as "Frida brows." Though Lyn tries to smile and dismiss the white people's objectification of her, this becomes increasingly difficult because she is not alone. There is another Latina at the party, Aurora—a housekeeper and Lyn's cultural collision counterpart—and she's just across the pool. In one of the series' most lucid and critical moments, Lyn watches from afar the way the white party goers treat Aurora as they make bigger and more disgusting messes, culminating in Aurora being called to clean up one man's projectile vomit. When a white girl pretends to feel bad about it, the Australian shrugs it off saying, "That's her job." As Lyn's discomfort grows, it's as if you can see her being pulled between shores, one foot precariously in the sands of whiteness as a space she thought she could escape to, the other in the mire of what it means to be Latina within white supremacy, which sees Aurora and Lyn as things ready for objectification, subordination, and extraction. In the final scene, Lyn and Aurora take the same bus home, silent and mortified. Lyn's beauty and stolen credit cards may have gotten her invited to the party, but, in the end, like Aurora, she's objectified, used up, and glanced over. She's not seen as a real person, but as an outsider.

Through Lyn, *Vida* engages in questions around the subjectivity of one who's been reduced to an object by the dominant culture. Prior to this episode, Lyn flits like a butterfly, between people, between neighborhoods, from job to job, from purpose to purpose. She doesn't seem to have a clearly defined self: in relying on her looks, chameleon-like, she becomes whatever her admirers need her to be. In this moment, however, because of the presence of—and particularly—the witnessing of Lyn by Aurora, Lyn stops and looks at herself through a different kind of mirror. For once, Lyn seems aware of—or at least as though she might be awakening to—what it means to be an object to others while being a subject to herself. Aurora's gaze means something to Lyn and affects her because they share a facet of identity. And because she is seen by another Latina, witnessed by her, she cannot continue hiding from herself. This doesn't mean that Lyn becomes demonstrably more Latina-identified (whatever that means) or that she could have a conversation with Mari about gentefication or feminism. Instead she has a moment of understanding about how her identity affects where she stands in the world. She sees how racism and sexism are woven into the fabric of the world, and, perhaps, how she is wrapped up in it.

Thus, what in traditional screenwriting would be deemed surface-level detail or characterization becomes essential and deep character work in *Vida*. Lyn's observable qualities have consequences, most especially because on many levels Lyn is someone who is reduced to her observable qualities by everyone she encounters. Being Latina makes Lyn's experience at the party fundamentally different from the experience of the white girl who raves about her eyebrows and connects her to Aurora. At the same time, Saracho avoids the trap of reducing Lyn and Aurora to one essentialized or archetypal image. This is in keeping with series like

Gentefied and *On My Block* that challenge a "monolithic understanding and image of Latinxs."[24] For Saracho, this is part of her creative ethos: "I don't like archetypes. I like messy. I like pores. I like to see the barnacles."[25] The messiness of identity, personality, and position within society is why you cannot whittle a character down to an essence: because no one is just one thing. We are good and mediocre and bad. We are heroes and demons and also totally inconsequential. Lyn and Emma are Latina and women and sexual and abandoned daughters and adjacent to whiteness and completely left on their own to deal with all of these things because they don't cling to any one part of their identity enough to get to go and be a part of any one community. They don't even have family to rely on; too often they barely have each other. In this way, the mess is essential to the storytelling, and it is generative of story, not constrictive. *Vida* demonstrates that screenwriters need not use conflict to hollow out one's characters, but, rather, can focus on a character's layered complexity and richness to generate conflict and tension. For Lyn and Emma, to become one thing—be it virtuous or confident or properly queer or properly Mexican—is impossible. They will always be in the borderlands.

Narrative Engine as Orientation Device

In *Vida*, perhaps more than any other series or film I've considered in this book, character is so deeply threaded with narrative that it is difficult to unravel the two for analytical clarity. At the same time, there is a logic—albeit an intuitive one—that guides the connection between narrative and character that screenwriters can learn from. In rejecting typical half-hour formats that introduce a disruption to the status quo only to have order restored by the end of the episode, *Vida* sidelines linear progression, pivotal turning points, and the transformation imperative for something akin to an emergent narrative, where, in keeping with adrienne maree brown's liberationist theory of "emergent strategy," one "notices the way small actions and connections create complex systems, patterns that become ecosystems and societies."[26] In such an "emergent" narrative, writers attend to the specifics of character and place: how they interact and how they grow and change in relation to one another. Essentially, the series eschews a plot-oriented story engine fueled by relentless conflict in favor of organic eruptions birthed from a deep awareness of the characters' identity, history, environment, interdependence, and relationality. It's screenwriting as "alchemy," a term Saracho used several times in our interview to explain the amorphous and difficult process of creation, of "lingering in the essence of things."[27] For those seeking a new paradigm, of course, such an approach undoubtedly feels nebulous. But there is a creative ethos at play that can serve as a guide.

With *Vida*, rather than imagine the climax-driven, dramatic arc of narrative progress that traditionally propels us through three-act structure, it's more helpful to imagine something akin to a network or a constellation: a space where characters are connected through proximity, where what seems random and, perhaps chaotic, takes on a shape if you look thoughtfully enough for the pattern to emerge. Or, to add movement to the shape, *Vida's* narrative operates like a cloud of atoms in which characters suddenly swerve, bouncing off one another and the world in surprising and unpredictable ways depending on their orientation, history, identity, and personal proclivities. Like Anzaldúa's "chocques," such collisions bring new life, new combinations, and new worlds into being. In reimagining the shape of narrative in this way, we shift towards an imaginary that moves beyond the static linear line of progress and evokes constellations (of relations) and collisions (and, thus, momentum and aftermath), all within a given space. In this way, significant plot points and narrative momentum are generated by the unique ways that the characters interact in relation to one another within specific cultural spaces. In short, *Vida's* narrative emerges through relationality and orientation to one's place in the world.

For Saracho, *Vida's* structure is maintained conceptually through the grounding force of the lode star. Organized around Emma and Lyn's sisterly bond, the series "was always a love story between both of them. More than an engine, it was the North Star."[28] In considering the sister's relationship as the series' North Star, Saracho allows us to think about the narrative engine as more of an orientation device than a destination. One looks to the North Star, not to build a spaceship to travel there, but to situate oneself within one's present environment. At most the North Star tells the traveler which direction they are facing, but can't tell the traveler how soon they'll reach that destination, nor how far they must travel to get there. Recalibrating to consider the story engine as lode star brings many generative storytelling possibilities to the fore that ask the writer to create within a constellated as opposed to linear space. In Chapter 3, I asked screenwriters to consider what it might look like to organize a narrative around something like friendship or love. Love as North Star provides one such answer in that it highlights that contrary to traditional romance narratives that set the conquest of the love object as a narrative destination, love—whether familial, platonic, or romantic—is relational, not destinational.

Emma and Lyn's sisterhood is never positioned as a goal, nor as a relationship that needs to be worked on: it simply exists in all of the troubled and lovely ways that a sibling bond can. When Emma and Lyn return home for their mother's funeral in the pilot episode, it is clear that they haven't done much to maintain this relationship. At the same time, they know and accept one another in ways that the familiarity of the sibling bond allows. When Emma gives Eddy a hard time about the decisions she's making regarding her late wife's funeral, Lyn interjects: "She's dead. Can that please override your cuntyness just for today?" Lyn knows Emma— her faults as well as her gifts. And Emma knows that, too, as I can't imagine another character getting away with calling her "cunty." They are connected not only by blood, but a shared history as children whose father disappeared into thin air and as young adults whose mother has just died. Here Saracho is worth quoting at length,

> It's a bond that's been created from a shared experience, but also there's respect for the blood bond that we have in Latinidad. "My dad disowned me; I don't talk to my sisters; but we have this blood bond anyway." So honoring

that. Even when you think your mother kicks you out because you're queer, there's a love bond to come back and honor her death and honor her legacy. That's messy: it's not a positive thing all the time, this love bond by blood. And then the shared experiences that they did have growing up—the sisters and the mom—that happens when you grow up in a certain time or place. It is watermarked in you.[29]

Over the course of three seasons, neither Lyn nor Emma sets her sights on improving, exploring, or working on their relationship. In fact, most of the time they're off pursuing their own interests, with Lyn concocting plans to seduce Johnny or booking acts for the bar and Emma entering various trysts via dating apps to avoid committed relationship entanglements while claiming one day to be selling the bar only to keep it the next. But, in the end, whether they're watching themselves dance with their mom in decades-old home videos, drinking tequila on the rooftop while scheming plans for the bar, or forgiving one another for the umpteenth time—as we see in the final episode after Lyn breaks Emma's heart by hiding a rekindled relationship with their abusive and homophobic father—they always circle back to one another one more time before, inevitably, swerving off on their own next adventure.

A lode star need not be a relationship, of course. A film or series could circle around a theme, motif, or place, as well. If we return to the theme of gentefication, which simultaneously returns us to the significance of place, we can see how the narrative thrust of *Vida* diverges from traditional plotting in multiple ways. Mari's story arc contains the bulk of the gentrification theme. Orientated towards community and activism, while Mari's goal is to end gentrification in her neighborhood and protect her community, the obstacles she faces are not always directly linked to that goal. While some of the obstacles she encounters are the expected antagonisms from developers, real estate agents, and the gentefying sisters, the ones that take her off course are related to the fact that she is a young woman living in a patriarchal culture. If in traditional screenwriting, conflict fuels narrative as outer want gives way to inner need, Mari's storyline provides an alternative to that model in that not only is her primary goal impossible, but the most significant challenge she faces is not directly related to her activism.

As I relayed earlier in this chapter, Mari is the resident local activist, who regularly challenges Emma and Lyn, defaces "chipster" (chicano and hipster) businesses with graffiti, and uses her vlog to rail against developers and real estate agents. In season one, she hooks up with Tlaloc (Ramses Jimenez), the leader of her local activist group, Los Vigilantes. He records the encounter without her consent and sends the video to Los Vigilantes group chat. This starts a chain reaction that extends into season two and includes Mari confronting Tlaloc, Tlaloc playing dumb and acting like it was an accident, all the way to Johnny (her brother) seeing the video and punching Tlaloc to Mari's father seeing the video and disowning her. If Mari thought that the "Warby Parker bitch" with a vlog or Nelson, the upwardly mobile Latino developer, were her biggest obstacles, those gentrifiers were nothing compared to the devastation of being disowned by her father, especially since Mari is her father's primary caretaker. In the aftermath, betrayed by her community and family on account of patriarchal and heteronormative double standards around female sexuality, Mari goes to live with the other community exiles: her other sworn enemies Emma and Lyn.

While one could argue that white-supremacist patriarchy fuels capitalism, and, thus, gentrification, within Mari's constellated world, she is not oriented against patriarchy per se, but rather against the continuation of settler-colonial capitalism. Therefore, when the leader of Los Vigilantes assaults her and her father subsequently disowns her, there is not a clear connection between her ultimate goal and the blow she received from those closest to her. Again, we are in a messy territory, where the boundaries and borders that normally maintain clarity and order are blurred. Being disowned by her father and betrayed by Tlaloc doesn't impact Mari's activism directly. Aside from feeling humiliated and betrayed, she doesn't question her intentions or her goals; she doesn't need to access new inner reserves. After all, what exactly is it that Mari is supposed to learn in order to grow, thrive, and achieve after being reduced to a mere woman in a man's world? Is she supposed to become better equipped to handle the ever-present abuses of patriarchy? Her father expected chastity; her assaulter expected lenience: is she supposed to abandon her anti-gentrification activism on account that she can't abide safeguarding a neighborhood that would allow her sexuality and femaleness to result in her houselessness? There are no easy answers because there are no direct, binaristic correlations between Mari's wants, needs, nor the obstacles she faces to either. Similar to Lyn, whom she would never accept being compared to, Mari is repeatedly punished for being exactly who the people around her want her to be. And because she is family and community oriented, she is bound to be let down by those she loves most fiercely. What exactly is the solution to that? Abandoning them back? Finding a new family, a new community? These questions form the basis of much of the ongoing tension in *Vida*. Ultimately, Mari's political and familial orientation within white supremacist patriarchy provide ample fuel for myriad antagonisms without asking that she be reduced to a singular essence to solve a narrative problem.

Like Lyn and Emma, Mari enters the borderlands. Caught between two worlds, she appreciates Emma and Lyn's kindness, but doesn't switch allegiance. In fact, in the season two finale, Mari continues to protest the bar and doesn't intervene when Los Vigilantes gleefully douse "Coconut Barbie" in detergent. At most, Mari pivots and tries new tactics towards the same end. By the end of season three, Mari has quit Los Vigilantes and taken a job with a Buzzfeed-like organization with a social justice wing. She's skeptical, as she should be, but when they offer to her her own platform for her "La Pinche Chinche" videos, she takes the gig. And while embracing work in a corporation focused on "content creation" might seem like a transformative change for Mari and a possible happy ending, knowing *Vida*, had the series continued, most likely it would have brought more problems than solutions.

In *Vida*, as with a dog chasing a car bumper, it is in the moments that we catch up with the object of our desire that we realize that it has no relation to what we need after all. Unlike the tried and true screenwriting formulas that would have a character pursue an external goal as a means to achieve an internal need, the characters in *Vida* succeed in their external pursuits at their own internal peril. More radical still, no one gains a deep understanding of what it is that they need, or at least not in a way that is permanent. *Vida's* characters are constantly in flux. They progress and regress so often that it'd be absurd to claim that anyone has definitively transformed from season one through the end of season three. This is not the tried-and-true screenwriting guru's narrative arc, and yet it's hard to deny that this kind of character development and narrative feels familiar. Why? Because it feels like being alive. *Vida* proves that writing from the complicated intersections of identity and acknowledging how your identities place you in a world of hurt is one way to guard against the neutralizing and assimilationist bent of screenwriting norms, instead honoring complex lives in ways that are closer to the ways they are lived and experienced.

Notes

1 Jess King. Interview with Tanya Saracho. Personal, May 11, 2021.
2 Ibid.
3 During my interview with Tanya Saracho, instead of Latinx, she used the term Latine as a gender neutral term for Latino, Latina, and/or gender nonconforming people. Taking her lead, I will do the same throughout this chapter.
4 King, Saracho Interview.
5 Aymar Jean Christian and Khadijah Costley White, "Organic Representation as Cultural Reparation," *JCMS: Journal of Cinema and Media Studies* 60, no. 1 (2020): 143–47, 144.
6 King, Saracho Interview.
7 Ibid.
8 Ibid.
9 Christian and White, "Organic Representation," 145.
10 Podcast: New Hollywood. The Deadline Podcast, May 28, 2019. Produced by David Janove.
11 Ibid.
12 King, Saracho Interview.
13 T. Saracho, *Pour Vida*, Pilot Script, 12.
14 If *Breaking Bad* had acknowledged the role that white male privilege played in White's descent into ruthless amorality, one can only imagine how differently fans might have responded to the series. I can't help but wonder: would the overwhelmingly misogynist response to Skylar as resident series "bitch" have been so vehement if the series took a critical stance on the role Walter's white, male privilege played in his downfall?
15 Carmen Merport Quiñones, "Binging the Borderlands," *Public Books*, March 22, 2021, www.publicbooks.org/binging-the-borderlands/.
16 G. Anzaldúa, *Borderlands -: La Frontera* (San Francisco, CA: Aunt Lute Books, 2007), 100.
17 Ibid.
18 Saracho, *Vida*, 3.
19 Carmen Phillips, "Vida's Gay Vaquero Episode Breaks Emma's Heart, Asks Hard Questions About Who's Included in the Queer Community," *Autostraddle*, May 2, 2021,

www.autostraddle.com/vidas-gay-vaquero-episode-breaks-emmas-heart-asks-hard-questions-about-whos-included-in-the-queer-community/.

20 Anzaldúa, *Borderlands*, 100.

21 Juana María Rodríguez, *Sexual Futures, Queer Gestures, and Other Latina Longings* (New York: New York University Press, 2014), 24.

22 Carmen Phillips, "Vida's Gay Vaquero Episode Breaks Emma's Heart, Asks Hard Questions About Who's Included in the Queer Community," *Autostraddle*, May 2, 2021, www.autostraddle.com/vidas-gay-vaquero-episode-breaks-emmas-heart-asks-hard-questions-about-whos-included-in-the-queer-community/.

23 Saracho, *Vida*, 4.

24 Richard Mwakasege-Minaya and Juri Sanchez, " 'Beautifully Represented' or an Attack on Our Culture? Netflix's Gentefied and the Struggle over Latinidad/Es," *Jump Cut: A Review of Contemporary Media*, no. 60 (2021), www.ejumpcut.org/currentissue/Mwakasege-Minaya-Sanchez-Gentefied/text.html.

25 King, Saracho Interview.

26 Adrienne Maree Brown, *Emergent Strategy: Shaping Change, Changing Worlds* (Chico, CA: AK Press, 2017), 3.

27 King, Saracho Interview.

28 Ibid.

29 Ibid.

CONCLUSION

A Way Forward

I began writing this book in March of 2020 during the first week of the COVID-19 pandemic lockdown in the United States. Over the course of the past two years, the glaring systemic and structural problems fed by white supremacist, heterosexist capitalism have been brought to light in numerous ways. As of this writing, over 736,000 people have died from COVID-19 in the United States and over 4.9 million have died globally with many more millions infected. Of the sick, the dead, and the dying, the majority are from marginalized communities and countries, as it tends to be the most vulnerable who are the most negatively impacted in systems designed around human hierarchy. At the same time that people in Black, Latinx, and Indigenous communities in the United States are dying in record numbers, white people refuse to wear masks to protect others or themselves from infection, gathering in large groups at popular vacation destinations and staging armed protests to demand their freedom, which within capitalism means the right to an "easy" and comfortable life. This is whiteness at work, fed by narratives of the exalted individual who is licensed to wreak havoc on his community for his own personal gain. This is the legacy of white settler-colonial expansion and its myth-making container: the Hollywood Western and its many offshoots the action film, the gangster film, and the police procedural.

From mutual aid work to political activism to non-governmental organizations, there are many avenues to address the inequities that American culture is premised upon. As a filmmaker and educator who works in an industry that shapes the American cultural imaginary, my fight is over what appears on our screens and what those images teach us about who we are, where we've come from, where we're headed, and whose lives have value. Throughout this book, I've argued that screenwriting was not founded on equity, but rather the false god of universal neutrality. Therefore, to imagine liberation through the lens of screenwriting requires a convivial inquiry into how screenwriters can trouble hierarchy and systemic

DOI: 10.4324/9781003170310-13

inequality through examining and reinventing the craft itself. For those who love the craft, this should be a welcome endeavor. As Sciamma says, "I am a screen-writer because I like asking myself questions about screenwriting."[1]

Examination comes in many forms, a few of which I will outline here as the initial tracing of a path forward. The first stage, much of which this book has concerned itself with, is to line up the tomes recognized as the cornerstones of our craft and honestly assess the lenses through which the creators were looking. Doing so contributes to a quick understanding that our screenwriting paradigms were created by particular men with particular privileges and biases, and that those privileges and biases inform how they conceive of things as complex as a person's subjectivity and as seemingly basic as how to define "conflict" or "desire." The list extends beyond whiteness, maleness, and heterosexuality to include issues around ability, class, citizenship, religious affiliation, indigenousness, ethnicity, and more. These particularities—the ones obscured by McKee, Field, Vogler, Snyder, and those who've followed in their stead—are the key to transformation. An awareness of human uniqueness not only gives us the tools to chart new journeys, but begs us to interrogate our own biases and privileges so that we don't perpetuate them in the stories we tell.

In order to establish the appropriate critical framework within the field of screenwriting, film school curricula would be richer with the inclusion of more media and cultural studies classes so that students understand the myriad insidi-ous ways that bias manifests in media texts. Where film school coursework tends to contain little to no critical theory, classes in the field of Communications and Media Studies tend to incorporate queer, feminist, and anti-racist critique, which go a long way towards identifying systemic bias within texts through critical decod-ing practices. In the same vein, film schools would do well to incorporate critical theory courses geared towards creators to help identify, mitigate, and perhaps even eliminate bias before it enters a text in the first place. To be clear, this isn't to say that a writer can control the reception of their work, that texts aren't read in ways the creator never intended, or that bias and structural inequality can be eliminated with a few courses on critical theory. At the same time, I've seen marked differ-ences in work from students who have taken courses I teach on "The Female Gaze" and "Queer(ing) Narratives," which center feminist, queer, and critical race the-ory to challenge screenwriting and filmmaking norms. In those courses, students have consistently emerged with more socially conscious approaches to storytelling, which has resulted in some of the most innovative, adventurous, and beautiful screenplays I've read. Through thoughtful engagement with intersectional identi-ties, social context, and political and economic realities informed by critical theory, students produce texts that not only entertain but seek to remedy social harm, and even further, celebrate human difference. Finally, as I've demonstrated throughout this book, the fact that the ideology of white masculinity is codified in screenwrit-ing paradigms has real-world consequences. We leave this unexamined at our peril.

Within the studio system, studios should continue to hire screenwriters of diverse backgrounds and identities, while also putting inclusive supports in place for those same writers to navigate a system predicated on racial and gendered violence. It's also important that industry leaders widen the practice of hiring gender and/or critical race experts to work as consultants or sensitivity readers on film projects or as fixtures in writers' rooms. In a writers' room, a scholar or expert of this kind can add nuance and depth to the stories told, as evidenced by Johanna Johnson's decision to hire Black Lives Matter co-founder Patrisse Cullors as a story consultant, performer, and, eventually, writer for the series *Good Trouble* (Freeform). Cullors' deep knowledge and experience of organizing work not only informs Malika's (Zuri Adele) storylines, but helps portray the intricate distinctions between being an organizer and an activist in ways never before seen on television.[2] Writing teams regularly employ consultants to guide them on industry specific information related to police procedurals, space exploration epics, and medical dramas—why not bring in specialists on how racial and gender bias operate instead of relying on well-meaning writers to be experts on all facets of humanity? Much in the way film and television figureheads responded rapidly to innovation in entertainment tech, making room for streaming platforms and fewer in-theater transactions, they wouldn't have to wait to listen to angry viewers from underserved and underrepresented audiences clamoring to see themselves on screen. The watchers have megaphones now, and they're not going to relinquish their voices. So, why not welcome those voices into the production process instead of making it a marketing spin exercise on the other side? Storytelling shouldn't be a write first, apologize later scenario.

Developing a critical apparatus, however, is only the beginning. While I don't foresee the traditional paradigms disappearing anytime soon, those invested in radically altering the cultural imaginary must begin experimenting with new methods of screenplay development. This does not mean starting from scratch, but rather taking the current paradigms as points of departure. In the following section—distilled from the analysis offered throughout this book—I offer ten avenues towards liberation-minded interventions in screenplay writing. This is not a new paradigm, nor is it a comprehensive list of what's possible. But I hope it serves as a launching pad for radical change premised on an understanding that another world is possible: we just have to imagine it.

Ten Tactics Toward an Equitable, Inclusive, and Intersectional Screenwriting Practice

Tactic 1: Locate Your Unique Perspective

Objectivity is a ruse. Don't fall for it. You have a unique subjective experience, but you cannot draw from it and create with it unless you fully acknowledge it. What are your identities? What are the angles and perspectives only you can provide? Are you holding majoritarian identities that have allowed or encouraged you to assume that you understand and can write from the perspective of anyone? Whiteness, straightness, and cis-het privilege like to grant the bearers of these identities with magical binoculars and microscopes allowing for expertise on those of all other identities. When I suggest in my workshops and classes that there may be limitations to the characters you should create or the stories you tell, I'm often met with the refrain: "But what about my imagination?" And I have news for you: your imagination is informed by your lived experience and your observations of others, including the stereotypes and biases of those you spend time with and the media you consume.

Our uniqueness lies in the fact that we're the only ones who've experienced life from our unique vantage point, our unique positioning in the world. It has the potential to shape stories in ways that feel fresh and alive. Embrace your unique subjective experience and learn from it. Use it to inform how characters interact and behave, and allow it to guide you in the mentors and collaborators you seek out. Use it to explore how to more effectively infuse your scripts with emotion and affect in ways seldom, if ever, captured. We all see the world from a different vantage point. That perspective matters.

Tactic 2: Write Screenplays About Underrepresented and/or Misrepresented Characters

One of the first questions that screenwriters must ask: how do we rectify the legacy of erasure and harmful media stereotypes targeting women, BIPOC, queer and trans people, disabled people, and more? An equitable and inclusive media landscape would be full of intersectional characters with a variety of political, social, and economic backgrounds and perspectives. We would write screenplays about far more women (not just white ones), including women over the age of 45. We'd watch series about poor people. We'd see and hear people speak multiple languages. We'd see Indigenous elders and two-spirit people. We'd see Black aunties and Latino abuelos. We'd see disabled people, some with cognitive disabilities, others with physical ones who are completely at home in themselves. At the same time, because representation is disciplined through screenplay structure, representation is not enough. The structural and conceptual logics of screenwriting impact the way characters, worlds, and narratives are shaped. Screenwriters cannot simply plug intersectional characters into molds made to accommodate and perpetuate the symbolic power of cis, straight, white men. Ideally this would be done by those who share all or some of the primary identities of the main characters, which, in turn, means that a concerted effort to hire intersectional writers, directors, producers, studio heads, and the like is necessary.

Tactic 3: Create Characters with Complex Subjectivities and Agency

Hollywood's attachment to autonomous and exceptional heroes obscures alternate forms of agency in which a character might act upon the world as frequently as they are acted upon, or whose actions are not legible as agential. To write screenplays about characters with non-dominant identities requires an attention to how agency expresses itself outside of exerting dominance. Characters who quietly resist, acquiesce, endure, collaborate with others, or choose acts of subtle subversion can carry a narrative. This requires attention to drawing out how non-heroic acts impact not only the emotional, intellectual, and physical development of the character, but how they impact the world around them. Screenwriters can reorient the logic upon which characters are constructed based on their own unique experiences of self, agency, and relationality. A new imaginary needs an infusion of nuanced observation about how different people from all walks of life express agency and experience subjectivity.

Tactic 4: Embrace Your Character's Messy Contradictions

As series like *Vida* and *I May Destroy You* demonstrate, complex characters rife with contradictions are a narrative engine in and of themselves. The more screenwriters embrace the messy ambiguities of what it means to be alive in a world that is neither predictable nor permanent, the more that the obstacles a character encounters will be rooted in their uniqueness, and the more natural and authentic the narrative becomes. Characters like *Vida's* Emma and *I May Destroy You's* Arabella thrive on contradictions, their various identities, sorrows, and goals crashing into each other in different ways every episode. Although many a self-help guru or weight-loss program would have you think otherwise, human beings are not on linear, finite journeys toward figuring themselves out and "finding themselves," but instead are on lifelong adventures involving never-ending self discovery and self evolution that cannot be summed up in a 90-minute film. Thus, consider writing characters who reveal themselves and revel in the human messiness rather than smoothing out and ridding characters of their flaws in order to make them more in line with the mythical norm.

Tactic 5: Center Characterization

Characterization is not a cosmetic afterthought. A character's unique identity—gender, race, sexuality, and more—impacts how they move in the world, which is in constant call and response with how the world reacts to them. Write with an awareness that identity impacts—without overdetermining—narrative. Consider all aspects of a character's identity, including the ways that they experience subjectivity and temporality, as well as relationality, or how they experience different degrees of porousness and connection versus boundedness and alienation. So much flattening of human variety occurs under the rubric of the universal neutral.

Perhaps the most useful tactic towards understanding how your characters are impacted by their unique characteristics is to consider the implications of the various aspects of your character's identity and how that plays out in different settings and contexts. If writing a film about an Asian female news anchor, consider questions like: What is her relationship to her gender? Is she South Asian-American, Vietnamese-American, Chinese-American, and how does it matter? If she's Chinese-American, is she first generation? What is her relationship, if any, to China or to Chinese culture?

Is she a dual-language speaker? If so, what specific languages/dialects does she speak and in what contexts? What happens at the intersection of her Asian heritage and her gender? How much does her parents' immigration story impact her? Is she concerned about carrying out traditions or her family legacy? How does being a news anchor complicate any of the answers to these questions? Has it changed how she experiences time and/or space? What is her relationship to wealth and class? And, having considered these questions, what additional complications might naturally arise that could help propel the narrative or enrich the storytelling? Answering these questions—and this is by no means a comprehensive list—isn't just an obligatory background-building exercise, but helps the writer understand the complexities with which the character is encountering the world and vice versa.

Tactic 6: Deepen World-building Practices

World-building is important beyond speculative and historical genres. Characters exist in and are impacted by where they are in space and time. Consider the relationship between world and character. You and I might live in the same country, city, or even neighborhood, but because of who we are—our identities, our unique histories, our perspectives—the rules that we are subject to are probably different. Even if they are the same, we very well might react to them differently based on who we are. Focus on building a world that is dynamic and dimensional. Consider how the social, political, and economic context impacts your characters. Just as a film set in outer space is going to be markedly different than one set on Earth, a film like *Sorry to Bother You* demonstrates that a city like Oakland—when filtered through Riley's specific anti-capitalist lens—might feel unfamiliar to a white Oakland resident counting on an uptick in real estate prices due to gentrification.

World-building is more than just picking a city or employing intricate production design. It's about understanding the space that your characters are living in and walking through, understanding that every place has a community with collective hopes and fears, carrying the idea that history is alive and evolving, and that every wall in every story setting has eyes, an opinion, and surprises for your characters.

Tactic 7: Conflict is a Toxic Narrative Engine

My head spins when I think too much about the supremacy of conflict as screenwriting's fundamental story engine. Have we not created enough suffering in the world through the belief that conflict is a way of creating order or solving problems? Conflict forces narratives to revolve around domination, overcoming, violence, and bargaining, effectively reducing the number of paths a narrative can take to the well-worn roads of winning, achieving, eliminating, and conquering. It's time to explore other avenues toward generating narrative. As Sciamma shows, conflict is not the sole driver of tension, and it is tension, rather than conflict, that keeps audiences engaged and moves a story forward. Tension can come from things like desire, contradiction, and the unfamiliar. De-centering conflict impacts the role of the antagonist, as well. For when we don't focus on conflict, the need to vanquish one's foes also disappears. Consider what new relationships might become central in a narrative organized around healing, for example, with its ups and downs, as opposed to the linear and seemingly finite trajectory of conflict.

Tactic 8: Challenge the Transformation Arc

Other than the transformation of the central character, which requires a whittling down to one's essence by steamrolling the character's flaws, what other goals might a narrative have? If escalating obstacles generates an arc that culminates in a final, explosive release, what structural shape might a narrative organized around accept-ance, healing, grief, care, friendship, entropy, or pleasure take? Consider paths that bloom, weave, and meander, where the breadth of one's complexity and how that complexity interacts with the world takes precedence. Consider the primary goal of a narrative less as a winnowing down of self and more as a burgeoning of a complex, multi-faceted self that is integrated and whole. Rather than seeking to simplify a character to one small, sharp, shiny knifepoint of truth, consider instead growing your character to resemble a complex system of levers and pulleys, reacting and responding to each encounter, decision, and opportunity with the most sensitive of scales in order to determine the best (or best in the moment) possible interaction.

Tactic 9: Redemption is for Cis, White Men

Retire the redemption arc. Much harm has been done in the world on account of the redemption arc, which—because of the over-representation of white men in media—has meant that white males have been getting away with murder (or assault or other harm) on screen (and off) only to be forgiven, empathized with, and understood in the end. Too often redemption arcs are employed to gaslight audi-ences into letting white men off the hook for atrocities, rather than to give space for those harmed by those same atrocious acts. In line with movements geared towards healing justice, screenwriters would do well to refocus narratives on survi-vors rather than aggressors, for survivors don't need redemption. In centering the stories and lives of those who have traditionally experienced harm and oppression, we begin the process of turning the tide by radically re-imagining storytelling practices that eroticize violence through a metric of universal heroism. In place of the redemption arc, stories centered on restoring dignity and belonging, as well as stories that transform our relationship with self and others towards healing and integration can become the new norm.

Tactic 10: Transgress Boundaries and Forge New Desire Lines

Categorical thinking, while helpful for the purposes of analytical clarity, can lock screenwriters into a limited view of what's possible. Binaristic categories like male/ female, good/bad, and white/non-white force an "imagining against" scenario.

This is how whiteness, maleness, heteronormativity, ableism, and so many other forms of dominant normativities reify themselves.

It is time to imagine otherwise. The Wachowskis provide many possible paths for doing this work: in their queering of the hero's journey, wherein the hero "unbecomes;" in their expansive trans-genre storytelling, which moves beyond *Killing Eve*'s playful but faithful mash-up of the thriller and the rom-com to *Sense8*'s irreverent meshing of the police procedural and the melodrama; and in their unabashed embrace of narrative excess. The Wachowskis demonstrate that each element of the paradigm holds the clues to its own dismantling. Screenwriters can draw new patterns that depart from the old because we simply cannot expect to re-enact the same tropes, maintain the same logics of categorization, or trace the same paths if we want to arrive in new destinations.

A Final Word

If liberation from the oppressive impact of cis-centric, white supremacist, heterosexist patriarchy is our goal, to do our part as screenwriters and screenwriting instructors, we must reformulate screenwriting practice towards healing and community-building. As Audre Lorde reminds us, "the master's tools will never dismantle the master's house,"[3] which is why shunting characters with marginalized identities into unquestioned majoritarian-style scripts is not going to bring about transformative change. This will not be a small endeavor. In an industry in which all who practice are scrambling for crumbs of success, to even quietly suggest that the industry needs an overhaul can be daunting. But in order to effect industry-wide awareness that change is needed and possible, and then to create change itself, we must begin to critically examine not just who has the ideas, gets the jobs, writes the screenplays, directs the stories, delivers the lines, or pays the price of admission: we must examine the logic and structure of the screenwriting paradigms themselves. In this spirit, it is time to upend the craft.

Notes

1 Céline Sciamma, "Ready for the Rising Tide," *BAFTA Screenwriters' Lecture Series*, February 4, 2020, www.bafta.org/media-centre/transcripts/screenwriters-lecture-series-2019-celine-sciamma.
2 Kelsey Minor, "How Patrisse Cullors Helped Turn Zuri Adele into an on-Screen Activist," *Shondaland*, June 26, 2019, www.shondaland.com/watch/a28175137/patrisse-cullors-zuri-adele-activist/.
3 A. Lorde, *Sister Outsider: Essays & Speeches* (Berkeley: Crossing Press, 2007), 123.

REFERENCES

Ahmed, Sara. "A Phenomenology of Whiteness." *Feminist Theory* 8, no. 2 (2007): 149–68.

———. *Queer Phenomenology: Orientations, Objects, Others*. Durham, NC: Duke University Press, 2007.

———. *Willful Subjects*. Durham, NC: Duke University Press, 2014.

Alison, Jane. *Meander, Spiral, Explode: Design and Pattern in Narrative*. New York: Catapult, 2019.

Altman, Rick. *Film/Genre*. London: BFI Publishing, 1999.

Anzaldúa, Gloria. *Borderlands -: La Frontera*. San Francisco, CA: Aunt Lute Books, 2007.

Ashton, Hilarie. "In Defense of Fleabag Feminism." *Ms. Magazine Blog*, March 1, 2019. Accessed March 10, 2019. http://msmagazine.com/blog/2019/01/02/defense-fleabag- feminism/.

Babalola, Bolu. "The Innate Black Britishness of *I May Destroy You*." *Vulture*, August 4, 2020. www.vulture.com/article/i-may-destroy-you-black-britishness.html.

Banks, Miranda. *The Writers: A History of American Screenwriters and Their Guild*. New Brunswick, NJ: Rutgers University Press, 2016.

Barr, Merrill. "'Sense8' Failure in Structure Highlights the Biggest Problem with Netflix Programming." *Forbes*, June 10, 2015. www.forbes.com/sites/ merrillbarr/2015/06/10/sense8-failure-netflix/.

Bastién, Angelica Jade. "Let's Talk About That I May Destroy You Ending." *Vulture*, August 25, 2020. www.vulture.com/article/i-may-destroy-you-finale-ego-death-explained-analysis.html.

Benson-Allott, Caetlin. "How I May Destroy You Reinvents Rape Television." *Film Quarterly* 74, no. 2 (2020): 100–5. https://doi.org/10.1525/fq.2020.74.2.100.

Berlant, Lauren. *Cruel Optimism*. Durham, NC: Duke University Press, 2012.

Bernstein, Fred A. "A House Not for Mere Mortals." *The New York Times*, April 3, 2008. www.nytimes.com/2008/04/03/garden/03destiny.html.

Berrios, Maria, and Jakob Jakobsen. *Hospital Prison University Radio*, May 2018. https://soundcloud.com/hospitalprisonuniversityradio/conversation-with-frank-b-wilderson-on-fanon-etc/

Bordwell, David. *Narration in the Fiction Film*. Madison, WI: University of Wisconsin Press, 1985.

Braudy, Leo, Marshall Cohen, and Laura Mulvey. "Visual Pleasure and Narrative Cinema." Essay. In *Film Theory and Criticism: Introductory Readings*, 833–44. Oxford: Oxford University Press, 1999.

Brown, Adrienne Maree. *Emergent Strategy: Shaping Change, Changing Worlds*. Chico, CA: AK Press, 2017.

Bugbee, Teo. "'Music' Review: A Woefully Misguided View of Disability." *The New York Times*, February 11, 2021. www.nytimes.com/2021/02/11/movies/music-review.html.

Butler, Judith. *The Force of Nonviolence: An Ethico-Political Bind*. New York: Verso, 2020.

Butler, Judith, and Sara Salih. *The Judith Butler Reader*. Malden, MA: Blackwell, 2004.

Campbell, Joseph. *The Hero with a Thousand Faces*. Princeton, NJ: Princeton University Press, 2004.

Cavarero, Adriana. *In Spite of Plato: A Feminist Rewriting of Ancient Philosophy*. New York: Routledge, 1995.

———. *Inclinations: A Critique of Rectitude*. Stanford, CA: Stanford University Press, 2016.

———. "Towards a Theory of Sexual Difference." In *The Lonely Mirror*, edited by Sandra Kemp and Paola Bono, 190–221. London and New York: Routledge, 1993.

Christian, Aymar Jean, and Khadijah Costley White. "Organic Representation as Cultural Reparation." *JCMS: Journal of Cinema and Media Studies* 60, no. 1 (2020): 143–47.

Clarke, Stewart, and Stewart Clarke. "Phoebe Waller-Bridge Twists the Spy Genre with BBC America's Thriller 'Killing Eve'." *Variety*, April 13, 2018. Accessed February 12, 2019. https://variety.com/2018/tv/features/phoebe-waller-bridge-sandra-oh-killing-eve-1202742904/.

Coel, Michaela. *I May Destroy You*. "Am I Bleeding?" Pilot Script, 2019.

Cohen, C. J. "Punks, Bulldaggers, and Welfare Queens: The Radical Potential of Queer Politics?" *GLQ: A Journal of Lesbian and Gay Studies* 3, no. 4 (January 1997): 437–65.

Conor, Bridget. *Screenwriting: Creative Labor and Professional Practice*. London: Routledge, 2014. https://doi-org.ezproxy.depaul.edu/10.4324/9780203080771.

Crenshaw, Kimberlé. "Demarginalizing the Intersection of Race and Sex: A Black Feminist Critique of Antidiscrimination Doctrine, Feminist Theory and Antiracist Politics." *University of Chicago Legal Forum* (1989): 139–67.

———. "Mapping the Margins: Intersectionality, Identity Politics, and Violence Against Women of Color." *Stanford Law Review* 43, no. 6 (July 1991): 1241–99.

———. "Toward a Race-Conscious Pedagogy in Legal Education." *National Black Law Journal* 11, no. 1 (1988).

Davies, Hannah J. "I May Destroy You: Why Michaela Coel's Drama Is a True TV Gamechanger." *The Guardian*. Guardian News and Media, July 11, 2020. www.theguardian.com/tv-and-radio/2020/jul/11/i-may-destroy-you-why-michaela-coels-drama-is-a-true-tv-gamechanger.

DeLauretis, Teresa. "Film and the Visible." In *How Do I Look? Queer Film and Video*, edited by Bad Object Choices, 223–64. Seattle: Bay Press, 1992.

Duggan, Lisa. *Materializing Democracy Toward a Revitalized Cultural Politics*. Edited by Dana D. Nelson and Russ Castronovo. Durham, NC: Duke University Press, 2002.

Dyer, Richard. *White*. New York: Routledge, 1997.

Elrod, James. "'I Am Also a We': The Interconnected, Intersectional Superheroes of Netflix's Sense8." *Panic at the Discourse: An Interdisciplinary Journal*. www.academia.edu/39809616/_I_am_also_a_we_The_Interconnected_Intersectional_Superheroes_of_Netflixs_Sense8.

Ergi, Lajos. *The Art of Dramatic Writing*. Rockville, MD: Wildside Press, 1946.

Fidel, Manny. "How White Savior Movies Hurt Hollywood." *YouTube. Insider*, March 5, 2019. www.youtube.com/watch?v=0sdC6RxaY-Q.

Field, Syd. *Screenplay: The Foundations of Screenwriting*. New York: Bantam Dell, 2005.

Garland-Thomson, Rosemarie. "Misfits: A Feminist Materialist Disability Concept." *Hypatia* 26, no. 3 (2011): 591–609.

Gates, Racquel J. *Double Negative: The Black Image and Popular Culture*. Durham, NC: Duke University Press, 2018.

Gilbert, Sophie. "Killing Eve Is a Sign of TV to Come." *The Atlantic*, April 11, 2018. Accessed February 22, 2019. www.theatlantic.com/entertainment/archive/2018/04/killing-eve-review-bbc-america/557531/.

Gitlin, Todd. "Prime Time Ideology: The Hegemonic Process in Television Entertainment." *Social Problems* 26, no. 3 (1979): 251–66.

Goldberg, Jonathan. *Melodrama: An Aesthetics of Impossibility*. Durham, NC: Duke University Press, 2016.

Grant, Stan. "Black Writers Courageously Staring down the White Gaze—This Is Why We All Must Read Them | Stan Grant." *The Guardian*. Guardian News and Media, December 31, 2015. www.theguardian.com/commentisfree/2015/dec/31/black-writers-courageously-staring-down-the-white-gaze-this-is-why-we-all-must-read-them.

Grier, Miles P. "Why (and How) August Wilson Marginalized White Antagonism: A Note for Hollywood Producers." *Los Angeles Review of Books*, April 12, 2021. https://lareviewof books.org/article/why-and-how-august-wilson-marginalized-white-antagonism-a-note-for-hollywood-producers.

Grosz, Elizabeth A. *Volatile Bodies: Toward a Corporeal Feminism*. Bloomington, IN: Indiana University Press, 1994.

Gulino, Paul Joseph. *Screenwriting: The Sequence Approach*. London: Bloomsbury, 2013.

Halberstam, Jack. "Looking Butch: A Rough Guide to Butches on Film." In *Female Masculinity*, 175–231. Durham, NC: Duke University Press, 2018.

———. *Trans: A Quick and Quirky Account of Gender Variability*. Oakland, CA: University of California Press, 2018.

Halberstam, Judith. *The Queer Art of Failure*. Durham, NC: Duke University Press, 2011.

———. *In a Queer Time and Place: Transgender Bodies, Subcultural Lives*. New York: New York University Press, 2005.

Hall, Stuart. "Encoding/Decoding." Essay. In *Culture, Media, Language*, edited by Dorothy Hobson, Andrew Lowe, Paul Willis, and Stuart Hall, 51–61. London, UK: Hutchinson, 1980.

Hartnett, Alison. "Escaping the 'Evil Avenger' and the 'Supercrip': Images of Disability in Popular Television." *The Irish Communications Review* 8 (2000).

Haynes, Todd, director. *Carol*. Film4, 2015.

Highsmith, Patricia. *Strangers on a Train*. New York: W.W. Norton, 2001.

hooks, bell. *Black Looks: Race and Representation*. Boston: South End Press, 1992.

———. "The Oppositional Gaze." Essay. In *Movies and Mass Culture*, edited by John Belton, 247–64. New Brunswick, NJ: Rutgers University Press, 2000.

———. "Power to the Pusssy: We Don't Wannabe Dicks in Drag." In *Outlaw Culture: Resisting Representations*, 9–23. New York: Routledge, 2015.

———. *Yearning: Race, Gender, and Cultural Politics*. New York: Routledge and Taylor & Francis Group, 2015.

Howard, David, and Edward Mabley. *The Tools of Screenwriting: A Writer's Guide to the Craft and Elements of a Screenplay*. New York: St. Martin's Press, 1996.

Howe, Elena Nelson. "Sandra Oh Layers in Her Ethnicity on 'Killing Eve' Because White Hollywood Does Not." *Los Angeles Times*, June 23, 2020. www.latimes.com/entertainment-arts/tv/story/2020-06-23/sandra-oh-layers-ethnicity-for-nuance-killing-eve.

Iglesias, Karl. *Writing for Emotional Impact Advanced Dramatic Techniques to Attract, Engage, and Fascinate the Reader from Beginning to End*. Livermore, CA: WingSpan Press, 2010.

Jenkins, Barry, director. *Moonlight*. A24, 2016.

Jenner, Mareike. "Telling Detection: The Narrative Structures of American TV Detective Dramas." *American TV Detective Dramas: Serial Investigations* (2016): 55–75.

Jung, E. Alex. "Michaela the Destroyer." *Vulture*, July 6, 2020. https:// www.vulture.com/article/michaela-coel-i-may-destroy-you.html.

Kafer, Alison. *Feminist, Queer, Crip*. Bloomington, IN: Indiana University Press, 2013.

Keegan, Cáel M. *Lana and Lilly Wachowski*. Champaign, IL: University of Illinois Press, 2018.

———. "Revisitation: A Trans Phenomenology of the Media Image." *MedieKultur: Journal of Media and Communication Research* 32, no. 61 (2016).

———. "Tongues Without Bodies." *TSQ: Transgender Studies Quarterly* 3, no. 3–4 (2016): 605–10. https://doi.org/10.1215/23289252-3545275.

King, Jess. "Interview with Tanya Saracho." *Personal*, May 11, 2021.

Leach, Jim. "The Landscapes of Canada's Features: Articulating Nation and Nature." Essay. In *Cinema and Landscape: Film, Nation and Cultural Geography: Film, Nation and Cultural Geography*, edited by Graeme Harper and Jonathan Rayner, 269–80. Bristol, UK: Intellect Books, 2010.

Lee, Kim. "Too Close, Too Compromised: Killing Eve and the Promise of Sandra Oh." *Los Angeles Review of Books*. Accessed February 12, 2019. https://lareviewofbooks.org/ article/ close-compromised-killing-eve-promise-sandra-oh/.

Levesley, David. "Netflix's Sense8 Isn't Perfect, but It's the Best Queer Show on TV." *Slate Magazine, Slate*, 22 June 2015. slate.com/human-interest/2015/06/in-sense8-netflix-has-created-a-queer-masterpiece.html.

Levy, Ariel. "Female Chauvinist Pigs." In *Female Chauvinist Pigs: Women and the Rise of Raunch Culture*, 89–117. Collingwood, VIC: Black, 2010.

Li, Sijia. "Netflix by Netflix: On 'Sense8'—Los Angeles Review of Books." *Los Angeles Review of Books*, May 16, 2017. https://lareviewofbooks.org/article/netflix-by-netflix-on-sense8.

"Lilly Wachowski and Lana Wachowski." *YouTube*, uploaded by DePaul Visiting Artist Series, May 2, 2014. www.youtube.com/watch?v=AR0KJ00cEZ8.

Loofbourow, Lili. "The Male Glance." *VQR Online*, March 5, 2018. www.vqronline.org/ essays-articles/2018/03/male-glance.

Lorde, Audre. *Sister Outsider: Essays & Speeches*. Berkeley: Crossing Press, 2007.

Malaver, Laura (Lau). "'I'm La Porqueria': Reading Affective Embodiments in Vida/Laura (Lau) Malaver." *ASAP/J*, October 4, 2020. https://asapjournal.com/im-la-porqueria-reading-affective-embodiments-in-vida-laura-malaver/.

Mann, Michael, director. 2004. *Collateral*. Los Angeles, CA: Paramount Home Entertainment, 2004.

Manne, Kate. *Down Girl: The Logic of Misogyny*. London: Penguin Books, 2019.

———. *Entitled: How Male Privilege Hurts Women*. New York: Crown, 2020.

Maras, Steven. *Screenwriting: History, Theory and Practice*. London: Wallflower, 2009.

Marling, Brit. "I Don't Want to Be the Strong Female Lead." *The New York Times*, February 7, 2020. www.nytimes.com/2020/02/07/opinion/sunday/brit-marling-women-movies.html.

McKee, Robert. *Story: Substance, Structure, Style, and the Principles of Screenwriting*. New York: Regan Books, 1997.

McRuer, Robert. *Crip Theory Cultural Signs of Queerness and Disability*. New York: New York University Press, 2006.

Mincheva, Kilyana. "Sense 8 and the Praxis of Utopia." *Cinephile* 12, no. 1 (2018): 32–39.

Minor, Kelsey. "How Patrisse Cullors Helped Turn Zuri Adele into an on-Screen Activist." *Shondaland*, June 26, 2019. www.shondaland.com/watch/a28175137/patrisse-cullors-zuri-adele-activist/.

Morales, Aurora Levins. *Medicine Stories: History, Culture and the Politics of Integrity*. Cambridge, MA: South End Press, 1998.

Morrison, Toni. *Playing in the Dark: Whiteness and the Literary Imagination*. New York: Vintage Books, a division of Random House, Inc, 1992.

Mulvey, Laura. "Visual Pleasure and Narrative Cinema." In *Film Theory and Criticism: Introductory Readings*, edited by Leo Braudy and Marshall Cohen, 833–44. New York: Oxford University Press, 1999.

Muñoz, José Esteban. *Cruising Utopia: The Then and There of Queer Futurity*. New York: New York University Press, 2009.

Murdock, Maureen. *The Heroine's Journey*. Boston, MA: Shambhala, 1990.

Mwakasege-Minaya, Richard, and Juri Sanchez. "'Beautifully Represented' or an Attack on Our Culture? Netflix's *Gentefied* and the Struggle over Latinidad/Es." *Jump Cut: A Review of Contemporary Media*, no. 60 (2021). www.ejumpcut.org/currentissue/Mwakasege-Minaya-Sanchez-Gentefied/text.html.

Nellis, Ashley, and Marcy Mistrett. "The Color of Justice: Racial and Ethnic Disparity in State Prisons." *The Sentencing Project*, January 10, 2019. www.sentencingproject.org/publications/color-of-justice-racial-and-ethnic-disparity-in-state-prisons/.

Nichols-Pethick, Jonathan. *TV Cops: The Contemporary American Television Police Drama*. New York: Routledge, 2012.

North by Northwest. Directed by Alfred Hitchcock. United States: MGM, 1959.

Nussbaum, Emily. (@EmilyNussbaum). "I Enjoyed KILLING EVE. But I'm Fascinated That It Isn'T Getting Any Flack for Suggesting—Basic Instinctishly—That Lesbianism and Murder Are Two Great Tastes That Go Great Together." May 28, 2018, 10:05 a.m. Tweet.

Palmer, Jerry. *Thrillers: Genesis and Structure of a Popular Genre*. New York: St. Martins Press, 1979.

Parker, Ian. "The Real McKee." *The New Yorker*, October 13, 2003. https://www.newyorker.com/magazine/2003/10/20/the-real-mckee.

Parsemain, Ava Laure. "'I Am Also a We': The Pedagogy of Sense8." *The Pedagogy of Queer TV* (2019): 215–37. doi:10.1007/978-3-030-14872-0_10.

Phillips, Carmen. "Vida's Gay Vaquero Episode Breaks Emma's Heart, Asks Hard Questions About Who's Included in the Queer Community." *Autostraddle*, May 2, 2021. www.autostraddle.com/vidas-gay-vaquero-episode-breaks-emmas-heart-asks-hard-questions-about-whos-included-in-the-queer-community/.

———. "Vida's Season Two Is a Triumph of Unapologetically Queer and Latinx Storytelling." *Autostraddle*, May 2, 2021. www.autostraddle.com/vidas-second-season-continues-its-unapologetic-queer-and-latinx-storytelling/.

Powers, John. "How Chloé Zhao Reinvented the Western." *Vogue*, March 22, 2018. https://www.vogue.com/article/chloe-zhao-the-rider-vogue-april-2018.

Price, Steven. "Character in the Screenplay Text." Essay. In *Analysing the Screenplay*, edited by Jill Nelmes, 201–16. London: Routledge, 2011.

Quiñones, Carmen Merport. "Binging the Borderlands." *Public Books*, March 22, 2021. www.publicbooks.org/binging-the-borderlands/.

Radish, Christina. "J. Michael Straczynski Talks Collaborating with The Wachowskis on SENSE8." *Collider*, September 25, 2019. collider.com/sense8-j-michael-straczynski-talks-collaborating-with-the-wachowskis/.

Rich, Adrienne. *Blood, Bread and Poetry: Selected Prose, 1979–1985*. London: Virago Press, 1987.

———. "Compulsory Heterosexuality and Lesbian Existence." *Signs* 5, no. 4 (1980): 631–60. www.jstor.org/stable/3173834.

Riley, Boots. "Sorry to Bother You Director Boots Riley Takes a Ride Through Oakland's Changing Landscape." *Vanity Fair*, July 2, 2018. www.vanityfair.com/hollywood/2018/07/sorry-to-bother-you-boots-riley-oakland.

Rodríguez, Juana María. *Sexual Futures, Queer Gestures, and Other Latina Longings*. New York: New York University Press, 2014.

Romine, Taylor, and Evan Simko-Bednarski. "Judge in Rape Case Removed After Asking Accuser If She 'Closed Her Legs'." *CNN. Cable News Network*, May 28, 2020. www.cnn.com/2020/05/28/us/nj-judge-removed-assault-trnd/index.html.

Ruiz, Raúl. *Poetics of Cinema: 1*. Paris: Editions Dis Voir, 1995.

Ruti, Mari. *The Ethics of Opting Out: Queer Theory's Defiant Subjects*. New York: Columbia University Press, 2017.

Samer, Rox, ed. "Sense8 Roundtable." *Spectator* 37, no. 2 (2017): 74–88.

San Filippo, Maria. *The B Word Bisexuality in Contemporary Film and Television*. Bloomington: Indiana University Press, 2013.

Saracho, Tanya. *Pour Vida*. Pilot Script, 2016.

Sartwell, Crispin. "Western Philosophy as White Supremacism." *The Philosophical Salon*, May 27, 2019. https://thephilosophicalsalon.com/western-philosophy-as-white-supremacism/.

Sedgwick, Eve Kosofsky. "Queer and Now." Essay. In *Tendencies*, 1–20. Durham, NC: Duke University Press, 1993.

Sciamma, Céline, director. *Portrait of a Lady on Fire*. Paris: Pyramide Films, 2019.

———. "Ready for the Rising Tide." *BAFTA Screenwriters' Lecture Series*, February 4, 2020. www.bafta.org/media-centre/transcripts/screenwriters-lecture- series-2019-celine-sciamma.

Shacklock, Zoë. "Queer Kinaesthesia on Television." *Screen* 60, no. 4 (2019): 509–26.

Shome, Raka. "Race and Popular Cinema: The Rhetorical Strategies of Whiteness in City of Joy." *Communication Quarterly* 44, no. 4 (Fall 1996): 502–18.

Slotkin, Richard. *Gunfighter Nation*. New York: Atheneum, 1992.

Smith, Stacy L. "Inequality in 1,300 Popular Films: Examining Portrayals of Gender, Race/Ethnicity, LGBTQ & Disability from 2007 to 2019." September 2020. https://annenberg.usc.edu. http://assets.uscannenberg.org/docs/aii-inequality_1300_popular_films_09-08-2020.pdf.

Smith, Stacy L., et al. *Comprehensive Annenberg Report on Diversity in Entertainment*. Los Angeles, CA: USC Annenberg, 2016.

Sobchack, Vivian. *Carnal Thoughts Embodiment and Moving Image Culture*. Berkeley, CA: University of California Press, 2011.

Soloway, Joey. "Joey Soloway on The Female Gaze." Lecture, Toronto International Film Festival, Canada, Toronto, September 11, 2016. Accessed February 22, 2019. www.youtube.com/watch?v=pnBvppooD9I.

Sorry to Bother You. Film. U.S.: Annapurna Pictures/Focus Features, 2018.

Spady, Sam. "Reflections on Late Identity: In Conversation with Melanie J. Newton, Nirmala Erevelles, Kim TallBear, Rinaldo Walcott, and Dean Itsuji Saranillio." *Critical Ethnic Studies* 3, no. 1 (2017): 90.

Staiger, Janet. "Blueprints for Feature Films: Hollywood's Continuity Scripts." Essay. In *The American Film Industry*, edited by Tino Balio, 173–94. Madison, WI: University of Wisconsin Press, 1985.

Stanford, Eleanor. "How Michaela Coel Shaped 'I May Destroy You'." *The New York Times*, July 21, 2020. www.nytimes.com/2020/07/20/arts/television/i-may-destroy-you-influences.html.

St. Félix, Doreen. "Michaela Coel on Making 'I May Destroy You'." In *Episode. The New Yorker Radio Hour*. New York: WNYC Studios, July 14, 2020.

Sutherland, Jean-Anne, and Kathryn M. Feltey. "Here's Looking at Her: An Intersectional Analysis of Women, Power and Feminism in Film." *Journal of Gender Studies* 26, no. 6 (2017): 618–31.

Tolentino, Jia. "The Pleasurable Patterns of the 'Killing Eve' Season Finale." *The New Yorker*, May 29, 2018. Accessed February 12, 2019. https:// www.newyorker.com/culture/on-television/the-pleasurable-patterns-of-the-killing-eve-season-finale.

Toropin, Konstantin, and Hollie Silverman. "Minnesota Supreme Court Overturns a Felony Rape Conviction Because the Woman Voluntarily Got Intoxicated." *CNN. Cable News Network*, March 31, 2021. www.cnn.com/2021/03/30/us/minnesota-rape-conviction-overturned/index.html.

VanDerWerff, Emily. "I Watched Netflix's Sense8 and Don't Know If It's a Travesty or a Whacked-out Masterpiece." *Vox*, June 10, 2015. www.vox.com/2015/6/10/8756283/sense8-review-netflix.

VanHemert, Kyle. "The Secret Sauce Behind Netflix's Hit, 'House of Cards': Big Data." *Fast Company. Fast Company*, July 9, 2018. www.fastcompany.com/1671893/the-secret-sauce-behind-netflixs-hit-house-of-cards-big-data.

Vogler, Christopher. *The Writers Journey: Mythic Structure for Writers*. Studio City, CA: Michael Wiese Productions, 2007.

Wachowski, Lana, and J. Michael Straczynski, creators. *Sense8*. Los Angeles, CA: Netflix, 2015.

Wallace, Michele. *Invisibility Blues*. London: Verso, 1990.

Waller-Bridge, Phoebe, creator. *Killing Eve*. New York: BBC America, 2018.

Warner, Kristen J. "Plastic Representation." *Film Quarterly* 71, no. 2 (2017).

West, Traci C. *Wounds of the Spirit: Black Women, Violence, and Resistance Ethics*. New York: New York University Press, 1999.

"WGAW Inclusion Report 2020." *wga.org*. Accessed October 17, 2021. www.wga.org/uploadedfiles/the-guild/inclusion-and-equity/2020_WGAW_Inclusion_Report.pdf.

Whatling, Clare. "'In the Good Old Days When Times Were Bad' the Nostalgia for Abjection in Lesbian Cinema Spectatorship." In *Screen Dreams: Fantasizing Lesbians in Film*, 79–116. New York: Manchester University Press, 1997.

White, Rosie. "Introduction." In *Violent Femmes: Women as Spies in Popular Culture*, 1–11. London: Routledge, 2007.

"Why The Matrix Is a Trans Story According to Lilly Wachowski | Netflix." *YouTube*, August 4, 2020. www.youtube.com/watch?v=adXm2sDzGkQ.

Wilderson, Frank B. *Red, White & Black: Cinema and the Structure of U.S. Antagonisms*. Durham, NC: Duke University Press, 2010.

Williams, Linda. "Film Bodies: Gender, Genre, and Excess." *Film Quarterly* 44, no. 4 (1991): 2–13. https://doi.org/10.2307/1212758.

Yancy, George. *Black Bodies, White Gazes: The Continuing Significance of Race*. London: Rowman & Littlefield, 2008.

Yates, Reggie. "Michaela Coel: 'If You Don't Show It, It Can Be Erased'." *Other. British GQ*, October 26, 2020. www.youtube.com/watch?v=SZ_0_DEe_2A.

Yeoman, Kevin. "'Sense8' Series Premiere Review: Beautiful Nonsense." *ScreenRant*, June 5, 2015. screenrant.com/sense8-series-premiere-review/.

INDEX

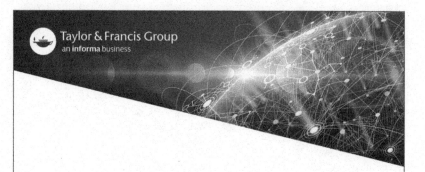